Making Decentralization Work

Making Decentralization Work

Democracy, Development, and Security

edited by
Ed Connerley
Kent Eaton
Paul Smoke

Viva Books
New Delhi | Mumbai | Chennai | Kolkata | Bengaluru | Hyderabad | Kochi | Guwahati

First Indian Edition 2011

VIVA BOOKS PRIVATE LIMITED

- 4737/23 Ansari Road, Daryaganj, New Delhi 110 002
  E-mail: vivadelhi@vivagroupindia.net, Tel. 42242200
- 76, Service Industries, Shirvane, Sector 1, Nerul, Navi Mumbai 400 706
  E-mail: vivamumbai@vivagroupindia.net, Tel. 27721273, 27721274
- Jamals Fazal Chambers, 26 Greams Road, Chennai 600 006
  E-mail: vivachennai@vivagroupindia.net, Tel. 28290304, 28294241
- B-103, Jindal Towers, 21/1A/3 Darga Road, Kolkata 700 017
  E-mail: vivakolkata@vivagroupindia.net, Tel. 22836381, 22816713
- 7, Sovereign Park Apartments, 56-58, K. R. Road, Basavanagudi, Bengaluru 560 004
  E-mail: vivabangalore@vivagroupindia.net, Tel. 26607409, 26607410
- 101-102 Mughal Marc Apartments, 3-4-637 to 641, Narayanguda, Hyderabad 500 029
  E-mail: vivahyderabad@vivagroupindia.net, Tel. 27564481, 27564482
- Beevi Towers, First Floor, SRM Road, Kaloor, Kochi 682 018, Kerala
  E-mail: vivakochi@vivagroupindia.net, Tel: 0484-2403055, 2403056
- 232, GNB Road, Beside UCO Bank, Silpukhuri, Guwahati 781 003
  E-mail: vivaguwahati@vivagroupindia.net, Tel: 0361-2666386

www.vivagroupindia.com

Published by arrangement with

Lynne Rienner Publishers, Inc.
1800 30th Street, Suite 314
Boulder, Colorado 80301
USA

ISBN : 978-81-309-1526-5

Published by Vinod Vasishtha for Viva Books Private Limited, 4737/23, Ansari Road, Daryaganj, New Delhi - 110 002. Printed and bound by Raj Press, R-3, Inderpuri, New Delhi - 110 012.

S0000 / S1000

Contents

Acknowledgments

The preparation of earlier versions of five chapters in this book was supported by the Office of Democracy and Governance of the US Agency for International Development (USAID). Draft versions of these papers were blind peer-reviewed in a two-day workshop held at George Washington University. Written and/or oral comments were provided on one or more papers by Robert Aten, Andrew Green, Arnold Harberger, Jerry Hyman, Kai Kaiser, Krishna Kumar, Brian Levy, Barbara Nunberg, Mark Payne, Janine Perfit, Andrew Selee, Paul Smoke, Peter Solis, Ernesto Stein, Tjip Walker, and Brian Wampler. Other workshop participants also contributed ideas that have improved these chapters. The editors are grateful to USAID for its support and to all who participated in the workshop. We are especially grateful to Neil Levine and Pat Fn'Piere, director and deputy director of the Governance Division of the Office of Democracy and Governance, who initiated and supported the efforts that produced these papers.

Two anonymous reviewers for Lynne Rienner Publishers provided extensive comments on the manuscript. The insights provided by these reviewers significantly improved the content of the volume.

We note with deep regret the premature death of Omar Azfar on January 21, 2009. He was a prolific writer on the political economy of development, with particular emphasis on the economics of corruption and decentralization. He enriched all who came in contact with him.

Lynne Rienner and the staff of Lynne Rienner Publishers have our gratitude for the highly professional guidance they provided throughout the process of publication.

Finally, we thank the chapter authors for their persistence and patience in responding to requests for changes to chapters.

—the Editors

1

Democracy, Development, and Security as Objectives of Decentralization

Kent Eaton and Ed Connerley

That decentralization seems to be occurring just about everywhere is one of its most distinctive features in the contemporary period. Over the past few decades, scholars and development practitioners alike have documented the remarkable reach of this trend, asking why otherwise very different countries in disparate regions are nevertheless endorsing a common shift toward more decentralized styles of governance. Indeed, in the first decade of the twenty-first century, it became increasingly difficult to identify countries whose leaders had not debated, adopted, or implemented some type of decentralizing changes.[1] Widespread experimentation with these changes constitutes a trend that now seems even more extensive than the roughly simultaneous trends of democratization and economic liberalization.

Just as significant as the extensive reach of the decentralization trend, though far less widely recognized, is the fact that political actors have embraced decentralization as a means toward many different ends. The effects of decentralization ripple across a country's economy, society, and polity. And as a result, it can be useful to those who are seeking to advance a broad array of economic, social, and political goals. More specifically, three overarching goals—democracy, economic development, and public security—have convinced governmental and nongovernmental actors around the world to support decentralization. Consider the following sets of cases. In Brazil, the Philippines, and South Africa, democratic reformers in the 1980s and 1990s enlisted decentralization as a type of reform that could facilitate the transition to and consolidation of democratic rule. In roughly the same period in Chile, China, and Vietnam, it was the promotion of market-oriented economic models, and not democratization, that elicited the support of national politicians for decentralization policies. In contrast, in Colombia, Ethiopia, and Sudan, decentralization appealed to those who sought to end their countries' internal armed conflicts and restore public security. These and other cases suggest that decentralization is remarkably flexible in the appeal that it holds out for actors who are motivated by quite different substantive goals.

Even as decentralization undoubtedly has been adopted in the pursuit of some very different goals, has it worked? Does decentralization actually help a country democratize, develop, or stabilize? Under what conditions does decentralization succeed in producing the benefits that have motivated its widespread adoption and generated such enthusiasm? Though the decision to decentralize is still fairly new in some countries, enough time has now elapsed to begin to assess in a tentative fashion how well decentralization has fared, which is the task we pick up in this book. As decentralization "ages," more and better quality evidence is now available about the performance of decentralized institutions. The chapters in this volume sift through this accumulating evidence in order to identify and analyze some of the critical problems that have emerged in the attempted transition to decentralized governance. Rather than offer a comprehensive survey of decentralization, which would be beyond the scope of any single book given its complexity and multifaceted quality, our more limited goal is to focus attention on several of the core dilemmas that decentralizing efforts have encountered so far. By focusing on what happens in the aftermath of the decision to decentralize, this volume complements but seeks to move beyond the already sizable existing literature that explains why policies of decentralization were adopted in the first place (Bird and Vaillancourt 1998; Falleti 2005; Garman, Haggard, and Willis 2001; Manor 1999; O'Neill 2005; Smoke 2003; Smith 2008).

There are three main points of departure for this volume. First, we take seriously the point that decentralization is a possible means toward other desirable ends—including chiefly democracy, development, and security—rather than an end in and of itself. Since decentralization is successful only when it succeeds in promoting these ends, it should be judged accordingly. The chapters in this volume present a frank and not always positive picture of the dynamics that decentralization has set in motion. Among other negative outcomes, decentralization can increase local corruption, weaken national political parties, and reinforce the authoritarian rule of subnational elites. Thus, while decentralization has definitely produced positive outcomes in many cases, in others it has either failed to solve the problems that motivated its adoption, created qualitatively new problems, or both. For example, decentralization has generated new forms of conflict between national and (now more independent) subnational governments while, at the same time, it has worsened discord between subnational governments that are not equally well positioned to perform the enhanced roles they are now expected to play.

Second, precisely because the various pressures that have led so many countries to decentralize are still in place, we argue that decentralization is likely to continue to find powerful advocates into the foreseeable future. In recent years, scholars have pointed to a variety of different factors that may explain why decentralization has become so widespread, including pressures for fiscal austerity, broad donor support for decentralization, strong public opposition to centralized rule, and a spate of formal transitions to political democracy (Litvack, Ahmad, and Bird 1998; Manor 1999; Montero and Samuels 2004). The debate over what has caused many and varied countries to decentralize is by no means resolved, and we do not enter into this debate in the chapters that follow. We do note, however, that most of the causal factors highlighted by scholars point to the continued salience of decentralization as a governance trend. With respect to economic causes, the current global economic crisis will likely encourage national governments to look harder for ways to transfer responsibilities to subnational governments, along with the blame for any associated decline in the quality and quantity of services. With respect to political causes, growing awareness of the limitations of recent transitions to liberal representative democracy have increased support for a more direct and participatory style of democracy that depends intimately on decentralization. Admittedly, in several key cases, it is important to note that frustration with some of the shortcomings of decentralization has already generated strongly recentralizing reactions. For example, in Argentina, Brazil, and Colombia, national governments in recent years have sought—with mixed success—to restore macrolevel economic stability by reversing transfers of fiscal authority to subnational governments (Eaton 2004a; Eaton and Dickovick 2006). Despite these and other forms of backlash against decentralization, in the short to medium term we will continue to live in a decentralizing era (Snyder 2001).

Third, if decentralization can often come up short (Point 1), but remains very much alive as a policy idea (Point 2), then it becomes urgent to study past decentralization episodes with a view to identifying how decentralizing policies and processes of implementation can be strengthened in the future. When it succeeds, decentralization by definition disrupts the deeply embedded relationships and networks that previously sustained decades—if not centuries—of centralized rule. It is a mistake, therefore, to conceive of decentralization as a one-shot deal. The design, legislation, and implementation of policies of decentralization are really only the beginning of a long process of institutional and organizational change. Successfully navigating this process requires closely studying and learning from earlier implementation efforts, particularly mistakes and difficulties encountered. For this reason, the purpose of this volume is not to argue against decentralization based on some of the negative findings that have begun to appear in the literature by academics and practitioners. Rather, our goal is to inform future interventions in support of decentralization by exploring important debates about past interventions and by showcasing some of the important trade-offs that decentralization usually generates. By focusing attention on how local governments underperform or misbehave in the wake of decentralization, we are by no means assuming a benign central government—nor do we intend to offer here a theoretical justification for recentralization. Instead, according to our position, examining some of the trade-offs, dilemmas, and challenges that are posed by decentralization offers the best hope for "making decentralization work."

As an opening to the chapters that follow, this introductory chapter is organized around the three main goals that decisionmakers most commonly cite when they decide to decentralize: democracy, development, and security. What is the logic of the hypothesized connection between decentralization and each of these stated goals? What does the emerging, though still incomplete, empirical record tell us about the relative success of decentralization as a means toward these distinct ends? After exploring these questions in the following sections, we then close with a discussion that introduces the volume's subsequent chapters.

Decentralization and Democracy

Democrats like decentralization for a number of reasons. First, democracy requires that governmental decisionmakers be held accountable for the decisions they make, a requirement that may be easier to satisfy when governments are local. According to this accountability argument, while it can be quite difficult to monitor the behavior of national politicians, voters face lower costs when they seek to gather information about how local politicians are making use of governmental resources. Second, frustration with the transitions to democracy that took place at the national level in the 1980s and 1990s have led many democrats to contemplate decentralization as a set of changes that can deepen democracy by multiplying the sites for political contestation. Precisely because authoritarian practices and behaviors often survived national transitions to democracy, democratizers have hoped that devolving power to local spheres could help eliminate the vestiges of authoritarianism (Diamond and Tsalik 1999; Eaton 2001). In some cases, advocates of democratization have endorsed decentralization in the explicit attempt to prevent possible relapses into authoritarianism by undermining the centralized practices that sustained nondemocratic rule.

Does the available evidence bear out these theoretical expectations? Though the impact of decentralization on democracy is complex, a number of patterns can be identified and analyzed. First, while democrats around the world have championed subnational elections in the attempt to improve accountability and attack authoritarianism, the mere introduction of elections is insufficient. Whether the shift from the appointment to the election of subnational officials substantially improves their ability to act independently of the national government depends on a host of additional factors. Beyond the holding of regular subnational elections, for example, the timing of national and subnational electoral contests and the rules governing ballot structure are critical institutional variables (Jones 1997; Jones and Mainwaring 2003). Where national politicians agree to introduce separate elections to constitute subnational governments, but insist that these elections be held on the same day as national contests, the simultaneity of these elections undercuts the likelihood that local contests will turn on local issues. Likewise, electoral rules can be written in ways that deny voters the right to cut their ballots, preventing them from using different criteria to reward or penalize different parties at the national and subnational levels. Furthermore, as Gary Bland shows in Chapter 3, rules permitting the arbitrary removal of subnational elected officials by the national government are easily as important as the decision to introduce subnational elections. Where national politicians can remove subnational politicians they do not like, subnational elections are unlikely to generate outcomes not sanctioned by the center.

In addition to the design of rules governing ballot structure, electoral calendars, and the removal of subnational officials, internal party dynamics powerfully shape the impact of decentralization on democracy. Although in theory the introduction of subnational elections encourages local politicians to shift their attention from national patrons to local voters, the extent to which this shift takes place in practice depends on how power is distributed within the political parties to which they belong (Willis, Garman, and Haggard 1999). Decentralization in the polity often depends on decentralization in the party. According to the experience of countries that have decentralized via the introduction of subnational elections, the degree of change generated by these elections may be limited when national party leaders play a preponderant role in determining who can use the party label to run in local elections. Whether subnational officials are elected by proportional representation in multimember districts or by the plurality rule in single-member districts, national control over candidate selection can undercut decentralization if these officials are chiefly focused on pleasing national party leaders. This type of center-regarding behavior in countries that now hold subnational elections points toward a possible tension between democratization and decentralization. Whereas the literature on democratization has highlighted the challenges that weak and undisciplined parties can pose for democracy (Mainwaring and Scully 1995; B. Powell 1982; Sartori 1976), the literature on decentralization suggests that strong and disciplined parties can make a mockery of decentralization (Willis, Garman, and Haggard 1999; Montero and Samuels 2004).

Summarizing the discussion so far, a variety of factors can reduce the political independence of subnational officials from the center, even when these officials are now elected in their own right and no longer appointed by the national government. Fearing that elections are insufficient as mechanisms that can generate downward accountability to voters, decentralizing legislation in many countries has been designed explicitly to empower civil society. In countries such as Bolivia, Indonesia, and the Philippines, for example, decentralization involved not just introducing or strengthening subnational elections, but adopting changes that expand the ability of local civil society actors to influence the greater range of decisions that are now made locally. As much as the contemporary move toward decentralization has sought to create or reinvigorate the institutions of representative democracy at the local level (e.g., municipal councils and provincial legislatures), it has also innovated by creating and strengthening institutions of direct democracy, including stakeholder councils and participatory budgeting fora (Fung 2006; Van Cott 2008). According to Derick Brinkerhoff and Omar Azfar in Chapter 4, decentralization can have the biggest impact when it goes beyond the introduction of subnational elections to empower community groups at the local level. As these and other authors emphasize, however, attempts to expand civil society participation in the context of decentralization are not separable from the party system; indeed, some of the most successful participatory innovations—including in the Brazilian case of Porto Alegre—have depended fundamentally on the sponsorship of political parties that hope to reap electoral benefits from successful participatory experiences (Goldfrank 2007; Heller 2001; Rhodes 2003; Wampler 2007).

Despite the justified enthusiasm for civil society, recent research by political scientists suggests that advocates of decentralization need to consider carefully the relationship between civil society and democracy. In the 1990s, Robert Putnam's influential study of variation in the quality of civic life between Italy's democratic north and authoritarian south encouraged scholars to view the impact of civil society on democracy in mostly positive terms (1993). Although many scholars found additional support for the argument that attributes higher-quality democracies to more thickly organized civil societies, others argue—in a variety of distinct national contexts—that the effects of dense civil society networks are not always positive (Armony 2004). According to Sheri Berman (1997), the deepening of civil society organizations may lead not to the deepening but rather to the breakdown of democracy, as occurred when civic associations developed strongly antidemocratic inclinations in Weimar Germany. In Bolivia, according to Harry Blair (2001), the national government selects which civil society organizations get to sit in on local oversight committees, and the representativeness of the organizations that it picks can often be questioned. According to Ashutosh Varshney's research on India (2002), while civil society organizations that bring together individuals of different ethnicities can reduce violence, local civil society groups that organize along ethnic lines can worsen ethnic conflict and undermine democracy. Particularly in developing countries that are characterized by significant degrees of ethnic and religious diversity, those who design decentralization should ask whether membership in local civil society organizations is likely to replicate or cut across membership in different societal groups. More generally, as Jesse Ribot, Ashwini Chhatre, and Tomila Lankina argue in Chapter 5, decentralization in some localities has strengthened the position of customary and religious authorities whose approach to governance may be more despotic than democratic.

According to the discussion in the preceding paragraphs, electoral rules, internal party dynamics, and the representativeness of civil society organizations all shape (and potentially limit) the impact that decentralization can have on democracy. In addition to the challenges posed by these factors, scholars have emphasized the significance of subnational authoritarian enclaves that can interrupt the purportedly positive consequences of decentralization for democracy. In many developing countries that have completed the national transition to democracy but that contain enclaves of persistent authoritarianism at the subnational level, decentralization has the unfortunate effect of transferring power and authority from units of government that are more democratic to units of government that are less democratic or nondemocratic. Though the earlier literature on democratic transitions devoted little sustained attention to these specifically subnational obstacles to democratization (Przeworski, O'Donnell, and Schmitter 1986), with time the importance of such obstacles has become all too clear. Particularly where local authoritarianism appears to be alive and well, rather than begin by asking whether there is sufficient political will to decentralize on the part of national politicians, some preliminary assessment is needed of how decentralization would influence authoritarian practices by subnational politicians.[2] At the very least, it is now possible to dismiss as naive the view that subnational elections alone will eradicate subnational authoritarian enclaves.

Recent scholarship on territorial politics and democracy has largely confirmed earlier concerns by Jonathan Fox (1994) and others that decentralization might make it easier rather than harder for subnational leaders to defend the nondemocratic practices that sustain their rule. Paul Hutchcroft, for example, argues that, "where powerful local bosses effectively challenge the authority of the central state," centralization rather than decentralization may offer a better way to promote democracy (2001, 24, 43).[3] Guillermo O'Donnell and his coauthors maintain that the more widespread abuse of civil rights in the hinterlands of developing countries makes it difficult for citizens to participate effectively in local governments, which in turn facilitates the dominance of entrenched local elites (O'Donnell, Cullell, and Iazzetta 2004). According to Pranab Bardhan and Dilip Mookherjee (2000), these elites may actually have an easier time capturing local politics because elite interests are more homogenous at the local level and because the informational and organizational costs that confront these elites are lower at the local level than at the national level. The familiar reality of elite capture leads Richard Crook and Alan Sverrisson to conclude their survey of decentralization by arguing that "central intervention is nearly always needed to ensure progressive or pro-poor outcomes" (2001, 4).

This concern about the authoritarian quality of subnational governments within nationally democratic regimes is not restricted to any one developing region. In Africa, Mahmood Mamdani argues that decentralization in the absence of an effective state has amounted to accommodation with local strongmen and has resulted in a kind of "decentralized despotism" (1996, 17).[4] According to Catherine Boone, many of those who have benefited the most from decentralization in Africa are "local notables" whose power derives from hereditary or spiritual authority and/or land tenure relations (2003, 32). John Sidel's work suggests that one of the most ambitious decentralization experiments in Southeast Asia—that of the Philippines—has made it easier for family clans to defend their exclusive control over local politics (1999, 129). In Indonesia, Michael Malley states that "allegations of vote buying mar the election of nearly every governor, *bupati* and mayor" (2003, 103). In Latin America, Edward Gibson (2005) argues that authoritarian enclaves below the national level may persist not because national democratic authorities are powerless to eradicate them, but because these authorities derive important benefits from authoritarian subnational officials who often control voting blocs that can be critical in national elections.

If patently nondemocratic practices in a given country are uniform in all subnational jurisdictions, then making the decision not to decentralize would be an easy one. In most countries, however, what is striking is the degree of heterogeneity across the landscape of subnational governments in the quality of democracy and in the opportunities for democratic local governance to take root. More often than not, the subnational realm is a complicated patchwork of local authoritarianism mixed in with reformist municipalities and states or provinces that have used decentralized resources to make significant strides in broadening participation and enhancing accountability. In fact, this heterogeneity is now a common theme in the literature on decentralization. For example, Tim Campbell (2003) documents how, in a sea of traditional clientelistic practices at the local level, some mayors have nevertheless responded to decentralization by governing in transparent and responsive ways. Alan Angell, Pamela Lowden, and Rosemary Thorp (2001) likewise contrast the democratic and nondemocratic responses of mayors to common changes such as the introduction of direct elections and revenue sharing.

The existence and uneven distribution of subnational authoritarian enclaves creates tremendous difficulties for the design of decentralization. In most cases, subnational governments that are dominated by authoritarian practices will have just as many rights and responsibilities as more democratically oriented subnational governments. To the best of our knowledge, in no country does decentralizing legislation differentiate the amount of resources and responsibilities that are transferred to subnational governments on the basis of a systematic assessment of their democratic credentials. In fact, when differential treatment is introduced, it is often to favor the less economically developed subnational areas that are often more likely to suffer from authoritarian political environments.[5] Given the persistence of subnational authoritarian enclaves, those who design future interventions in support of decentralization will want to develop better indicators of the quality of local democracy across subnational jurisdictions. In practice, the heterogeneity of subnational governments with respect to the quality of democracy may well be an argument for asymmetry in the devolution of resources and authority.[6]

Decentralization and Development

Relative to democracy, economic development in the twentieth century was a much more heavily cited rationale for the adoption of decentralizing measures. For that reason, the literature linking decentralization and development is quite vast. Although scholars have identified a number of causal mechanisms through which decentralization might improve development outcomes, two have loomed especially large in the scholarship and we showcase them here. First is the argument that decentralization improves the mix and quality of goods and services provided by governmental actors, thereby raising the well-being of individuals and groups. To date, international donors have emphasized this mechanism in their support for local service delivery improvement projects, the "bread and butter" of donor-funded decentralization activities. Second is the relatively newer argument that decentralization under certain conditions can encourage growth-promoting behaviors by subnational officials who compete among themselves for investment and thereby improve national development outcomes.

Historically, most efforts to enhance development through decentralization have been informed by the theoretical work of Charles Tiebout and Wallace Oates. Tiebout's hypothesis holds that, when there are multiple governmental jurisdictions offering varying "packages" of public goods and the taxes that support them, citizens and firms will seek out jurisdictions offering a combination of goods and taxes that closely match their individual preferences by "voting with their feet" (1956). Furthermore, jurisdictions will, in theory, both learn from each other's efforts and compete with each other to offer desired combinations of public goods, services, and taxes, thus improving the welfare of citizens. In addition, expenditure decisions can be tied more closely to real resource costs in smaller jurisdictions, and greater service delivery innovation is possible when there are many local governments.[7] In formal game-theoretic simulations, Tiebout's expectations are frequently supported, but results in empirical research concerning (mostly US) metropolitan areas are mixed, with some studies supporting a "race to the top" interpretation of interjurisdictional competition while others support a "race to the bottom" conclusion.[8] Thus, it may not be entirely surprising that efforts to accelerate development through decentralized governance in developing countries also achieve mixed, uncertain impacts. In contrast to Tiebout, Oates's theory of fiscal federalism (1972) does not require perfect mobility; whether and how citizens hold their representatives accountable within their jurisdictions can affect the mix of goods and services provided by government. For both Tiebout and Oates, defining an efficient decentralized structure is a complex process because optimal service area may vary greatly for different public goods and may not correspond exactly to the boundaries of existing political jurisdictions.

Increasingly, advocates of decentralization as a development-promoting measure have argued that it is not enough merely to transfer additional responsibilities for the provision of goods and services in the hopes that subnational governments will behave in the ways anticipated by Tiebout and Oates. Subnational governments are frequently hard pressed to accomplish welfare-enhancing services that are not understood and valued by citizens. With respect to these services, decentralization support has begun to encourage subnational governments to engage citizens more directly in "coproduction" in a number of dimensions. For example, coproduction of learning outcomes by parents is especially important for public education (G. Davis and Ostrom 1991). In resource-poor environments, production of desired public sanitation outcomes is greatly facilitated when a large majority of residents refrain from casual disposition of household wastes (Ostrom 1996). Targeting both government officials and citizens assures attention to both the "supply" and "demand" aspects of public service delivery, and hopefully ensures both that valued services are provided and that citizens' expectations for services are consistent with the resources and capacities of governments. Especially important in coproduction schemes are participatory processes that are designed both to give citizens voice in local decisionmaking and to reveal citizens' preferences for local government services and policy positions (Fung 2006; Goldfrank 2007). Given the special challenges faced by marginalized groups, together with accumulating evidence of elite capture subsequent to decentralization, donor-sponsored activities geared toward boosting the participation in these processes of previously underserved groups have become especially common.

Over time, scholars and practitioners have come to argue that the theoretical linkages between decentralization on the one hand and development on the other depend on community empowerment as an intervening variable. In Chapter 4, for example, Derick Brinkerhoff and Omar Azfar put community empowerment at the center of their analysis. According to these authors, growing awareness of the significance of community empowerment raises important questions of sustainability. As they argue, the effectiveness of the community empowerment approach should be measured not by the effectiveness or durability of particular project processes and mechanisms, but by the learning, capacities, and altered incentives retained by involved communities and subnational governments. Even as ever greater attention has been placed on the urgency of empowering communities, other scholars note that more extensive forms of citizen participation vis-à-vis service provision are not a panacea. In fact they may, as Jonathan Hiskey argues in Chapter 2, generate new problems. According to Hiskey, increasing citizen oversight of elected representatives encourages them to act as delegates (doing only what the voters tell them to do), but may in equal measure diminish their potential to act as trustees (doing what they believe to be in the voters' best interests). Drawing on Hannah Pitkin's work (1967), Hiskey maintains that both delegate and trustee roles are appropriate for local elected representatives, and that some degree of insulation may enable local officials to make decisions about service provision that are ultimately better for the development prospects of the localities they govern.

Regardless of the important debate, highlighted in this volume, over the appropriate dimensions of citizen participation, scholars who study the relationship between decentralization and development agree on the importance of capacity. Though the capacity of subnational governments was more often assumed a priori rather than investigated empirically in the earlier literature on decentralization, with time problems of capacity have become undeniable. If it is to enhance development outcomes, decentralization must involve not just formally shifting authority over goods and services to subnational officials, but engaging in capacity-building efforts to help subnational governments actually provide these goods and services (Oates 1999; Shah and Thompson 2004). Improvements in subnationally provided goods and services depend on technical assistance, which is typically sponsored by external donors, national governments, or associations of subnational governments, and which is designed to help subnational officials plan, manage, deliver, and account for local public goods and services.[9] To date, these efforts have been targeted most commonly at multiple-service local governments rather than single-purpose bodies such as utility, water, and school boards (though the latter may hold out real promise as sites for service provision in the future).

In addition to improving individual well-being by improving the quality of governmental goods and services and the capacity of subnational governments to provide them, scholars have increasingly focused on a second causal pathway linking decentralization and development. According to this more recent wave of theorizing, decentralization generates development because it can create new growth-promoting incentives for subnational officials. Associated with the institutionalist turn taken in recent years by the disciplines of both political science and economics, this new scholarly interest in the institutional incentives faced by subnational officials has yet to directly inform donor activities on a large scale, though this may be changing. According to this new literature, appropriately structured decentralized governments can serve as an effective constraint on potentially predatory central governments and their officials. The most well-developed version of this argument is the influential work on "market-preserving federalism" (MPF) by Barry Weingast (1995, 2006).

Briefly stated, MPF requires that there are multiple levels of government, with each level having a defined set of autonomous authorities.[10] Included among the authorities defined for subnational governments is primary responsibility for regulation of the local economy and the authority to provide significant local public services. National government policies and enforcement activities must guarantee a single, nationwide common market that enables factor and product mobility across subnational jurisdictional boundaries. All governments, but especially subnational governments, must be subject to hard budget constraints. Accordingly, only the national government may create and manage a monetary system and all levels must live within prudent, defined, and delimited spending restraints, particularly and specifically restraints on intergovernmental transfers and borrowing. Finally, authority must be institutionalized in a manner and degree that prevents unilateral modification of the characteristics of the federal system by, on the one hand, the national government or national officials and, on the other hand, significant groups of subnational governments or subnational officials.[11] Proponents of MPF argue that, through the competitive interactions of subnational governments engendered in this structure, governmental systems offer incentives to citizens to save, invest, and produce as well as incentives to officials to refrain from confiscation of citizens' wealth.[12]

The national case study literature featuring MPF explanations of political and economic events over time is, however, somewhat mixed and contentious.[13] The purported impact of federalism on economic outcomes has generated a fair amount of disagreement in the empirical literature. Writing over a decade ago, Gabriela Montinola, Yingyi Qian, and Barry Weingast (1995) focus on federalism as the factor that explains how China, in the absence of the rule of law, could nevertheless produce sustained market-based economic growth. According to these authors, the delegation of authority to the provinces encouraged provincial officials to compete with each other to attract and retain investors, a dynamic that limited acts of predation by the government and that encouraged pro-market policies.[14] Others have disputed the beneficial impact of federalism. For example, with reference to India, Susan Rose-Ackerman and Jonathan Rodden question "whether market-preserving federalism can in fact solve the 'fundamental political dilemma of an economic system,'" and argue that the Chinese experience should not be used to promote calls for "radical decentralization and deregulation in the name of efficiency" (1997, 1524). More recently, Erik Wibbels's work on Argentine federalism (2005) has shifted the analytical focus from competition between subnational units to the degree of political competition within subnational units, concluding that political competition generates growth-enhancing policies by politicians who fear the fiscal shadow of the future.[15]

But market-preserving federalism does not exhaust the various arguments that link more robust subnational governments with better development outcomes. Subnational governments that aim to promote economic growth over time can exercise their inherent governmental powers in a collaborative, strategic process to promote local economic development (LED). Such efforts are "collaborative" when they involve cooperation with local firms and communities and they are "strategic" when they are based in systematic knowledge of the relative advantages and disadvantages of the locality. The need for, and advantages of, planned LED have increased with the globalization of markets. A first, minimal step in LED may be an effort by the involved subnational government to eliminate unnecessary constraints on business activity imposed by local regulations, as suggested by the MPF literature. But, moving beyond MPF, these steps can be followed by efforts to provide local public goods and services in accordance with the comparative advantages of the locality and articulated aspirations of citizens and producers (Swinburn 2006; USAID 2006). Finally, the autonomy of subnational governments may be closely linked, other things being equal, to their ability to raise own-source revenues, which in turn reflects local markets and productive activities. If subnational government own-source revenues are not closely linked to local markets and productive activities, subnational governments may have little direct incentive to enhance local economic growth (Shleifer and Vishny 1998).[16]

To summarize, as is the case with decentralization as a democracy-promotion measure, the evidence linking decentralization and development is highly indeterminate. On the one hand, the literature has documented numerous modest successes in specific short-term interventions to improve citizen welfare and subnational public services. In some cases, local governments after decentralization are more regularly soliciting citizen input in the identification of spending priorities, with associated improvements in individual well-being. On the other hand, decentralization has also transferred responsibilities over critical goods and services to subnational governments that are often poorly prepared to provide them, and that frequently escape the control of all but the wealthiest of local citizens. Clearly, decentralization does not always generate the type of self-sustaining, competitive local governance systems that enhance human welfare.

Decentralization and Security

The study of decentralization as a goal-driven set of changes has focused chiefly on democracy and economic development. During the long years of the Cold War, decentralization was far less relevant to the pursuit of security goals given the predominance of interstate over intrastate security challenges. In most regions of the world, US-Soviet competition had the effect of keeping a lid on territorial conflicts within developing countries. In the two decades since the demise of the Soviet Union, however, the number and severity of intrastate conflicts appears to have increased, and these conflicts in turn have received far greater attention from security experts (Brown 2003; Lake and Rothchild 1996; Snyder 2000). As a result of this underlying shift in the content of salient security threats, decentralization has come into greater focus as a possible conflict prevention or conflict mitigation strategy (Bland 2007a; Brinkerhoff 2007).

As is the case when democracy and development are the overarching goals, security goals can theoretically be advanced by decentralization through a number of causal mechanisms. In conceptualizing these mechanisms, the distinction between devolution and deconcentration as different forms of decentralization is paramount. As it is commonly defined in the literature on decentralization, devolution requires the introduction of subnational elections so that subnational officials do not owe their jobs to national-level actors (Manor 1999). For many groups with grievances against the national government, winning subnational elections may be far less daunting than winning representation in the national government via national elections, particularly where national electoral rules establish thresholds that make it more difficult to gain national-level representation. Groups that can compete successfully in subnational elections and exert influence in subnational offices may consequently be more willing to abide by national electoral results that disfavor them.

While decentralization as devolution requires subnational elections, other forms of decentralization including deconcentration may deserve attention in highly adverse security environments. Defined as the strengthening of the subnational offices of national line ministries, rather than the separate election of subnational governments, deconcentration can extend the presence of the national government throughout the national territory, which in most postconflict cases is a necessary precondition for improved security. In fragile states, deconcentration can be deployed as an important state-building exercise.

Decentralization may have security implications in all developing countries, but it deserves special consideration in those developing countries that are also gripped by internal armed conflict. In these settings, the decentralization option may have special advantages and disadvantages, as Joseph Siegle and Patrick O'Mahony demonstrate in Chapter 6. In recent years, many countries that have emerged or are trying to emerge from periods of internal armed conflict and civil war have turned to decentralization and related forms of institutional engineering in the hope that these changes can help consolidate the peace. Particularly where high levels of centralism played a contributing role in the initiation of conflict between subnational groups, it makes a great deal of sense to consider seriously these reforms—whether they are called decentralization, devolution, federalism, or territorial autonomy. In these cases, the generic pressures and incentives to decentralize that face most countries in the world today are combined with the additional belief that territorial reforms can prevent the reinitiation or continuation of conflict. Decentralization and related reforms have received significant attention in such disparate cases of post-conflict negotiation and constitution writing as Afghanistan, Angola, Bosnia, Colombia, Cyprus, Ethiopia, Iraq, Mozambique, Nigeria, South Africa, Sudan, and Sri Lanka.

Where decentralization is proposed as a possible solution to armed conflict, however, institutional engineers need to proceed with as full an appreciation as possible of the special opportunities and risks that decentralization can pose in these environments. With respect to the former, political, administrative, and fiscal decentralization can all bolster the confidence of former combatants who are worried about the defense and promotion of their interests in the postconflict period. By multiplying the number of elected offices, political decentralization can be an effective response to demobilizing groups who believe they would have a difficult time successfully competing for national offices. In turn, when policies of administrative and fiscal decentralization are successful in shifting real governing authority downward, they can lower the importance and the desirability of holding the highest-level national offices, competition over which may have fueled conflict in the past (Bland, Chapter 3). If significant resources and responsibilities are attached to subnational offices, combatants may respond positively to the offer to lay down their arms and run for local office instead.

According to the research of a number of experts on civil wars, institutional reforms like decentralization that shift power downward have in practice played an important role in bringing armed conflict to an end. For example, one attempt to uncover the conditions that explain the durability of peace in thirty-eight civil war settlements found that the inclusion of territorial autonomy in a postconflict settlement dramatically reduced the likelihood of its failure (Hartzell, Hoddie, and Rothchild 2001, 199). According to these scholars, "by increasing the influence of policymakers at the subnational level while diminishing the powers of policymakers at the center, groups should gain an increased sense that they possess a means of protecting themselves from the exercise of central authority" (2001, 192). Likewise, in her study of forty-one civil wars between 1940 and 1990, Barbara Walter argues that "allowing factions to maintain some regional autonomy offers them an important fallback position if they do lose control of the central government" (1999, 142). In addition to highlighting the advantage of limits placed on central authority, David Lake and Donald Rothchild found that decentralization, regional autonomy, and federalism "provided insurgent militias with an important incentive for responding positively to the government or third-party mediator's proposals for settling the conflict" (1996, 61).[17]

The potential risks associated with decentralization in postconflict settings, however, are also significant. In the worst case scenario, the very reforms that are designed to end the armed conflict can actually facilitate and finance its continuation. In countries that are emerging from especially prolonged periods of armed conflict, we should expect considerable limits on the central state's ability to exercise in practice its formal monopoly over the use of force. In these settings, it is likely to be difficult for central authorities to ensure that subnational groups abide by the terms of the decentralizing agreement. The specific cause for concern is that representatives of these groups can run for subnational offices and appropriate the greater resources that are now under the control of these offices without giving up violence. If the writ of the central state does not reach very far in a particular locality, then decentralized resources can finance the resumption and continuation of armed conflict even if representatives of armed groups do not themselves hold governing positions. In vast stretches of Colombia, for example, the threat and practice of violence enables both guerrilla organizations and paramilitary groups to influence what mayors do with decentralized resources (Eaton 2006b). Decentralization may be strongly ill advised where: (1) security agents who are responsive to the central government do not operate throughout the national territory; (2) national prosecutors, attorneys general, and representatives of the judiciary are not able to monitor the legality of governmental acts by subnational authorities; and (3) subnational officeholders are the targets of threats and acts of violence.

Where the central state in postconflict settings *does* have sufficient strength to enforce the disarmament of combatants, this strength has implications for the design of fiscal and administrative decentralization. On the one hand, the devolution of important tax bases to subnational governments may be a better way of accommodating the anxieties of subnational groups than the reliance on fiscal transfers from a central government they may not fully trust. On the other hand, control over subnational tax bases in many cases has served to incite secessionist struggles (Siegle and O'Mahony, Chapter 6). With respect to administrative decentralization, transferring the authority to set independent education policies—and not just operate schools—may be indicated where the prior conflict had important ethnic, linguistic, and religious components.

If, in contrast, the central state is too weak to prevent the illicit use of decentralized resources, decentralization may worsen rather than end armed conflict.[18] The potential dangers of decentralization in postconflict settings have encouraged reformers to consider the more cautious, sequential approaches that, in less difficult environments, would likely be dismissed as insufficient or superficial.[19] The critique advanced by Jonathan Hiskey in Chapter 2 of "all at once" approaches to decentralization appears to be particularly germane in postconflict settings. For example, with respect to administrative tasks, the urgency of the need to restore public services as part of the so-called peace dividend may increase the appeal of administrative decentralization that takes the form of deconcentration rather than devolution. The line agencies of central government ministries may well have a leg up on local governments in the attempt to restore essential services quickly. Having line agencies take the lead in providing basic governmental services is likely to have a depressing effect on the capacity of local governments, but the need to provide such services in the aftermath of armed conflicts is often critical. On a related note, sequences that privilege political decentralization may undermine the security environment in some settings. According to Dawn Brancati (2006), for example, political decentralization can encourage ethnic conflict and secessionism by promoting the development of regional (as opposed to national) parties.

In response to the uneven presence of the central state, another option facing decisionmakers who would like to use decentralization to enhance security is the asymmetric treatment of subnational governments located in different parts of the national territory. In other words, in addition to considering sequences of decentralization that privilege the administration of services or that postpone the introduction of subnational elections, it may be desirable to sequence decentralization *spatially*. According to this distinction, subnational governments at the same hierarchical level (e.g., the intermediate or local level) do not necessarily receive the same mix of rights and responsibilities from the central government.[20] Instead, under asymmetric approaches, political, administrative, and fiscal authority is transferred to only those jurisdictions in which representatives of the central government are able to monitor and prosecute any illegal use of this authority.[21]

Organization of This Volume

From a number of different angles and disciplinary perspectives, the following chapters of this volume are all engaged with the significant debates over decentralization that we have introduced above. Some of the chapters that follow remain tightly focused on one of the several goals that decentralization has been adopted to achieve. For example, in Chapter 6 Joseph Siegle and Patrick O'Mahony systematically explore the impact of decentralization on security outcomes, and in Chapter 3 Gary Bland emphasizes the impact of decentralization on political democracy via the introduction or strengthening of subnational elections. Other chapters offer arguments about decentralization that apply across each of the three goals that are reviewed above: democracy, development, and security.

For example, in Chapter 2 Jonathan Hiskey applies a principal-agent framework to the study of decentralization in order to gain analytical leverage on the problems that decentralizing policies often confront, whether they are adopted to enhance democracy, development, or security. According to Hiskey's argument, students of decentralization must take seriously the extent to which local political environments vary across the subnational units of a given country. Variation in the local political environment powerfully shapes the likelihood that voters (e.g., the "principals" in his model) will be able to monitor and control subnational elected and appointed officials (e.g., their "agents"). Even where these officials are elected, the heterogeneity of local populations due to such factors as ethnic diversity and income disparities can make it difficult for voters to hold officials accountable. Hiskey's adoption of the principal-agent approach also enables him to make innovative arguments about the impact of decentralization on both democracy and development. With respect to democracy, Hiskey argues that decentralization enhances democracy when it helps principals to hold their agents accountable, which may or may not translate into measurable improvements in the quality of service delivery. With respect to development, Hiskey maintains that decentralization can actually undermine economic development if it limits the insulation and independence that local elected officials need in order to make the types of decisions that would advance developmental goals. Thus, according to Hiskey, efforts to make decentralization work will need to pay much more attention to the possible tension that exists between decentralization's various goals.

In Chapter 3, Gary Bland assesses one of the most striking features of the decentralization trend: the introduction of elections to select subnational officeholders. While decentralization in this political dimension potentially makes elected officials independent from the national government (which no longer appoints them), Bland demonstrates the frequency with which subnational elections are proving to be insufficient. According to Bland's survey of subnational electoral practices in fifteen illustrative countries in Africa, Asia, Eastern Europe, Eurasia, Latin America, and the Middle East, the impact of elections is strongly mediated by each country's party system. Specifically, Bland documents the regularity with which subnational elected officials are kept under the control of national party patrons due to internal party discipline and national control over subnational candidate selection. Bland also reminds us that, in addition to studying the content of rule changes that introduce subnational elections, we need to pay attention to rules that often enable national politicians to dismiss those officials who are elected in ostensibly separate subnational electoral contests (e.g., President's rule in India and federal interventions in Argentina). According to Bland, attempts to make decentralization work will need to look beyond electoral law changes to include a more sophisticated sense of internal party dynamics.

Whereas Bland focuses closely on electoral rules and party systems, Chapter 4 by Derick Brinkerhoff and Omar Azfar shifts to the study of how nonelectoral practices affect the ability of decentralization to meet its various goals. According to the hypothesis posited by Brinkerhoff and Azfar, the impact of decentralization on outcomes like "democracy" and "service delivery" depends critically on "community empowerment" as an intervening variable. As a result of their extensive survey of decentralization programs, the authors find numerous cases in which the transfer of authority downward has opened up new opportunities for empowerment, in the form of both "state-centered" and "society-centered" mechanisms. However, the chapter by Brinkerhoff and Azfar also documents critical problems that stand in the way of community empowerment, including elite capture, the incomplete implementation of decentralization frameworks, and the persistent preference by many citizens for clientelism. Just as significantly, these authors show that communities in civil society have achieved the best results when their efforts have been supported and defended by politicians and party organizations in political society—at both the local and national levels. Making decentralization work, according to Brinkerhoff and Azfar, requires increasingly that we think beyond the civil society—political society divide.

Whereas Bland in Chapter 3 focuses on local elected institutions and Brinkerhoff and Azfar in Chapter 4 focus on local civil society, Chapter 5 offers an analysis that integrates local elected institutions and local civil society into a single conceptual framework. According to Jesse Ribot, Ashwini Chhatre, and Tomila Lankina, a broad array of local institutions and organizations have received additional powers and resources as a result of decentralization. Nowhere is this more critical than in the natural resource activities included in the survey that these authors conduct in their chapter. But in numerous cases, governments, international development agencies, and large nongovernmental organizations (NGOs) have supported forms of decentralization that sideline and circumvent local elected institutions in favor of nonelected actors, including private bodies, customary and religious authorities, and local NGOs. Decisions by donors, the national government, and national NGOs to "recognize" these other local actors means that fledgling local governments often receive few public powers—despite decentralization—and that they increasingly face competition for legitimacy from parallel authorities. According to Ribot, Chhatre, and Lankina, this recognition of parallel authorities can take place through a variety of mechanisms that are common under decentralization, including project-based partnerships, engagement through contracts, and participation in dialogue and decisionmaking. Thus, although decentralization purports to strengthen democracy, in many countries it has channeled public resources into private bodies or autocratic authorities, with the result that the scope for citizen engagement and the quality of the public domain are both substantially diminished. As these authors warn, efforts to make decentralization work must ensure that it does not have the unintended effect of trapping individuals in customary systems they cannot influence.

Turning toward the use of decentralization as a security-enhancing measure, in Chapter 6 Joseph Siegle and Patrick O'Mahony conduct a theoretical and empirical review of the relationship between decentralization and internal conflict. Through the quantitative analysis of ethnic conflicts since 1995, Siegle and O'Mahony cast serious doubts on the merits of decentralization in conflict settings. First, these authors find that factors other than decentralization are more powerful in explaining ethnic conflict outcomes. Second, by disaggregating "decentralization" into different types of changes, they find that these different changes generate different outcomes. For example, they find that higher levels of subnational expenditures and employment are linked to lower levels of ethnic conflict while subnational governments that have significant tax revenue and residual governing authority often strengthen societal divisions and fan secessionist aspirations. According to Siegle and O'Mahony, then, the study of how decentralization can work as a conflict-mitigating strategy needs to proceed on the basis of a more finely grained understanding of decentralization as a phenomenon that involves many different types of component changes.

As the chapters that constitute the core of this volume remind us, decentralization has been adopted in a range of diverse contexts and toward a variety of distinct goals. This variation underscores the importance—but also the myriad challenges—of developing universal indicators that can be used to evaluate decentralization around the world, which is a task that Kent Eaton and Larry Schroeder take up in Chapter 7. According to Eaton and Schroeder, scholars working from a number of separate disciplinary bases have generated useful indicators of decentralization in its three main dimensions: political, fiscal, and administrative. This chapter brings together in a single place those indicators that have been most consistently emphasized by political scientists, economists, and public administration experts. But it also questions the disciplinary approaches that have dominated the development of indicators in recent years and that make it difficult to determine how decentralization functions across its different dimensions. Eaton and Schroeder conclude that figuring out whether decentralization is working as a means toward democracy, development, or security will require the more integrated use of political, fiscal, and administrative indicators.

In Chapter 8, Paul Smoke concludes the volume by bringing into the discussion a topic that has been neglected in the literature on decentralization, despite its importance: implementation. According to Smoke, scholars in this literature have focused in detail on questions of design, debating the relative merits of different designs for decentralization processes without sufficiently exploring the many obstacles that arise in the implementation phase. From the perspective of both national and local governments, he surveys the most significant challenges that threaten successful implementation, including the need to build rapidly the capacity of subnational governments that have suddenly taken on new roles, and the difficulties of coordination not only among central government agencies, but also among external donor. Drawing on evidence from Cambodia, Indonesia, Kenya, and Uganda, Smoke argues for the importance of adopting a flexible and pragmatic approach to the implementation of decentralization. In the end, making decentralization work will require a much more strategic view of implementation, whether democracy, development, or security is the overarching goal that motivated the initial decision to decentralize.

Notes

The opinions expressed in this chapter are solely those of the authors and do not necessarily reflect those of the US Agency for International Development or the US government.

For helpful comments on this chapter, we are grateful to Paul Smoke and two anonymous reviewers.

1. For two cross-regional edited volumes that survey these changes, see Oxhorn, Tulchin, and Selee (2004); and Smoke, Gomez, and Peterson (2006).

2. In addition to questioning support for decentralization where it reinforces subnational authoritarian enclaves within nationally democratic regimes, it is important to note more generally that the relationship between national regime type and decentralization can be quite complex. For example, national governments in China in the 1980s and 1990s and in Latin America in the 1960s and 1970s adopted changes that had important decentralizing effects despite the authoritarian character of these governments (Montinola, Qian, and Weingast 1995; Eaton 2006a). On regime type and decentralization, see Montero and Samuels (2004).

3. See Smoke (2003, 11) for the rival argument that local elite capture must not be used to validate continued centralization.

4. For the Ugandan case, see Reinikka and Svensson (2004).

5. Latin America is a case in point, where traditional political patrons in less developed regions have used clientelism to reinforce their undemocratic control over marginalized groups—in contrast to the more competitive political environments that have emerged in the more economically developed regions centered around national capitals. See O'Donnell, Cullell, and Iazzetta (2004); and Gibson (2005).

6. For an argument in favor of asymmetric decentralization, see Rowland (2001).

7. We are grateful to Paul Smoke for his help drafting this section.

8. See Harrison (2006), especially chapter 1, for a detailed exploration of the effects of interjurisdictional competition among Canadian provinces.

9. The fact that substantial capacity-building efforts are required suggests that the circumstances of developing countries may frequently and substantially diverge from the assumptions incorporated into Tiebout's hypothesis.

10. Kasper (1995) describes "competitive federalism" and its presumed results in terms similar to market-preserving federalism.

11. This account of the essentials of market-preserving federalism is based on Weingast (2006).

12. See Inman (2008) for a quantitative study of seventy-three developed and developing countries that validates and refines previous assertions concerning the superior economic and political performance of appropriately structured federal systems.

13. See, for example, the excellent symposium in *Virginia Law Review* 83 (7) (1997).

14. For alternate views that challenge the MPF explanation for China's transition toward markets, see Wedeman (2003) and Thun (2004).

15. More fundamentally, Montero's (2002) work on subnational industrial policy in Brazil questions the emphasis that MPF places on markets by showing how some subnational states (e.g., Minas Gerais) intervened in the private sector in ways that enhanced long-term prospects for development.

16. Shleifer and Vishny (1998) argue that Polish local governments have been much more successful than Russian local governments following the breakup of the Soviet Union because Polish local governments believed (correctly) that success in local economic development would result in significant increases in local government revenues, whereas Russian local governments believed (correctly) that local effort would not be rewarded by central authorities.

17. See P. Collier et al. for the argument that "federal systems combined with two-chamber parliaments" can help protect minorities in postconflict settings (2003, 124).

18. Decentralization in these settings is especially dangerous because it can be difficult to take back resources and responsibilities once they have been transferred.

19. For example, de Silva argues that in the regions of Sri Lanka that have been most affected by the armed conflict, "innovative local government institutions" are more promising than the adoption of more radical and potentially destabilizing reforms (2000, 203).

20. In the Philippines, for example, subnational governments in the Autonomous Region of Muslim Mindanao received additional powers and

resources as part of an attempted political settlement to the armed conflict in that region (Gutierrez et al. 2000).

21. In Colombia, President Alvaro Uribe has introduced a form of asymmetry by replacing democratically elected mayors with military officials in those select municipalities where the central government has been unable to prevent the violent appropriation of decentralized funds.

2

The Promise of Decentralized Democratic Governance

Jonathan T. Hiskey

> We are all witnesses to how tragic can be the consequences of centralization as the means for maximizing values chosen by one or a few powerful men. But it does not follow that the opposite value, decentralization, is an absolute good.
>
> —James W. Fesler 1965, 538–539

> Decentralization is rapidly replacing God, Country and Motherhood in popular favor.
>
> —Norman Furniss 1974, 958

As has been the case in previous periods of decentralization reform, the most recent widespread adoption of decentralization strategies across the developing world holds much promise, but also the potential to fall victim to excessive expectations. In this chapter, I examine one critical dimension of this strategy: the altered relationships, responsibilities, and expectations of citizenries and their local government officials that accompany what have come to be known as democratic decentralization reforms (Blair 2000; Dauda 2006; Johnson 2001). Through the lens of agency theory, I highlight potentially difficult trade-offs in achieving the goals of decentralization that may lie embedded in the new principal-agent relationships between citizens and elected officials that such reforms create. I then examine certain community-level socioeconomic and political characteristics that may influence how these trade-offs manifest themselves differently within a single country. Though myriad other actors and factors affect, and are affected by, decentralization reforms, I confine my focus to those arguably most directly involved in efforts to "bring government closer to the people"—citizens and their newly empowered local agents.

Democratic Decentralization and the Dual Transition

Across the developing world, countries continue their struggle to move beyond the seemingly interminable stage of political and economic transition toward a stable, effective democratic political system and an economy resistant to the recurring crises that have plagued so many for so long. This era of political and economic reform, often referred to as the developing world's "dual transition," is now entering its third decade and has become for many a period marred by unfulfilled promises and expectations. Growing dissatisfaction with market reforms gone awry has revealed itself in the numerous electoral victories over the past several years of candidates opposed to the wholesale adoption of neoliberal reforms. Similar disappointment with the political side of the developing world's dual transition is also evident as more and more citizens in emerging democracies are beginning to question the merits of democracy, at least as it has manifested itself in their country.

Into this world of dual dissatisfaction, decentralization reforms have entered, seen by many as a solution to both sources of citizen discontent.[1] Proponents view decentralization as a remedy for the poor performance of overly centralized governments in such areas as basic service delivery and local economic development. Additionally, by bringing government closer to the people and empowering citizens with oversight and occasionally policymaking capacities, decentralization will serve to deepen citizens' commitment to democracy and play a critical role in the inculcation of the democratic values and behaviors.

Perhaps as a consequence of the severity of the many political and governance problems that have plagued a majority of developing countries for decades, the current wave of decentralization reforms suffers somewhat from the same unrealistic expectations and conflation of goals highlighted by Furniss (1974) and Fesler (1965) over thirty years ago. As Pranab Bardhan notes, "decentralization has undoubted merits and strengths. However, the idea of decentralization may need some protection against its own enthusiasts" (2002, 187). One possible by-product of the oftentimes overly optimistic expectations associated with decentralization reforms may be a growing dissatisfaction among citizens with the strategy as it almost inevitably fails to fulfill its many promises.

Indeed, though much of the development community continues to push with great enthusiasm for greater decentralization, citizens in at least some developing countries appear somewhat skeptical of the strategy in recent years. Results from the 2006 AmericasBarometer reveal these doubts about the decentralization strategy.[2] In response to an item asking respondents whether they think their local government or the central government should be given more responsibilities and money, close to half (48.5 percent) preferred giving more power to their national government while only 37 percent wanted their local government to have more development responsibilities. Not surprisingly, less than a third of these respondents considered the services delivered by their local government to be "good" (25.7 percent) or "very good" (3.3 percent). In the 2008 round of the AmericasBarometer survey, these figures improve slightly, with only 42 percent of respondents supporting a shift in power toward their central government. Clearly, we must interpret these data with caution, as they offer only a fairly simple snapshot of public views toward decentralization and do not reveal what citizen's views were ten or twenty years ago on these issues. If citizen support for decentralization matters, however, then the fact that there appears to be such tepid support for empowering local government suggests that the strategy may be approaching a crossroads in many countries.[3]

Even more disconcerting for decentralization proponents are growing indications that the very problems the strategy theoretically purports to attack, such as corruption and inferior levels of local-level governance, seem to remain central obstacles across much of the developing world. The World Bank's Governance Matters Project reports, for example, that Bolivia's governance scores have been on relatively steady decline from 1996 to 2007, a period of time during which the country implemented a wide range of decentralization reforms (World Bank 2008b). From the same AmericasBarometer survey cited above, we see that in 2006 more than 15 percent of Latin American respondents reported being victimized by a corrupt government official within the previous twelve months. Country-level victimization rates are even more striking, with 37 percent of respondents in Mexico experiencing at least one incident of corruption, 30 percent in Peru, and an overwhelming 50 percent in Haiti. Even in Chile, the country with the lowest percentage of corruption victimization reports, one in every ten respondents reported being a victim of local corruption.[4] These troubling levels of corruption victimization are leading many to declare corruption as "one of the most significant threats to deepening democratization in Latin America (and indeed much of the democratizing Third World)" (Seligson 2006, 381). The fact that the forms of corruption uncovered by the AmericasBarometer project tend to be local in nature is particularly problematic given the emphasis of decentralization on improved governance at the local level. In his assessment of 2004 corruption trends in Latin

America, Mitchell A. Seligson found that "corruption victimization among those who carried out some transaction with local municipal governments (for example, asking for a permit) was commonplace" (2005, 283). Findings such as these lend support to John Gerring and Strom Thacker's (2004) argument that link decentralized political systems to higher levels of corruption. More to the point of this chapter, however, are the troubling trends in governance across countries that have pursued decentralization strategies of one form or another in recent years. Such patterns at a minimum should raise important questions about our current frameworks for understanding, designing, and evaluating decentralization reforms. Though a systematic empirical analysis of the impact decentralization reforms have had on levels of local governance or citizen satisfaction with local government is far beyond the scope of this chapter, I do seek to highlight certain implications that decentralization reforms hold for citizens as principals and local elected officials as agents, and how local context may affect the outcomes of these relationships. In the process, it becomes clear that in some cases, and certain socioeconomic and political contexts, there is at least the potential for the goals of citizen participation and improved governance to be at odds with one another.

A focus on the import of principal-agent relationships at the local level is by no means novel. Indeed, Elinor Ostrom offers a series of seminal theoretical and empirical treatments of the issues surrounding the establishment of successful common pool resource (CPR) institutions across a wide range of communities as well as extensive work on how these principles apply more generally to decentralization reforms (e.g., 1990, 2005). Though consistent with Ostrom's concerns for how institutions shape individuals' "opportunities and constraints . . . the information they obtain, the benefits they obtain or are excluded from and how they reason about the situation" (2005, 3), my purpose here is employ a principal-agent perspective to cast certain features of decentralization in a different light, emphasizing the importance of local context in the process. What this perspective calls attention to are the tensions that can arise between the democracy and governance goals of the strategy. These tensions notwithstanding, this chapter also shares Ostrom's position that "a political system that has multiple centers of power at differing scales provides more opportunity for citizens and their officials to innovate and to intervene so as to correct maldistribution of authority and outcomes" (2000, 42). Recognizing the merits of "polycentrism," I offer a means with which to identify and perhaps mitigate some potentially necessary trade-offs between the dual goals of democracy and improved governance that often come attached to decentralization reforms.

Beyond Ostrom's work, many have highlighted the utility of agency theory in studies of the relationships between voters and politicians (Keech

1995), and legislators and bureaucrats (e.g., Luppia and McCubbins 1998). Despite the widespread use of this approach in the study of various issue areas, such a perspective does not often inform work on the altered nature of relationships between citizens and their local officials that occurs with decentralization. Indeed, much of decentralization concerns changing one or more of a society's principal-agent relationships dealing with the task of governance. Whether in the form of enhancing citizens' powers to select their agents (e.g., introduction of elections for local officials) or granting local officials more policymaking autonomy from the central government, a basic component of this strategy is to restructure the network of principal-agent relationships that exist between citizen and state. The goals of such reforms are twofold—to improve government's performance and to give citizens a greater stake in their political systems—and, as a consequence, to produce a stronger, more vibrant democracy. The value of analyzing decentralization reforms with the tools of agency theory, then, comes from the explicit attention such an approach places on the duties and responsibilities that a decentralization reform implies for citizens and local officials, the wide variance in the capacity of those actors to fulfill their new responsibilities, and the trade-offs that such changes in these principal-agent relationships may bring with them.

The chapter proceeds as follows. Following a brief discussion of how decentralization may be understood in principal-agent terms, I turn to an examination of several elements of agency theory that seem essential in identifying the potential trade-offs and tensions inherent in decentralization's efforts to enhance democracy and governance outcomes. Following this section, I then apply the basic elements of agency theory to an analysis of how various local socioeconomic and political contexts may affect the outcome of decentralization reforms. I conclude with a discussion of the implications these insights may hold for the design and implementation of future decentralization reforms around the country.

Decentralizing Principals and Agents

Though decentralization reforms come in many shapes and sizes, my focus here is on those reforms that enhance the oversight role of citizens and the development responsibilities of local government—reforms, then, that are motivated by the principle of downward accountability. Often referred to as "democratic decentralization" (Blair 2000; Smoke 2001; Dauda 2006), such reforms include the implementation of elections for local officials, the establishment of citizen oversight councils, and greater local government involvement in such basic service areas as water, sanitation, and electricity.

Common to all of these reforms is an alteration of local principal-agent relationships, where principals theoretically gain more leverage over those agents most directly responsible for such critical areas as basic service provision. Using this defining characteristic as a point of departure, I argue that these reforms are usefully understood through the lens of agency theory. That is because inherent in such a shift in the direction and degree of accountability that local agents have to citizen principals is a change in the responsibilities that both have in carrying out the duties such reforms assign to them. Perhaps by understanding the nature of these new responsibilities, and the varying capacities and willingness of the relevant actors to carry them out, we can better identify points of local stress in the decentralization agenda.

Decentralization and Agency Loss

The core issue of any principal-agent relationship concerns "agency loss," defined by Arthur Lupia (2001) as "the difference between the consequences of delegation for the principal and the best possible consequence. Agency loss is zero when the agent takes actions that are entirely consistent with the principal's interests. As the agent's actions diverge from the principal's interests, agency loss increases" (3376). Lupia then describes the foundational propositions concerning variation in these losses across principal-agent relationships as "agency loss is minimized when two statements are true. The first statement is that the principal and agent *share common interests*. . . . The second statement is that the *principal is knowledgeable* about the consequences of the agent's activities" (3376). In essence, these two conditions identify the motive and opportunity (to use Lupia's terms) for agency loss to occur. A core assumption underlying democratic decentralization reforms is that they can address both of these areas in an effort to minimize agency loss. It thus is worthwhile to examine how such reforms might affect the matching of interests between citizens as principals and local officials as agents, and the degree of knowledge the former gain about the activities of the latter in order to better frame subsequent discussions of conditions conducive to successful decentralization outcomes.

Agent Selection

Given the centrality of elections in the principal-agent relationships of most concern for this chapter, certain widely recognized conditions should ideally hold in order to most effectively minimize agency loss with respect to the quality of local governance. To the extent that these conditions do not hold, the expected changes in governance quality may be less likely to occur. One such condition is a level playing field for all candidates to local office. Additionally, a candidate selection process that draws candidates from the community itself, rather than from a national or state party's pool of candidates, becomes essential. Similarly, a campaign process and media capable of informing the public about candidate preferences (e.g., through radio or public fora in communities with low rates of literacy) become critical to lessening the possible agency loss that stems from the agent selection process. Central to these ideas is a focus on increasing the level of information available to citizens regarding the degree to which the competing candidates or agents for local office share their interests.

A related concern is the fact that communities rarely have a single interest with respect to a certain policy. This "multiple principals" problem is particularly troublesome in highly unequal communities, a feature common to many developing countries. Local elections oftentimes produce abysmally low voter turnout, and therefore may further distort the effectiveness of the elections as a mechanism for aggregating community preferences. The reliability of elections as an indicator of community interests tends to be even more problematic in poor, rural communities where, as Craig Johnson (2001) and others have pointed out, "agrarian institutions may be structured in a way that prevents poor people from participating" in politics and "the costs of political action . . . may deter them from pursuing or sustaining coherent political movements" (525). Finally, as many have argued, elections, even in the best of conditions, most often serve the role of either rewarding or punishing the incumbent's performance rather than sending any clear prospective message that carries meaningful policy content (e.g., Key 1966). Several decentralization scholars also have recognized the many ways in which local elections may not match the theoretical expectations underlying the decentralization strategy (Blair 2000; Dauda 2006). In viewing elections as a method designed to achieve maximum interest compatibility between principal and agent, it becomes readily apparent how far short they fall of this ideal in the best of circumstances, and what particular contextual features of a community may influence how and why they fall short.

Agent Oversight

I now turn to an examination of some of the issues involved with the second determinant of agency loss: opportunity. The opportunity for an agent to work against the interests of the principal relates most directly to the level of oversight the principal is able to exert over the agent. At one end of an oversight continuum would be a principal with full information regarding the agent's tasks and one who is able to monitor all of the agent's activities. This situation should produce near complete agent compliance with the principal's demands. But what is the downside? The principal must once again expend tremendous costs in information-gathering and monitoring efforts to ensure full agent compliance. At the other extreme is a situation where the principal has no information concerning agent performance and spends no time or energy monitoring the agent, creating tremendous opportunity for agency loss to occur.

These theoretical extremes suggest the dilemma faced by the principal; namely, the trade-offs inherent in the choice of how to minimize agency loss. How much, and in what ways, should the principal expend resources in order to bring agency loss to an acceptable level? This dilemma is made worse by the informational asymmetries inherent in most principal-agent relationships. The tendency for agents to have far greater expertise than principals with respect to the agent's task(s) makes control of the agent by the principal all the more costly. Once again, these costs are in large part a function of the availability and accessibility of information, and it is in this area that decentralization efforts can make an impact. The burden of information costs for principals may lead many citizens, particularly those with limited information-gathering skills, to withdraw from local government, allowing rent seekers to corrupt the decentralization process.

From these two features of the principal-agent dynamic—information and monitoring costs—other trade-offs also emerge with respect to the behavior of the agent. The first concerns how agents behave under different oversight conditions. An oft-cited example of this is the impact that varying term lengths have on the behavior of politicians, with those elected to longer terms in office, and thus more insulated from voters, often displaying a far more moderate, pragmatic approach to policymaking than their colleagues with shorter terms in office who seem always to have the next election in mind. William R. Keech maintains that longer terms allow for "slack between principal and agent [that] can be used constructively as well as perversely," highlighting the potential problems and tensions that certain decentralization reforms can bring to local principal-agent relationships (1995, 149). Craig Johnson concurs, citing evidence from across the developing world that suggests an "underlying tension between the autonomy that governments require to plan and implement coherent policy and the participatory spirit of representative democracy" (2001, 524). To the extent that decentralization reforms tend to emphasize citizen oversight at the expense of agent independence, they may induce more short-sighted, electorally driven behavior on the part of agents interested in the next election campaign. Though such an outcome is by no means certain, and local elections and other forms of citizen oversight may have such positive effects as strengthening citizens' attachment to the political system, it is by no means a given that bringing government closer to the people will be beneficial for both democracy and government performance.

The Goals of Decentralization

Decentralization proponents generally see improved government performance as a central goal of decentralization reforms. Regardless of whether the actual reform in question concerns political, administrative, or fiscal powers, at least one of the underlying objectives of these reforms tends to be related to an "improvement in governance," a term that includes such performance-related indicators as basic service delivery, transparency, and levels of government corruption. The theoretical underpinning for this expectation of improved governance relates directly to the above discussion of principal-agent dynamics, where agency loss is reduced when interest compatibility and monitoring capability increase. The oft-cited phrase "bring government closer to the people" essentially implies an enhancement of interest compatibility between principal and agent and the ability of principals to monitor agents through greater flows of information between agent and principals (e.g., Azfar 2006; USAID 2000).

A second typical goal of decentralization involves the strengthening of the country's democracy through the creation of more transparent local political institutions and the inculcation of stronger citizen support for and participation in democratic procedures of government. Proponents view the devolution of powers to local governments and the creation of mechanisms that allow for greater citizen participation in local affairs as holding "great potential to stimulate the growth of civil society organizations . . . ; prevent widespread disillusionment with new policies from turning into a rejection of the entire democratic process . . . ; [and] boost legitimacy by making government more responsive to citizen needs" (Diamond 1999, 124–125). These posited benefits of decentralization rest on the proposition that a citizen's experience with local government is a critical determinant of his or her views of the larger political system (Vetter 2002).

A wealth of empirical research does in fact suggest that the local government, and one's experiences with local officials, has a significant impact on more general views of the political system. Jonathan T. Hiskey and Mitchell A. Seligson (2003) found a significant connection between citizens' experiences with decentralization and their more general level of system support in the case of Bolivia. Unfortunately for proponents of decentralization, in this case, flaws in the institutional design of that country's

Popular Participation Law had a negative impact on citizen support for the political system, even after controlling for the sizable effect that citizens' evaluations of their local government services had on these more general, system-level attitudes. The fact that Bolivians responded as much to the process of governance (in this case, the widespread removal of popularly elected mayors through questionable procedures) as they did to governance outcomes (such as service delivery) is indicative of the need to design and evaluate decentralization reforms with both process and outcome criteria in mind, rather than conflating the two. For as I discuss below, and as was the case with some municipalities in Bolivia, improvements in democracy and governance may not occur simultaneously under decentralization programs.

Effective service delivery will almost certainly make citizens more satisfied with those government institutions and officials responsible for the service in question. If improvements in service delivery or other areas of governance occur following a set of decentralization reforms, such success likely will also engender broader support for decentralization. Such specific forms of support, based on "the satisfactions that members of a system feel they obtain from the perceived outputs and performance of the political authorities" (Easton 1975, 437), are vulnerable to short-term fluctuations. Improved service delivery, and local governance more generally, is without question a desirable outcome of decentralization and such improvements, if sustained for a long enough period of time, will undoubtedly strengthen citizen support for the system that produced those improvements. What is unclear, however, is whether decentralization reforms can engender any forms of support for democracy that do not rely so heavily on development outcomes, but rather on the democratic process of enhanced citizen involvement as principals in the political process.

Rather than associating democracy so closely with the improved provision of services, decentralization reforms and their advocates might emphasize more strongly the procedural benefits of decentralization that allow for citizens to better identify and address agent failure by making this as a centerpiece of decentralization, even in the context of less than optimal government outcomes. In such a scenario, citizen dissatisfaction with government performance might be directed more at the failings of the agent, rather than at democracy and the decentralization strategy itself. That is, from this view, one somewhat paradoxical but no less important, measure of decentralization's success is the enhanced ability of principals to identify the failings of their agents. What the principal-agent perspective therefore provides is a way to begin understanding the basis on which the distinction can be made between the performance of decentralization institutions and the performance of the agents and principals that occupy those institutions. Indeed, the most immediate "benefit" that may come from a decentralization reform is not improved service, but rather the ability of citizens to exercise their newly established power as principals who can directly hold accountable those local agents responsible for problems in service delivery. While this heightened accountability may or may not eventually lead to improved service, the ability to "throw the bums out" can have positive effects on levels of citizen support for democracy and the decentralization reforms that helped them more effectively identify who the bums were.

Decentralization's goals of increasing citizen involvement in politics as principals and improving local governance face a dilemma, then, brought about by the fundamental tension between levels of principal oversight and levels of agent independence. In some cases, a decentralization reform that seeks to strengthen the oversight capacity of citizens may in fact make achieving the development goals of the reform more difficult. For certain areas of local government responsibilities, it may be necessary to insulate agents from their local principals in order to achieve specific policy outcomes. Gary J. Miller's (2005) analysis of US base closures during the 1980s and 1990s offers a clear example of this tension between enhanced principal oversight capacities and effective agent performance. Base closures were at once critical for US budgetary and strategic needs and disastrous for the electoral chances of individual members of Congress representing districts in which the closings occurred. In such a situation, the various members of Congress collectively were unable to carry out this essential task and thus created an autonomous "base closing commission" to perform the task, essentially protecting the members of Congress from themselves (2005, 222). In doing so, Congress created an agent that was not "demonstrably responsive to the incentives created by Congress. . . . but rather by creating a kind of perverse agent who was designed to be insulated from Congress and to deny the particular reelection demands of its members" (2005, 223). Though far removed from the local principal-agent relations between citizens and officials created by decentralization reforms, this example highlights the potential tensions between extensive principal oversight and agent effectiveness in certain policy areas.

From a more general perspective, this raises the classic delegate-trustee distinction between the roles political representatives serve, and whether decentralization reforms favor one type of representation over the other. A trustee model of representation essentially sees a representative democracy as one where the people elect representatives and, once elected, those representatives are expected to do what they think is best for their constituents. As Edmund Burke famously notes, "if we do not permit our members to act upon a very enlarged view of things, we shall at length infallibly degrade our national representation into a confused and scuffling bustle of local agency" (1774). A delegate model, on the other hand, sees elected representatives as individuals who do only what their constituents tell them to do.

Though both perspectives have advantages and disadvantages, decentralization reforms that emphasize high levels of citizen oversight and involvement in their agents' activities tend to create incentives for local agents to act almost exclusively as delegates, rather than achieving a balance between the two types of representation. In her seminal work on this issue, Hanna Pitkin (1967) establishes that a successful resolution of this representation dilemma in fact rests on a set of institutions that allow elected officials to perform both as trustees and delegates over the balance of their terms in office.

If decentralization reforms do indeed tip the balance toward a more delegate form of representation, this puts the onus on citizens to clearly and effectively identify their policy priorities and communicate those to their elected agents. And though this is certainly possible in some policy sectors, in other sectors, citizens may be unwilling or unable to identify their long-term policy interests. When combined with the multiple principals problem, we have a situation where agents begin to act as delegates for a very limited number of principals that may not represent the majority of citizens. Thus, in emphasizing participatory mechanisms of interest articulation and oversight at the expense of more indirect oversight mechanisms that allow for some measure of agent autonomy from their principals, some decentralization reforms may undermine efforts to pursue more beneficial long-term development strategies.

The benefit, of course, is that by increasing citizen participation in local government, and agent responsiveness to those citizens, individuals are introduced to the process of democracy and begin to learn the art of compromise that a democracy requires—a lesson that, at once, can strengthen citizen support for democracy and demonstrate how difficult democratic policymaking can be. As Jean-Jacques Rousseau, John Stuart Mill, and many others have argued, these lessons may be critical in instilling a democratic civic culture that is less vulnerable to the inevitable ups and downs of government performance (see, e.g., Pateman 1970). Carol L. Dauda (2006) offers a highly nuanced account of how these ideas manifested themselves in the context of decentralization reforms carried out in Uganda and South Africa. As discussed in the preceding section, support for democracy emerges from an appreciation of the process as the best possible, though perhaps not most efficient, means of arriving at a development policy that allows all citizens a role in establishing the collective interests of the community and monitoring the agents contracted by the community to perform the duties of government.

Decentralization reforms, then, might offer a mix of designs that encourage not only participatory forms of democracy, but representative forms as well, where agents are insulated from the short-term pressures of principals. Such reforms might include lengthier terms of office for some elected officials, the promotion of a merit-based, autonomous civil service at the local level, and the creation of institutional checks and balances within local government itself, rather than relying exclusively on citizen participation as a check on local officials. As Gary Bland discusses in Chapter 3, these checks may include such features as the division of powers between town council and mayor, the creation of autonomous technical oversight committees, and information disclosure and reporting requirements for local officials that enhance interinstitutional accountability as well as to the general public. Through the intentional mixing of institutional incentives, a balancing of the trade-offs of decentralization can be achieved and progress can be made toward realizing both development and democracy returns.

Decentralization, Local Democracy, and Development

Relying on the basic insights from agency theory, it becomes clear what types of local environments will help, and what types will hinder, attainment of the goals of decentralization. In a vibrant local democracy that is making progress in economic and human capital development, decentralization reforms that emphasize citizen involvement will find a far more receptive populace than one living under the thumb of a local political boss. In a democratic setting, *ceterus peribus*, principals will be more willing, if not more able, to fulfill the roles assigned to them by the decentralization strategy. This engaged set of principals, however, may dictate a mix of decentralization policies that lean toward greater autonomy for local agents. Given greater elite competition in a more democratic political environment, relatively greater autonomy for agents may be less subject to abuse, or agency loss, than it would in a nondemocratic setting. In the latter environment, where citizens lack a history of democratic experience, an initial emphasis on citizen empowerment as principals may be more productive, even with the risk that such high levels of principal involvement might induce more short-sighted agent behavior.

Political Factors

Citizens living in an authoritarian or pseudodemocratic local political regime, however, may be less willing or able to carry out the tasks that decentralization reforms assign to them (Hiskey 2003). A well-developed local clientelist system may even lead citizens to view themselves as the agents of a local political boss and, thus, tacitly participate in the perversion of decentralization reforms into tools that allow for the continuation of the boss's undemocratic regime. The fact that these types of political environments overlap more often than not with poor, rural sectors of a country makes all the more likely the possibility that decentralization may have a series of unintended negative outcomes if implemented equally across a country with little regard for subnational variations in political environments.

Jonathan Fox and Josefina Aranda, in their study of Mexico's demand-based National Solidarity Program (PRONASOL) in the state of Oaxaca, concluded that project outcome was highly contingent on whether "local governments are already democratic and responsive to their citizens. Where these prior conditions do not hold, however, decentralization could actually reinforce authoritarian rule at the local level" (1996, 2). From a general perspective, local political strongmen who rule with impunity will be more likely to use their positions of power for personal gain than those who must answer to the electorate. This commonly cited problem of elite capture will also lead to an environment where corruption and abuse of power prevail and the rule of law is weak. As Michael Coppedge points out in his description of political bosses, "a cacique [political boss] necessarily was, or became, not just the most powerful figure in the community, but also the wealthiest. Indeed, it is hard to escape the impression that this was the whole point of being a cacique in the first place" (1993, 264). Mitchell A. Seligson and John A. Booth identified nearly three decades ago a similar pattern in Central America, where levels of citizen participation were significantly lower in one-party towns, because "local 'power elite' domination of municipal government strongly discourages the participation of the public" (1979, 104). In this context, then, efforts to transfer to local agents more fiscal or administrative powers likely would not produce the expected benefits of decentralization because citizens would be largely disengaged from their local political system to begin with, allowing the newly empowered agents to diverge farther from the interests of principals.

Similarly, Jonathan T. Hiskey and Shaun Bowler found that citizens in Mexico who lived in one-party dominant towns during the country's democratic transition of the 1990s were almost three times as likely to view elections as fraudulent when compared to the views of citizens living in competitive electoral environments during that period (2005, 67). The authors then establish a link between one's views of the electoral system and "a citizen's willingness to engage in democratic politics" (2005, 67). From these findings emerge a clear connection between the local political environment and the degree to which citizens will be receptive to becoming more active principals in the local political process. If such reforms occur in an "authoritarian enclave" (Fox 1994, 182), they should be accompanied by explicit efforts aimed at disrupting the malaise of citizen disengagement common to undemocratic towns.[5] While the prospect of assessing a target community's local "political regime" may be a highly sensitive one for reform proponents, the consequences of not carrying out such an assessment and empowering local authoritarian "agents" may severely undermine the development and democracy goals of decentralization.

Further benefits of a democratic local political environment for attainment of decentralization's goals include the enhancement of the accountability mechanisms embedded in competitive local elections. In a study of demand-based poverty alleviation efforts in India, John Echeverri-Ghent concludes that "political competition is essential to the effective diminution" of patronage and corruption, leading to a more positive outcome of community-based antipoverty projects (1992, 1414). These results, again, can be traced to the network of principal-agent relationships that exist before decentralization reforms arrive.

A democratic local environment also allows for more effective "preference matching" (Azfar 2006) and increases the likelihood of respect for the rule of law by local officials and citizens alike (Beer and Mitchell 2004). Widespread acceptance of electoral results also decreases the chances for postelectoral instability, thus offering a relatively effective, peaceful mechanism for citizens to express their approval or discontent with their agents. Such "conflict management" institutions have been shown to be critical factors in an assortment of economic development processes (Rodrik 1999). Instability and societal conflict, for example, increase the risks associated with investment, thus diminishing the flow of capital into areas with conflict-inducing political institutions (Comeau 2003). Where citizens have a means of control over elected officials through the presence of viable electoral alternatives, the increased level of uncertainty among local political elites should enhance the responsiveness of these elites to the concerns of the citizenry. As Kaare Strom put it, "innovation and anticipation are born of competition and reflect efforts to escape a situation where failure is so perilously close. . . . These dynamics may in the long run be the greatest benefit of political competition" (1992, 391).[6] In sum, there is quite a bit of theoretical and empirical evidence in support of the notion that outcomes of decentralization reforms are at least partly a product of the existing political environment into which they enter.

In contrast to these positive theoretical and empirical assessments of the relationship between local-level political environments and decentralization outcomes, Merilee Grindle is far less sanguine about the benefits of local democracy for decentralization, suggesting that a democratic local environment may in fact make the governance goals of decentralization reforms more difficult to achieve. She found in a study of decentralization reforms in thirty municipalities across Mexico that "democratization of elections does not necessarily lead to less conflictive politics, easier decision making, or better functioning governments" (2007, 83). These findings serve as an important reminder that, even under the best of political conditions, decentralization faces tremendous challenges in achieving governance goals such as improved service delivery, making all the more important the need to separate these goals from those that seek to deepen democracy through decentralization. And given the tremendous variation in subnational political environments throughout the developing world, understanding the relationship between these local environments and decentralization reforms is increasingly important as more and more countries continue implementation of the decentralization strategy (e.g., Gibson 2005).

Socioeconomic Factors

Other potentially important preconditions that may affect the outcomes of decentralization reforms include economic and social inequalities, both within and across communities targeted for reform. In a revealing and insightful World Bank "Project Appraisal Document" related to a Bank loan to the government of Mexico, the author offers an assessment of problems evident in previous decentralization efforts funded by the Bank: "Most of the reform process in the sector and subsequent policies and programs have, at least initially, been carried out nationally and homogeneously, without much consideration for the extreme regional diversity and income disparity characterizing the rural sector" (2002, 3). These socioeconomic divides and their consequences can also be identified and better understood through a principal-agent perspective. Given that a community represents multiple principals, all of whom theoretically should have an equal voice in the selection and monitoring of the community's agents, extant economic and social inequalities within a community may dramatically affect the ability of all principals to gain equal access to the information-gathering and agent-monitoring mechanisms created by decentralization. This may in turn produce agents whose interests match the interests of only a select few of the community's principals.

Another consequence of preexisting inequalities within a community concerns the varying capacities of principals to communicate with agents and perform their oversight duties. If a decentralization reform creates citizen councils charged with the monitoring of agent activities, then such a reform should also seek to ensure that intracommunity variations in the human capital skills required to perform such duties do not produce a council wholly unrepresentative of community interests. Related to this issue are variations in the capacities of local officials charged with the implementation of development policies. As Bardhan notes, this problem "is especially severe in many developing countries, where the quality of staff in local bureaucracies—including basic tasks like accounting and record keeping—is very low. Even their more professional and technical people suffer from the disadvantages of isolation, poor training and low interaction with other professionals" (2002, 189).[7] Such gaps in technical capacities within and between communities may make subregional development gaps worse after decentralization reforms unless these issues are recognized and addressed. The first step, then, is to assess the socioeconomic characteristics of the community prior to implementation of the reform.

A glance at data drawn from a survey of most of Mexico's municipal presidents in 2002 reveals how glaring the need is for such capacity-building efforts. Recognizing that Mexico is among the most advanced developing countries makes all the more surprising the finding that over half of the mayors surveyed had no more than a high school education, and only 4 percent of the municipal governments they headed had access to the Internet in 2000. This striking technology deficiency is all the more glaring when looking only at rural and semirural towns, where only thirty-six of more than 2,000 reported having an e-mail account, and only six had Web pages.[8] Though clearly not fully adequate as proxies for a municipality's capacity level, these data highlight the tremendous need for attention to the capabilities of agents and principals when designing and implementing reforms.

This discussion is only a small first step in outlining some of the essential community characteristics that would seem critical to identifying the type of decentralization reforms that would best suit a particular locality. Bardhan concurs with this assessment, arguing first that "the extent of [elite] capture of local governments relative to that of the central government is a critical determinant of the welfare impact of decentralization" (2002, 194) and that elite capture is in part a function of

> levels of social and economic inequality within communities, traditions of political participation and voter awareness, fairness and regularity of elections, transparency in local decisionmaking processes and government accounts, media attention and other factors. These factors vary widely across communities and countries, as documented in numerous case studies. (194)

Accepting the relationship between a community's socioeconomic level and the chances of elite capture, the question then becomes how to design decentralization reforms that take into account these socioeconomic differences. As Peter Blunt and Mark Turner found in the case of Cambodia, "decentralisation has faltered due to a lack of fit with Cambodia's sociocultural and institutional context" (2005, 75). They conclude that "pragmatism, based on a thorough and realistic assessment of context, rather than ideology, should inform the character and pace of governance reform" (86). What the principal-agent perspective offers is a way to begin to understand which of these conditions may be important in shaping the nature of the newly altered relations between citizens and local officials in the context of decentralization.

Discussion

The perspective put forth in this chapter highlights the need to carefully consider the characteristics of the target community and the intended goals of the reform when analyzing or designing decentralization reforms. Through a focus on agency theory, we can begin to formalize the abundance of decentralization research that in one way or another identifies issues similar to the ones raised here. In research on decentralization efforts across Africa, for example, Ragnhild Muriaas found that decentralization reforms implemented before a stable democracy had been established at the national level produced a series of negative economic and political development consequences because the reforms ran into existing power structures at the local level that were resistant to the changes brought by the reforms (2005, 2). In an entirely different setting, Ralph M. Kramer found the same problem in his study of the US Community Action Program, an antipoverty initiative of the Lyndon B. Johnson administration driven by the mandate for "maximum feasible participation." Kramer concludes that the idea of neighborhood-based self-help could only succeed if the entrenched local power elite allowed community organizations to "become politicized" (1969, 273). Viewing these latter conclusions from a principal-agent perspective, he is essentially suggesting that, in contexts where citizens lack the ability (because of entrenched and powerful agents) to become active principals in both decisionmaking and oversight processes, decentralization will not work until those obstacles are removed or diminished.

The principal-agent perspective also points us toward the importance of the central government and its capacities and motivations surrounding a particular decentralization reform package. This consideration is particularly relevant to cases of ongoing civil conflict or in transition or postconflict states, where the central government is ill equipped to provide the necessary resources to the target community and where citizens are either unwilling or unable to take on the responsibilities of active involvement in policymaking and oversight activities. In this context, a careful assessment, community by community in some cases, of the capacities of principals and agents to carry out the tasks of decentralization becomes especially important.

Elements of a successful decentralization reform package, then, can be found through analysis of their potential impact on four critical variables: (1) the role citizens or principals are expected to play in the particular reform sector (e.g., oversight or decisionmaker); (2) the balance struck between agent independence and accountability for newly empowered local officials; (3) the availability and accessibility of relevant information that allow citizens to carry out their roles as principals; and (4) the gap between the responsibilities placed on principals and agents by the reform and their respective abilities to fulfill those duties.

As Edward Fiske points out in his analysis of the decentralization of education responsibilities, "the critical question becomes: what levels of government are best suited in any given set of particular circumstances to carry out what functions of the educational system?" (1996, 8). In order to determine the most appropriate level of government for the delivery and monitoring of a particular government function, the characteristics of the target population (e.g., urban or rural, level of education); the policy sector (e.g., education or electricity); and the capacity of the principals and agents at the affected levels of government all need to be examined.

In order to develop sufficient understanding of these characteristics, a variety of instruments may be usefully applied before designing a reform for a particular community or region. These include the application of surveys to the local communities, the sponsoring of public fora in order to gauge citizens' capacities and interest in carrying out responsibilities of oversight and policymaking, and the holding of capacity-building workshops and training sessions for citizens and their prospective agents in order not only to improve the skills of those who will potentially be involved in the policy sector, but also to lay the groundwork for high levels of principal-agent communication and interaction during the policy design and implementation stages. The Food and Agriculture Organization (FAO) report on lessons from its rural decentralization projects offers a similar recommendation concerning the role of capacity building:

> FAO's experience indicates that it is not always easy to involve all groups of society in development activity. That is why FAO emphasizes

training citizen organizations and government administrators, in order to instill a real culture of decentralization. There are three conclusions drawn by FAO in regard to training:

1. For training to be integrated into the participatory approach, it has to target not only managers of support institutions, but also citizens and their organizations.
2. No training effort can be useful if its themes and pedagogical methods do not give priority to knowledge and organizational abilities of grassroots actors, and if knowledge and abilities of local populations are not taken into account.
3. Decentralization increases the need for training just as training increases the chances of success of decentralization. (FAO 2006)

Once again, analysis of the specific tasks that a reform requires of the relevant principals and agents is an effective approach to determining who should receive training and what type of training should be provided.

A somewhat dated, but still relevant, report on the decentralization experiences of Bangladesh in the 1980s reveals the consequences of a reform package that did not pay sufficient attention to the demands placed by decentralization on the relevant principals and agents:

> Decentralization policies can hardly avoid conflict in the process of implementation, and they are not a panacea for the administrative, political, or economic problems of developing countries. Their application does not automatically overcome shortages of skilled personnel, but initially creates a greater demand for them. Decentralization, in a resource poor country, may lead to greater dependence on the center by local administrative units and, as a corollary, local government units may act as bureaucratic instruments of the center rather than as generators of alternative values, performance, and aspirations. (Shawkat Ali 1987, 799)

Sylvia Bergh, in her review of decentralization research, also notes the consequences of reforms designed without consideration of the target population:

> Weak administrative capacity at local levels may result in services being delivered less efficiently and effectively than before. [Also] decentralisation may allow functions and benefits to be captured by local elites instead of increasing accountability at the local level (e.g., leading to a "decentralisation of corruption"). (2004, 781–782)

It is with this pessimistic prospect that decentralization may, in some cases, do more harm than good that this essay ends. For the central thesis posited in the preceding pages is that to avoid such a scenario, consideration of the principals and agents involved in a reform, and their institutional and socioeconomic environment, is essential. Underlying this focus on principals, agents, and their varying socioeconomic and political environments is the absolute necessity to recognize the implications for decentralization reforms of the immense intranational variation that exists within most developing countries. These subnational variations require a move away from the notion that a single decentralization reform can be implemented successfully across the myriad localities within a country. Also critical to this most basic goal of any reform (do no harm) is to have a clear conception of what the specific goals of the reform are, and where the priorities lie with respect to those goals. For example, is an increase in citizen participation more or less important than efficient delivery of services? Though this clearly is not always an either-or question, policymakers and decentralization proponents who do not at least recognize the possibility of tensions between the many goals of decentralization risk being less able to effectively design or evaluate a particular reform that does perhaps implicitly prioritize one goal over another.

Notes

1. See the World Bank's views on the potential benefits of the decentralization approach in Burki et al. (1999). See also Bardhan (1996), Bergh (2004), Faguet (1997), Smoke (2001), and Oxhorn, Tulchin, and Selee (2004). For a more comprehensive assessment of the decentralization "paradigm" as it developed in Latin America, see Eaton (2004a), Campbell (2003), Dietz and Meyers's edited volume (2002), and Nickson (1995).

2. The AmericasBarometer is a product of the Latin American Public Opinion Project (LAPOP) at Vanderbilt University. These data are drawn from the 2006 survey that conducted over 30,000 interviews across nineteen countries in Latin America and the Caribbean. Complete information on the survey instrument and data is available at http://www.vanderbilt.edu/lapop/.

3. For a more detailed analysis of these data, see Montalvo (2009).

4. The survey asked respondents the following questions: "(1) Did any police officer ask you for a bribe during the last year? (2) During the last year, did any public official ask you for a bribe? (3) During the last year, to process any kind of document (such as a license, for example) did you have to pay any money above that required by law? (4) At work, did anyone ask you for an inappropriate payment during the last year? (5) Did you have to pay a bribe in court during the last year? (6) In order to receive attention in a hospital or a clinic during the last year, did you have to pay a bribe? (7) Did you have to pay a bribe at school during the last year?"

5. See Gibson (2005) for the most well-developed account of the persistence of subnational authoritarianism in nationally democratic regimes.

6. See also Careaga and Weingast's analysis of the role of electoral competition and good governance in Rodrik (2003).

7. See also Bardhan and Mookherjee (2005) for further development of these issues.

8. These data are drawn from a survey carried out by the Mexican government agencies Secretaria de Desarollo Social (SEDESOL) and Instituto Nacional de Estadistica y Geografia (INEGI) entitled "La Encuesta Nacional a Presidentes Municipales 2002 INEGI-SEDESOL." In addition to the author's analysis of these data, an internal report produced by INDESOL and made available at http://www.indesol.gob.mx/docs/4_fomento/Porque.swf (accessed February 3, 2008) also was used as the source for the data reported.

3

Elections and the Development of Local Democracy

Gary Bland

Over the past three decades, much of the developing world has undertaken reform to decentralize the state and enhance the responsiveness and effectiveness of local governance.[1] Local elections have in almost all cases been a part of the process. Developing countries have explicitly recognized that local elections—particularly in those countries that have not held them recently or ever—are central not only to the success of decentralization, but also to the larger democratic transition of which the reforms are often a part. Indeed, particularly during a transition, one not infrequently sees reform of the electoral rules governing local elections with each election cycle.[2] In the era of the "third wave," if a country is serious about building a durable democratic system the local populace needs to be given a voice in determining who governs their communities.

Making decentralization work fundamentally (albeit not exclusively) requires determining how citizens can most effectively acquire that voice and make use of it to ensure that their locally elected officials are held accountable for their policy decisions. Achieving a measure of local autonomy that can be effectively representative of the local jurisdiction requires much more than allowing citizens to cast ballots, however. A variety of inherently political features of the larger institutional context bear directly on the ability of local officials to exercise the popular will. The objective of this chapter is to consider the most important of these features, propose a model for a minimally effective level of political decentralization, and, through a brief assessment of several illustrative country cases, consider how well the model—my argument for the "ideal"—holds up.

When considered within the context of democratization, "decentralization" is best defined as a multidimensional process of transferring power to popularly elected local government. It is the explicitly political realm of decentralization that is my concern in this chapter.[3] Here, "political decentralization" refers to the enhancement of local autonomy through political reform, primarily reform of the electoral or political party system to enhance local political pluralism and the provision of effective means of public participation in decisionmaking.

In this chapter, I propose a set of five conditions that must be instituted for a local system to be considered minimally politically decentralized, or what I refer to as "local electoral democracy." To illustrate my conceptual argument, I select a group of fifteen countries for investigation and review. My principal concerns in selecting the cases were balancing geographic diversity (Africa, Eastern Europe, Latin America, the Middle East, and Asia are equally represented) and, likewise, allowing for a diversity of country experience with democracy and decentralization; it is not meant to be a scientifically selected random sample. I find that the model does provide a useful conceptual framework for analyzing local electoral democracy in the developing world. Only a third of the fifteen countries meet all five local conditions. Among the group, serious weaknesses exist because locally elected officials are not protected from arbitrary removal from office, direct election does not occur, and local political parties cannot participate in local elections. The absence of other important features for the improvement of local autonomy, such as the separation of local and national elections, is also noteworthy.

The wealth of literature on elections, political parties, and decentralization tells us comparatively little about the operation and effects of electoral systems at the local level of government. Few publications, surprisingly, address the local level within a discussion of the national electoral system or examine the relative value of various local electoral reforms. To be sure, there appears to be a growing interest.[4] But even today one cannot easily locate, for example, a discussion of intergovernmental political change in the developing world as a result of the choices made around local electoral or related political issues.[5] This is puzzling, given the strong international interest in decentralization and the prominence of local electoral systems in intergovernmental reform efforts.[6] Especially in the developing world, it is easy to assume that, because there is often little divergence between levels of government as far as electoral systems are concerned, the local level requires little attention. To the contrary, specific features of local electoral systems require close examination because of the effects they can have on representation, accountability, and intergovernmental politics. These institutional characteristics can be viewed not only as fundamental to the achievement of minimally effective political decentralization, but also as primary elements of local electoral democracy.

In the section that follows, I review the importance of local elections, specifically addressing the general classification of electoral systems and their perceived local-level representational effects. In the next section, I examine the relationship between decentralization and intergovernmental electoral politics and political party systems. Turning to the model, I next propose a series of conditions for achieving a minimally politically autonomous local electoral system. When met, I argue, these institutional features provide sufficient political foundation for democratic local governance to flourish. I then consider a group of additional characteristics that warrant consideration in efforts to achieve local autonomy. In the next section, I provide the case studies, in essence, a reality check on the preceding discussion through a survey of fifteen local electoral systems across the five major geographic regions of the developing world. In the final section, I bring together the principal observations and conclusions, including a proposed typology of progress toward political decentralization. Ultimately, this chapter demonstrates that we can define a model for electoral democracy at the local level that is somewhat demanding, yet fits fairly well with the reality of local governance in the developing world.

Elections and Electoral Systems Viewed Locally

Local elections and the local governments that emerge from them are generally viewed as fundamental to democratic transition and consolidation in the developing world.[7] First, local elections allow for more tailored representation of local interests—school management, park cleanup, sewage systems, etc.—within each of the hundreds or thousands of politicoadministrative units into which the country has been carved. Second, local elections facilitate the representation and inclusion of minority groups in political life—be they former combatants, religious organizations, women, or long-marginalized indigenous peoples.

A third distinguishing feature is that local as opposed to national elections tend to be associated with a close relationship, based on physical proximity and greater contact, between the elected official and the constituency within the local jurisdiction. Fourth, local elections, particularly as they provide a training ground for new party leaders and independents, are intimately tied to the formation, functioning, and rejuvenation of national and local party systems. Finally, local electoral competition serves as a bellwether of voter attitudes and political trends in the national political system.

Local elections can have deleterious effects on an emerging democratic system, however. Some argue, if improperly convened, they facilitate a weakening or fragmentation of the national party system—or national unity overall. They also can be manipulated by religious leaders, wealthy candidates, or other influential figures in the locality. In such cases, the outcome—especially in the lowest-income and least-educated areas of a country—is elite, authoritarian dominance of the local government, perhaps in tacit alliance with national-level allies who resist breaking up their local electoral dominance (International IDEA 2003, 18; Gibson 2005, 128–129). Finally, when the ruling party utilizes state resources and manipulates the system to gain local victories, elections can lend legitimacy to a superficially democratic regime.

The three basic components of electoral systems, be they local or national, are district magnitude, ballot structure, and electoral formula. "District magnitude" refers to the number of seats to be filled in an election district. Districts with low magnitudes distribute seats less proportionally than districts with high magnitudes. Examples of low-magnitude districts include the election of a mayor with a plurality vote municipality-wide or election of the council in single-member, submunicipal districts or wards. In cases with larger magnitudes, as seen in proportional systems or municipality-wide council elections, more parties tend to compete (Farrell 2001, 6; Powell 2000, 23–24).

"Ballot structure" governs how the voters cast their votes. At the local level, a common concern is the nature and number of ballots. For example, if the mayor is elected separately from the council, two ballots may be used—one for each office. The appearance on the ballot of individual names or candidate photos as opposed to party labels may be an issue, and advocates of the former believe voters should know for whom they are voting so that they are better able to hold them accountable.

The "electoral formula" is the means of translating the votes into seats. Numerous formulas are used, but they also can be divided into three main groupings (Farrell 2001, 6). First, there are "majoritarian systems," which are distinguished by producing a majority winner even if the result reflects a disproportion between votes cast and the number of seats won. These systems are associated with single-member district voting and the desire to hold individual representatives directly accountable for their performance; clarity of responsibility is the watchword (International IDEA 2003, 19–20; Powell 2000, 50–51). At the local level, majoritarian systems are typically characterized by candidates that run at large municipality-wide or in submunicipal, single-member districts. In systems in which the council chooses the mayor, the question of how they are elected geographically can take center stage. The advantage of at-large election of the mayor is that the elected local official tends to be less parochial and more concerned with the community as a whole. Conversely, a major concern is that at-large candidates will all be drawn from—and pay closer attention to—

densely populated areas of the municipality because the votes are clustered in urban centers.

The submunicipal, single-member district election is used to ensure that all areas of the municipality have a representative on the council. Each ward has a single councilor to turn to, and no area of the municipality can feel entirely left out of the representative process. Some argue, however, that this system results in overrepresentation of rural areas; creates parochial representation as opposed to a municipality-wide perspective on local problems; and can allow candidates to win with a tiny proportion of the total municipal vote.

The second grouping is "proportional representation systems," in which the share of seats won by a party is roughly proportional to the number of votes it received, reflecting the political composition of the constituency. In the most popular example, parties present open or closed lists of candidates. At the local level, the proportional system provides for the political reflection of the social composition of the municipality, which is especially important when diversity of representation is an issue in large urban areas. A local council will likely operate on the basis of party coalitions in support of or opposed to the government, like a miniature parliament, and the mayor may not be directly elected.

"Mixed or semiproportional systems," which attempt to combine majoritarian and proportional characteristics, represent the final grouping. Mixed systems can have the best and worst characteristics of both types. They can create competition or tension between local officials elected proportionally and those elected by their own constituencies.

Intergovernmental Electoral Politics and Political Party Systems

Political party dynamics can reveal a great deal about the state of decentralization and the likelihood that centralizing or decentralizing trends will emerge. Efforts to enhance the political autonomy of local government through electoral reform or other measures automatically present a series of likely consequences. They can be positive and negative, depending on one's perspective, for all levels of government. Concerns about the effects of change are almost invariably rooted in the operation of intergovernmental party politics; that is, in the defining characteristics or structure of the political party system.

Though many factors influence a government's degree of decentralization, one of the most important variables is the degree to which the political party system is decentralized. In his seminal study, examining federal systems in the developed and developing world, William Riker reached the following conclusion:

> The federal relationship is centralized according to the degree to which parties organized to operate the central government control the parties organized to operate the constituent governments. This amounts to the assertion that the proximate cause of variations in the degree of centralization (or peripheralization) in the constitutional structure of a federalism is the variation in the degree of party centralization. (1964, 129)[8]

This relationship—the level of political control exercised by the center over the periphery—is fundamental to the discussion of elections, decentralization, and the development of democratic local governance.[9] Central control is generally exercised through two kinds of relationships: (1) the degree to which the same political party controls both the center and local levels of government; and (2) the degree to which each of the political parties at the national level controls its party membership at the local level of government (Riker 1964, 131; Shugart and Carey 1992, 175). Party nomination rules and informal nominating procedures are powerful tools (though certainly not the only ones) for control because they determine the relative influence of national party leaders on the selection of candidates. To the extent that local party leaders are influential in selecting candidates for the *national* legislative elections, the system tends to be decentralized. Intraparty dynamics force career-minded politicians to be more responsive to local interests in the legislature because local leaders help determine who gets on the ballot (Samuels 2000, 241–242; Willis, Garman, and Haggard 1999, 18). Conversely, to the extent that national party leaders make the determination on who runs in *local* elections, the systems tends to be centralized. Local leaders will be relatively more responsive to their national party counterparts because national politicians control who gets on the ballot. It may also be that, when national elites believe their national electoral prospects are diminished and that their allies can be successful in the local vote, they will preemptively decentralize in an effort to maximize the gains of office (O'Neill 2003).

Where the level of national control is strong, local elected officials tend to be *center oriented* because the success of their administrations and political careers largely depends on respecting the dictates of the national party leadership. In essence, local officials are beholden to their national counterparts. National party involvement at the local level would likely include enforcing the party line in council decisionmaking, using closed party-list systems, providing campaign resources, and especially selecting or approving local party candidates for office.[10] As evidenced in the country cases described below, when national party control is strong enough, local electoral system redesign will provide little opportunity for improved representation. Conversely, in diffuse party systems, discipline is weak and candidate selection is typically determined locally. Local political machines may deliver votes for national legislative candidates. In these instances, local elected officials can demonstrate a varying measure of independence from higher-level party leaders. They tend to be *locality oriented*, or focused on serving the interests of the local jurisdiction.

It is important to note that, while the nature of the party or electoral system produces important effects on the degree of centralization or decentralization, the evidence provided in this chapter and elsewhere demonstrates that the decentralization of political party systems is primarily the result of decentralization of the polity—reform of fundamental intergovernmental political (including the party system), fiscal, and administrative relationships. That is, political party rules, electoral incentives, and other characteristics of the party system tend to be the consequence of decentralization, not the prime motivation for it (Chhibber and Kollman 2004, 227; Montero and Samuels 2004, 21, 24). Decentralization itself alters the relative strength of the national legislator vis-à-vis the regional or local elected official. As elections begin to revolve around regional or local issues and as voters begin to vote for regional or local candidates on their own merits, the internal party organization will reflect the shift, and power within the organization will move from the center to the periphery (Hopkin 2003, 230). Depending on the nature and degree of decentralization, one can also expect the emergence of regional or local brokers in a system that was once centralized and dominated by the national brokers.

Defining Features of Local Electoral Democracy? A Proposal for Achieving Political Autonomy

In the liberal tradition,[11] decentralization is the transfer of power from the central government to popularly elected local governments (Lipset 1995, 335).[12] Decentralization may entail only the (re)establishment of local elections or it can involve a shift to the local level of a variety of new functions and financial resources in a country that has regularly convened local elections for decades. Decentralization involves three dimensions—political, administrative, and financial—that essentially represent the components of power, and basic progress along each dimension provides local government with sufficient authority for local democratic governance to develop.

Basic progress along decentralization's political dimension is, again, the basis for local electoral democracy, and it requires development of a minimum level of local political autonomy. Political autonomy is not simply a matter of according local officials increased freedom to act as they deem fit. Local officials must also face clear incentives to act on behalf of the residents of the community. The local constituency must be the lead actor in determining who the local leaders will be within a local system that can develop a political identity of its own.

It is important to emphasize that the achievement of local political autonomy, as it is viewed here, is predicated on the existence of a national democratic regime. Current consensus posits eight minimal conditions that define national democracy.[13] Though it is conceivable that elected and relatively responsive local officials can govern locally (and citizens can participate in positive ways) in the absence of democratic national institutions, local politics cannot be divorced from the national system. Authoritarian regimes deny the basic rights of citizenship, locally or otherwise.

The analytical challenge lies in determining what additional institutional features or conditions are required to achieve that minimum level of political autonomy.[14] How do we know when it appears? The crux of the issue is being able to provide for participation and contestation, the two dimensions of national democratization developed by Robert Dahl (1971), while also recognizing that an additional dimension—decentralization—is required for local democracy. Participation and contestation at the local level is fundamentally dependent on the control exercised by the national government; relinquishing a level of control provides the foundation for a successful local transition.

I posit that the following five characteristics of a local electoral system are required—again, at a minimum—to attain sufficient political decentralization:

1. Control over local government decisionmaking is constitutionally vested in officials elected by the citizens of the local jurisdiction;
2. Locally elected officials are chosen in frequent and fairly conducted elections in which coercion is comparatively uncommon;
3. An effective number of locally elected officials are directly elected;
4. The arbitrary removal of locally elected officials is effectively precluded; and
5. To achieve their various rights, including those listed here, citizens have a right to form relatively independent local associations or organizations, including independent political parties and interest groups.[15]

First (covering the first, second, and third criteria), constituent-oriented local representation requires not only regular, constitutionally guaranteed, free and fair local elections. It also entails the presence of direct election, which in practice typically means the direct election of the local executive or at least a majority of the local deliberative body. Direct election entails a popular election in which: (1) voters are entirely free to choose among individual candidates exclusively (i.e., an open party list) according to the particular office the candidate would assume if elected; and (2) the voters' choice is not subject to intermediation by a third party (i.e., an electoral college, council vote).[16] Thus, direct election accords the local elected official a fundamental measure of independent authority, not only vis-à-vis the local public, but also with respect to higher-level governmental authorities and his or her own political party. Local politicians have a stronger incentive to cultivate a personal reputation as opposed to a party reputation (Carey and Shugart 1995, 420–422).

Likewise, the locality benefits from increased clarity of responsibility. Popular elections that do not entail a significant measure of direct election, on the other hand, accord primacy in selecting candidates for local office to the political party and, thus, place in the parties' hands predominant influence over who represents the locality. Local elected officials who must rely on the party to get on the ballot are ultimately more responsive to the interests of their party leaders than to those of the community.[17]

Second, arbitrary removal of elected local officials (the fourth condition) violates the expressed will of the locality. By arbitrary, I mean procedures that are used or potentially used with some regularity, usually for a primarily political objective that does not in practice serve a clear local public purpose or the purpose for which they were intended. Many local government systems contain formal (i.e., a vote of the town council; a minister's discretion) or informal means for pressuring or legally removing local officials from office, absent of any public input, for purely political reasons. This is not to say that legitimate processes for removing corrupt and incompetent officials (public referenda, formal financial reviews, etc.) cannot be developed and effectively implemented; indeed, these are fairly common and are generally bulwarks of good governance. Because local and other pertinent institutions are weak and the level of politicization is high, such mechanisms for ensuring good governance can be used as fronts for the political manipulation of local administrations by party leaders or nonlocal interests.

In an electoral democracy, nationally, the general thrust of the fifth condition—local associational freedom—can be expected to hold. Political party organizing, civil society activity, and the formation of associations of one kind or another are usually conducted without much restriction. Even so, in such environments there is often effective or outright prohibition on creating local parties or on presenting independent candidates in local elections. Such limitations present an obstacle to the emergence of democratic local institutions. The established national parties typically do not want to cede their control over local authorities by allowing more competition and more options for prospective candidates at the local level.

Allowing the participation of independents or the establishment of local political organizations,[18] however, provides a strong inducement for pluralistic politics and competitive local elections. Such competition puts pressure on all political organizations, at the national level or otherwise, to respect local interests to win local office. Providing an opening for local parties and new political leaders—indeed, merely their potential emergence—softens central party control, engenders decentralization of the party system, and encourages a more decentralized central government (Riker 1964, 129–131). As we will see below, allowing local interests and candidates a voice in local elections appears to be a core issue in many developing countries.

Important Secondary Conditions for Local Political Autonomy

Although the specific characteristics described above are proposed as the minimum required for establishing political autonomy, several additional political characteristics of the system affect the quality of electoral democracies. Probably the most important is the separation of national, especially presidential, and local elections. Sufficiently separate election of national and local leaders (to be politically significant, most likely at least one year's separation) allows local concerns to predominate during the local electoral cycle. Separation raises the profile of local government, allows local leadership to function more independently of higher authorities, and further strengthens the tacit contract between the local elected official and the voter. Conversely, when national and local elections coincide or nearly coincide, local issues are invariably submerged and local candidates tend to respond to national party priorities.

The length of the term of office can be too short or too long to benefit democratic growth. A primary consideration is the time elected local officials need to develop a coherent team and plan of action and implement it, without continually having to worry about electoral politics. If a new mayor will need a year or so to get the administration going reasonably well, and at least the final six months will be largely driven, if not consumed, by the upcoming election, then a two- or three-year term is too short. On the other hand, a five- or more-year term, especially if unlimited reelection is permitted, may be an invitation for local bossism. Too much time between elections could reduce the local officials' sense of accountability to the electorate or become a temptation to abuse the power of incumbency to remain in office indefinitely.

Permission of reelection is another consideration. It would seem undemocratic to deny a popular local official with a strong record of performance the chance to continue serving the community. Yet a legacy of subnational authoritarian leadership would seem to warrant at least a limit on the number of times one can be reelected. Does a ban on reelection liberate local officeholders to pursue the public good without being tempted to abuse public power to remain in office, or does it invite the use of public office for maximum personal gain because a major performance incentive—the possibility of being reelected—has been removed?

Formal procedures for direct democracy remain popular. Though not strictly an electoral issue, such mechanisms do allow the public to circumvent their elected officials, depending on the situation, and may involve going back to the polls. Local communities can participate directly in municipal decisionmaking through referenda, petitions, oversight committees, plebiscites, and other vehicles. The success of such efforts remains an open question.

It is also important that any electoral system or election be considered in its totality. Other factors that are not directly related to accountability or representation can have important influences on the outcome of local elections. The general conduct of an election is often at issue. Campaign financing rules, which are often viewed in isolation from the electoral system, may favor large, centralized parties and make it more difficult for local candidates or new parties to compete (see the case studies below). The same holds, of course for media access because candidates can receive an unfair advantage through manipulative or unbalanced coverage.

Achieving Local Political Autonomy and Decentralization in the Developing World

I now apply the five criteria above to allow some comparing and contrasting across local (in this case, municipal) systems in the developing world. Three countries have been selected from each of the five major regions. Given the small sample and limited discussion of the cases, it is not meant to be representative of the developing world writ large. Nevertheless, one can develop a good sense of the import of these electoral variables and perhaps some idea of the commonalities across regions. Finally, it is worth noting that the same analysis can be done for the intermediate level of government (state, provincial, regional, etc.). Because space is limited, however, and because many unitary systems do not have elected intermediate-level governments, I have limited the discussion to municipal or municipal-equivalent level.

Asia

Indonesia is one of the two Asian nations—along with the Philippines—to push through a major and rapid intergovernmental reform in direct response to the fall of a discredited, highly centralized authoritarian regime (see Table 3.1). In the wake of Suharto's thirty-two-year reign, local democracy became one of the primary motives for passing two major laws (Laws 22 and 29) in 1999, the implementation of which began in 2001. A real fear of national disintegration was another major concern as provincial leaders and separatist movements threatened to break away unless their long-standing demands for greater autonomy were addressed (Hidayat and Antlöv 2004, 270–271). The two decentralization laws, which were amended and renumbered (Laws 32 and 33), defined significant new social service responsibilities for districts and municipalities. They also provided for a new intergovernmental fiscal framework that includes substantial subnational transfers. Thirty-two percent of government expenditures now occur subnationally (White and Smoke 2005, 10).

Electoral reform also has been a central component of Indonesia's decentralization, and reforms in 2003 and 2004 created open list proportional representation and direct election of local executives as of 2005. In 2008, respecting a Constitutional Court decision a year earlier, a new electoral law allowed independent candidates to run in local elections for the first time—a major reform that is expected to enhance local pluralism, though concerns have been raised about strict requirements. By the end of 2008, the first pair of independent candidates won in regional elections. As for other features of the system, council elections are held in conjunction with national votes, reelection is not permitted, and local elected officials are subject to removal for political reasons.[19]

The 1991 enactment of the Local Government Code remains the seminal decentralizing event in *the Philippines*. A dramatic reform, that law was primarily a reaction to the fourteen years of central control of the Ferdinand Marcos dictatorship, which came to an end in 1986 with the rise of "people power" under President Corazon Aquino. The code was aimed not only at involving local authorities in a range of new functions and provid-

Table 3.1 Local (Municipal or Municipal-Equivalent) Electoral Features for Asia: Indonesia, the Philippines, and Cambodia

Country	National Political Democracy	Elected Local Officials	Free and Fair Local Elections	Presence of Direct Election	Arbitrary Removal Precluded	Local Associational Autonomy	Separate Elections	Term of Office	Reelection Permitted	Direct Democracy Provisions
Indonesia	1999	Yes	Yes	Yes	No	Yes	No[a]	5	No	No
Philippines	1986	Yes	Yes	Yes	Yes	Yes	No	3	Yes	Yes
Cambodia	1993	Yes	Yes[b]	No	No	No	Yes	5	Yes	No

Notes: a. Local executives are elected separately.
b. Preelection violence and intimidation raised serious concerns about democracy in the 2002 vote.

ing substantial unconditional fiscal transfers, it was also designed to bring civil society into the process of governing and provide avenues for public participation such as the recall and citizen initiative (Angeles and Magno 2004, 227–233).

Given the heavily personalistic and clientelistic nature of the political system, local elections in the Philippines are wide open affairs: it is perhaps the only country that requires voters to write in their preferred candidates for every electoral office. Central political control is relatively weak, naturally (though national and local elections occur simultaneously and so local preferences are partially obscured by national political trends). Local political autonomy is considerable. There is some politicization of local governance such that local elected officials are subject to removal, but this is not extensive.[20]

Decentralization in *Cambodia* is in its infancy, and the motive for reform has been primarily political—a desire to increase state presence outside the capital and promote local democratic legitimacy. The enactment of the Commune Law in 2001, and the February 2002 and April 2007 commune elections, were the major reform efforts. The Commune Law provides a regulatory framework for communal government and establishes a broad mandate for social and economic development, including participatory planning. It does not provide, however, specific responsibilities for service delivery or significant fiscal resources. Government interest in further intergovernmental reform appears limited (Romeo and Spyckerelle 2004, 7–9).

In a country with such a traumatic history and a checkered, violent transition to democracy, competitive communal elections assume considerable importance for the emergence of democratic local governance. Yet as one would expect, the local electoral system reflects the lack of local political autonomy. A closed list system in which local parties and independents are precluded helps the three major parties—the governing party particularly—remain dominant. In 2002, the Cambodia People's Party won 68 percent of the commune seats; five years later it won 70 percent. The combined percentage of seats won by the Sam Rainsy Party and the National United Front for an Independent, Neutral, Peaceful, and Cooperative Cambodia (FUNCINPEC) fell from 32 percent to 26 percent during this period (UNDP 2007, 8; Romeo and Spyckerelle 2004, 8; Gallup 2002, 61–63). Considerably more parties and candidates participated, however. The failure to encourage independent candidates is viewed by reformers as a missed opportunity to promote local groups, encourage citizens to participate in the political process, and help ensure that elected officials are more constituent focused than party oriented. Elected officials also face expulsion for not following the party line (COMFREL 2006, 1–2).

Africa

Decentralization is now beginning in *Zambia*, a system that remains well centralized (see Table 3.2). A National Decentralization Policy was launched in 2004 and its implementation will require continued reform. Local government—the district councils—have taxing authority and, therefore, the ability to generate their own revenue. The central government provides grants to local governments—all transfers are provided on an ad hoc basis—to assist in covering water and sanitation, roads, and health care, among other services. Government policy is to eventually devolve a set of service delivery functions to the local level as capacity increases (Commonwealth Local Government Forum 2005).

Limited political autonomy further demonstrates the lack of progress toward subnational reform. The multiparty system is dominated by the ruling Movement for Multiparty Democracy, which controls the government machinery and assets. Councilors are elected by wards—a first-past-the-post system that tends to favor the ruling party—and the victors select the mayor, whose party affiliation is the primary consideration in the choice. Direct election of the local executive is another ostensible objective of the National Decentralization Policy (International IDEA 2004, 40–46).

It is extraordinary that the minister of local government has the authority to suspend councils (or individual councilors) and replace them with local administrations; such action has been taken. Moreover, members of parliament who represent the local district also sit on the local council. Given these controls and personality-driven local elections, it is not surprising that independent candidates and local political parties are allowed to run for election. Local political party leaders do have a lead role in selecting local candidates for office (Commonwealth Local Government Forum 2005).

In *South Africa*, passage of the 1996 constitution providing for comprehensive decentralization, enactment of a series of legislative reforms covering all intergovernmental dimensions, and the institution of municipal elections every four years reflect a strong commitment to the development of a local democratic system in the wake of apartheid. The extensive 1998 White Paper for Local Governments emphasizes the importance of local democracy. In 1999, the Municipal Structures Act established three types of municipalities based on size, allocated functions among the three types, and put in place local electoral rules. Various functions have been decentralized and local governments have significant taxing, borrowing, and revenue-generating authority.

South Africa's local electoral rules provide for considerable local political autonomy. South Africa uses a mixed system: half of the members

Table 3.2 Local (Municipal or Municipal-Equivalent) Electoral Features for Africa: Zambia, South Africa, and Benin

Country	National Political Democracy	Elected Local Officials	Free and Fair Local Elections	Presence of Direct Election	Arbitrary Removal Precluded	Local Associational Autonomy	Separate Elections	Term of Office	Reelection Permitted	Direct Democracy Provisions
Zambia	1992	Yes	Yes	Yes	No	Yes	No	5	Yes	No
South Africa	1994	Yes	Yes	Yes	Yes	Yes	Yes	5	Yes	Yes
Benin	1990	Yes	Yes	No	Yes	Yes	Yes	5	Yes	No

of municipal councils (metropolitan, local, and district) are elected by proportional representation through closed party lists and half are elected directly in single-member wards. National and local elections are separated; local officials cannot be removed and independent candidates are permitted (Hendrickse 2005, 1–3).

The African National Congress (ANC) won the historic elections of 1994 and has since been the dominant political force in leading not only the national government, but also most municipalities. The local political dominance of the ANC and of the national parties generally—coupled with the enforcement of the party line within the councils—has undermined local autonomy. So far, the country's local elections demonstrate that it will be some time before independent candidates—or officials who can more freely represent their constituents' interests—become established (Friedman and Kihato 2004, 177).

Benin's National Conference, convened in February 1990, opened the door to the successful transformation of the country from a Marxist-inspired, state-centered regime to a multiparty democracy with a market-based economy. In part a reaction to the previous system, decentralization—the free administration of communes by elected councilors—was a major recommendation of the National Conference. By the late 1990s through 2001, decentralization laws were enacted, including new electoral provisions, for the transfer of authority to the commune level.

Benin's communes are accorded a series of significant local functions, including responsibilities in health, education, water, and sanitation. They are also responsible for public infrastructure and the management of natural resources. Capacity needs and a lack of resources from the central government, despite the communal efforts to mobilize their own revenue, are major limitations. Decentralization remains a slow, gradual process in a system that remains fairly centralized.

The first local elections were held in December 2002. As a national party–driven system, Benin's commune councilors are elected by closed party list in a vote separate from the national elections, and the winning councilors select the mayor by majority vote. Coalitions of parties and independents are able to participate. A major concern is the weakness of public participation in local decisionmaking. Councils hold public sessions, but the agenda is rarely published in advance, and citizens do not have the right to address the meetings.[21]

Latin America

Despite the 1982 return to democratically elected government, *Bolivia* was the only country in Latin America that did not have a nationwide municipal system (see Table 3.3). The landmark 1994 Popular Participation Law (PPL) then established 311 municipalities across the national territory, and the following year elections were held in all of them. This law extended municipal jurisdiction to a wide variety of new service areas and accorded municipal governments the authority to set rates and collect property taxes. The PPL also established "vigilance committees" for civic control over municipal investment decisions and increased from 10 percent to 20 percent the amount of national income transferred to municipal governments each year. Another major reform allowed the participation of indigenous and citizens' groups, for the first time, in the 2004 municipal elections. Local pluralism increased dramatically.

Despite this progress, however, Bolivian municipal government faces limitations on political autonomy. National party leaders continue to exercise considerable control over their local counterparts; closed party lists are used in municipal elections. One of the more striking features of the municipal system is the degree of elected official turnover created by a constitutional provision allowing removal and replacement of mayors via a three-fifths council vote (Bland 2000, 75), though use of the provision has been somewhat restricted. The procedure also allows national political parties and other outside interests to manipulate the operation of municipal government.

Beginning in 1983 and continuing to the present, *Colombia* has transformed itself from a highly centralized country into one of the most decentralized in Latin America. One of the major rationales for the reform was a desire by successive governments and demands by civil society to open up the democratic system and allow Colombians—and guerrilla groups—to participate in public decisionmaking of consequence and thereby bring an end to the conflict.

Under new legislation, previously appointed mayors were directly elected for the first time in 1988. Decentralization in Colombia provided new mechanisms for community participation that include a popular referendum on the mayor's continuance in office, but elected municipal officials are not subject to arbitrary removal from power. As the decentralization process was in part an effort to open up the political system to former guerrillas and other community actors, the 1991 constitution provides for the participation of social movements and citizens' groups in politics, including municipal elections.

During the 1990s, nontraditional parties and coalitions made considerable municipal electoral gains at the expense of the Liberal and especially Conservative parties (Querubín, Sánchez, and Kure 1998, 129–131; see Hommes 1996). In addition, through a series of laws, decrees, and constitutional reforms, Colombia has substantially increased financial transfers

Table 3.3 Local (Municipal or Municipal-Equivalent) Electoral Features for Latin America: Bolivia, Colombia, and Costa Rica

Country	National Political Democracy	Elected Local Officials	Free and Fair Local Elections	Presence of Direct Election	Arbitrary Removal Precluded	Local Associational Autonomy	Separate Elections	Term of Office	Reelection Permitted	Direct Democracy Provisions
Bolivia	1982	Yes	Yes	No	No	Yes	Yes	4	Yes	Yes
Colombia	1958	Yes	Yes	Yes	Yes	Yes	Yes	3	Yes	Yes
Costa Rica	1952	Yes	Yes	Yes	No	Yes	Yes	4	Yes	Yes

to the municipal level and mandated the transfer of primary health care, education, water, agricultural extension services, and other functions to municipal governments.

Costa Rica quietly enacted a constitutional reform in 2001 that provided for innovative and significant political decentralization. The country is a long-established democracy—the oldest in Latin America—but one that has been highly centralized under the control of two major political parties. This legacy of centralization has produced increasing decomposition of the party system, eroding systemic legitimacy (low voter turnout and electoral gains by new parties), and little public confidence in the abilities of weak municipal government.

The 2001 reform was most interesting in what it accomplished on the political side. In addition to providing for a gradual transfer of fiscal resources and functions to the municipal level, the new municipal code includes the following: direct election of the mayor (and various other municipal positions); staggered local elections to be convened ten months after the national vote; allowance of independent parties to compete only in municipal elections; and several new mechanisms for direct democracy locally such as plebiscites, referenda, and open municipal meetings (Bland 2007b). The intergovernmental tensions created by the reform were reflected in the comments of a traditional party member, who remarked that "it is totally unjust and irrational. It's not designed to give representation to the minority parties, but to take it away from the majority parties" (Ryan 2004, 82).

The Middle East and North Africa

In the Middle East and North Africa (MENA), national political democracy does not exist in many countries and intractable centralization continues to be common (see Table 3.4). In some cases, however, there have been significant advances through the (re)introduction of democratic processes at the local level.

Morocco is a constitutional monarchy that has progressively pursued decentralization and subnational reform over decades. Though ultimate authority always rests with the king, Morocco can lay claim to a considerably open local political system when viewed within the regional context. Current law contains requirements for making local council deliberations and decisions public—and there appears to be increasing awareness of the importance of accountability—but citizen participation remains limited.

The local system is characterized by a variety of political parties operating within an environment—and on a council—characterized by shifting loyalties. Council election is by party list (direct election does not occur),

Table 3.4 Local (Municipal or Municipal-Equivalent) Electoral Features for the Middle East and North Africa: Morocco, Jordan, and Lebanon

Country	National Political Democracy	Elected Local Officials	Free and Fair Local Elections	Presence of Direct Election	Arbitrary Removal Precluded	Local Associational Autonomy	Separate Elections	Term of Office	Reelection Permitted	Direct Democracy Provisions
Morocco	No	Yes	Yes	No	No	Yes	Yes	6	Yes	No
Jordan	No	No	No[a]	N/A	No	No	N/A	4	N/A	No
Lebanon	No	Yes	Yes	No	Yes	Yes	Yes	4	Yes	No

Note: a. Half of the local councils are elected; these elections are held separately from the national vote; and reelection of those who are elected is permitted.

and then the council selects the mayor by majority vote. The 1976 Law on Municipal Organization (Municipal or Commune Charter) provides for the removal of the mayor after two years by a two-thirds vote of the council. In a system with a long six-year term, this provision has been used as a political tool and promoted instability in local leadership. Consequently, there has been interest in enhancing representation through reform to directly elect the mayor or otherwise provide stability to the executive position (World Bank 2001b, 6). It also bears mentioning that just one Islamic party was permitted to participate in the latest, 2003 local vote (and performed well).

Local governments are accorded appropriate local responsibilities in a series of public service areas, though their capacity to govern is seriously constrained by the *tutelle*—or the Ministry of Interior. Under the charter, the ministry must approve council decisions in a wide range of areas before they can go forward. Such central control is extensive and has a significant impact on the management of budget resources and execution of development projects. Local accountability is diluted; the attribution of accountability overall suffers (World Bank 2001b, 7).[22]

Jordan, another constitutional monarchy, is not one of the region's examples of progressive local democratic reform. Actual decentralization—as opposed to deconcentration—has minimal support within the central government, and the royal commission appointed in 2005 to study and make recommendations on decentralization is replete with conservatives who are unlikely to propose conclusive reforms. Jordan takes a technocratic approach in seeking to build the capacity of newly amalgamated local governments, based on the belief that the localities do not yet have the ability to take a leading administrative and developmental role.

Jordan's local governments have seen a continual erosion of their political autonomy and functions since the passage of the 1955 local government law. The 1955 law gave municipalities responsibility for all service delivery and provided for the direct elections of mayors and councils. Today, the intergovernmental system remains highly centralized, and the major functions of local governments are waste collection and street cleaning; street and road maintenance and repair; public lighting; and culture and sports. As of 1999, under the temporary law for municipal governments, mayors and up to half of the councils are appointed—concern about the potential local emergence of Islamic movements has played a role here. Such lack of representation locally undermines the already weak tradition of public participation in local decisionmaking.

The fragile democratization of *Lebanon* faces continuing hazards today, and the absence of a nationally independent democratic regime obviously constrains the prospects for municipal government.[23] After fifteen years of political instability (1975–1991), the Taif Agreement (1989) that brought an end to the civil war became the basis for progress at the local level. The agreement included a commitment to strengthening municipalities, and the Ministry of Municipal and Rural Affairs was created in 1993 to address municipal concerns and support the development of local governments (Atallah 1998, 4).

In mid-1998, for the first time in thirty-five years and after multiple postponements, municipal elections were successfully convened (and are now held every four years). Local electoral lists are fairly informal collections of family affiliations. Political parties do not control the process from the center, but rather establish alliances with influential local families and attempt to effectively manage their local ties (the mayor is chosen by a vote of the council). Despite the limitations on representation, the electoral process is viewed as important to social and political stability.[24]

The weakness of local government and the sector's fairly insignificant influence on national politics partially explain the fair amount of autonomy they hold. The small country is fragmented into more than 700 municipalities, and the large majority of them have too little financial or administrative capacity to collect revenue or provide services so they depend on central government transfer. A series of laws and decrees beginning in 1977 delineates municipal functions, and own-revenue sources either have been too restrictive, remain unimplemented, or have not produced much additional income. Many municipal projects have been taken over by the central government or private sector; indeed, in this sense the trend is toward further centralization (UNDP 2006, 3).

Eastern Europe and Eurasia

Armenia has a fairly solid basis for the establishment of democratic local governance, including the eventual development of fairly effective administrations for the provision of important public services (see Table 3.5). The constitution, adopted in 1995, four years after the achievement of independence, provides for the functioning and development of local self-governance. Local elections were held in 1996, 1999, and 2000, and now occur every four years. Decentralization reform, which was initially a result of pressure to comply with the European Charter for Local Self-Government, has produced a series of laws outlining local functions for social policy, local tax collection, urban transport, and other areas (Gimishyan and Manoukyan 2003, 38–43).

Armenia is also a classic case, however, of the gap that can exist between the enactment of legislation and actual implementation of reform. The new laws have not been enforced, and the political will to move forward

Table 3.5 Local (Municipal or Municipal-Equivalent) Electoral Features for Eastern Europe and Eurasia: Armenia, Bulgaria, and Ukraine

Country	National Political Democracy	Elected Local Officials	Free and Fair Local Elections	Presence of Direct Election	Arbitrary Removal Precluded	Local Associational Autonomy	Separate Elections	Term of Office	Reelection Permitted	Direct Democracy Provisions
Armenia	1996	Yes	Yes[a]	Yes	Yes	No[a]	Yes	4	Yes	Yes[b]
Bulgaria	1990	Yes	Yes	Yes	Yes	Yes	Yes	4	Yes	Yes
Ukraine	1991	Yes	Yes	Yes	Yes	Yes	No	4	Yes	No

Notes: a. The point that Armenia's local elections are free and fair is debatable. Armenia has a tradition of arbitrarily removing elected officials; although a recent reform formally prohibits removal, the practice likely will continue.

b. Recall legislation does exist, but it is so arcane as to be ineffective.

appears to be lacking. Some responsibilities newly assumed by local government have been reclaimed by the national level (Gimishyan and Manoukyan 2003, 39).

In addition, despite having a system with virtually all of the institutional features of open local elections, political autonomy is considerably restricted by undemocratic practices and the political control exercised by the central government. Pressure from the ruling party through the use of state resources, direct intimidation of opponents, widespread vote buying, and electoral fraud raise the question of the degree to which local elections are free and fair. Only recent amendments to the governing law on local government have precluded the common practice of impeaching mayors who ran afoul of the government. This is an important advance, though removal probably continues to occur. A few powerful families tend to be the power brokers in the local system. A growing concern is the emergence of oligarchs whose resources and influence with the government allow them to win local elections (Danielyan 2005).[25]

Bulgaria has experienced the emergence of a municipal government movement that began in 1991 as the country has instituted decentralizing reforms and sought to achieve European-level standards for local self-government. The movement reflects the progress of decentralization to the municipal level, which has included transfers of public services, considerable European Union funding for infrastructure investment, and, recently, a financial decentralization program. Though municipalities do not have tax powers, the program increased own-source local revenue from nearly one-fourth of total revenue in 2002 to nearly one-third 2 years later (Local Government Forum Working Group 2005, 1).

The local system has become much more politically diverse and autonomous and has allowed mayors an increasing presence within the national political life. Former mayors are amply represented in the national parliament—local government has become a path to a national political career, in competition with members of parliament.

Since 1991, as Bulgaria has transitioned from communism to democracy, local elections have been successfully convened every four years. Mayors are elected directly by the municipality at large, but the council is elected by closed party list. The two branches are consequently somewhat competitive; mayors claim to better represent the local public. As of the late 1990s, the council elections began to produce fewer party majorities and larger numbers of small parties. In elections four years later, as voter discontent with conventional politics increased, these trends were reinforced. Many parties and large numbers of independents won local representation, and local issues—not national party politics—dominated the campaign.[26]

Following a series of halting steps toward local democratic reform in the early 1990s, the 1996 constitution of *Ukraine* recognized and guaranteed the establishment of local self-government. Building on this framework, Ukraine ratified the European Charter of Local Self-Government the next year and, subsequently, a series of laws establishing the functions and financial basis for local (and regional) government. The 2001 Budget Code Reform, for example, allocated fiscal transfers by transparent formulas to 700 cities and provided the foundation for continued progress in the system of intergovernmental finance. Own-source revenue generation remains quite weak, however.

Constitutional reform agreed to in 2004—and implemented with the March 2006 parliamentary and local elections—transformed Ukraine from a presidential to a parliamentary system in which the elected president shares powers with the prime minister. Mayors continue to be elected directly by a plurality vote, but council elections in the large cities are run on a party-list system (small cities and villages elect councils in submunicipal districts via plurality vote). The party system includes some 120 parties, the effect of which is to make the local votes pluralistic (though under the new system, independents are no longer allowed to participate without joining a party). In the past, selective application of the criminal code has been used to remove elected executives from office, though this appears to be uncommon today.

The Orange Revolution and the new government that emerged from it represented the promise of democratic reform in Ukraine. Local government became a major focus and, by the fall of 2005, a draft package of reform of four local government laws was introduced. However, the initiative became caught up in delaying tactics and a power struggle between the presidency and parliament, and it remains on hold.[27]

Summary Results

This review of the local political features of the fifteen countries indicates a broad international consensus in favor of democratic local governance (see Table 3.6). Local democracy is typically a major feature or objective of transitional or consolidating national democratic systems and, in each of the twelve national democracies in this sample, local elections have followed fairly soon after the transition or after consolidating reforms. Only in the three MENA region cases is national democracy yet to be achieved. Despite the national constraints, only one of the three countries (Jordan) does not have popularly elected local officials (the mayor and half of the council are appointed).

Table 3.6 Totals of the Local (Municipal or Municipal-Equivalent) Electoral Features for the Fifteen Country Cases

	National Political Democracy	Elected Local Officials	Free and Fair Local Elections	Presence of Direct Election	Arbitrary Removal Precluded	Local Associational Autonomy	Separate Elections	Term of Office	Reelection Permitted	Direct Democracy Provisions
Total	12/15	14/15	14/15	9/15	7/15	12/15	10/15	8/15, 4 years; 5/15, 5 years	13/15	7/15

About two-thirds of this group of cases provides for a measure of direct election. Direct election is often viewed as a means to strengthen representation of the local constituency and improve the accountability of the elected officials to the public. It should be noted, however, that open party-list systems can be designed in ways to preserve the control of the major national parties. In Indonesia, for example, national parties have considerable leeway to determine who from their list of party candidates receives a council seat; it is not necessarily the candidate who received the most votes. Moreover, as seen in Zambia, single-district plurality (or ward) systems can benefit a dominant party determined to ensure its monopoly over the system. The dominant party often has advantageous access to state resources and simply needs to garner the most votes in a jurisdiction to win a seat.

This sample also illustrates a fairly strong desire for local associational autonomy—permitting independent candidacies, local political parties, and an open political system. Considerable value—as seen in four-fifths of the cases—is placed on the development of local political pluralism.

That more than half of the countries engage in the arbitrary removal from office of elected local officials is the clearest sign of the progress that remains for local political autonomy. Allowing local officials to exercise the authority vested in them by the community is at the heart of democracy, yet many local systems are lacking in this regard.

The four additional, facilitating features of a local democracy were also surveyed. Two-thirds of the countries provide for the separation of the national and local vote, thereby allowing local politics and issues some opportunity to develop an identity apart from the national political scene. The cases further indicate that either a four- or five-year term of office is the ideal for democratic representation and accountability: nearly all of the countries have chosen one of these two options as the length of term for their local officeholders. The three-year term in Colombia and the six-year term in Morocco are unique among the fifteen, and are probably less than ideal for democratic local governance. The former is probably too short for a stable local political system; the latter allows incumbents tremendous advantage and, because elections are so widely spaced, poses a risk to electoral accountability. The reelection of local officials appears to be widely accepted. In all but two of the country cases (the exceptions are Indonesia and Jordan), voters are given the ability to reward or punish their local officials on election day. Direct democracy provisions are much less popular, however, and seem to appear in the more progressive, participatory decentralization reform efforts.

Conclusion

Taking on a broad range of issues involving local elections, decentralization, and the democratization of local governance, this chapter argues that a minimum level of local political autonomy—of which the local election system is naturally a central feature—is necessary to enhance the representativeness and accountability of local government and, ultimately, to promote the development of a democratic national regime. Meeting that minimum measure of autonomy is achieved through political decentralization. Decentralization works, then, when citizens acquire voice and use their new political authority to ensure that their elected officials effectively represent them. Decentralization reform facilitates progress toward local democracy because it improves the opportunity for better representation of local interests, effective inclusion of minority groups in political life, closer ties between the local official and the community, development of the national and local political party systems, and national regime transition and consolidation.

In this chapter, I review from a local perspective how the three fundamental features of an electoral system combine to produce the three major types of systems. Majoritarian systems seek to produce a single winner who can be held more directly accountable to the electorate. Proportional systems aim to reflect the political composition of the electoral jurisdiction as a whole, and they better allow for minority representation. Mixed systems combine features of both types. Each type creates a series of incentives for elected leaders that significantly influence the nature of local politics, accountability, and representation.

The nature of the political party system is a prominent consideration in any examination of the progress of political decentralization or decentralization in general. The stronger the party system—the stronger its ability to control local party representatives—the weaker decentralization tends to be. Avoiding party fragmentation is an important concern. Instability is not infrequently the result of increasingly ossified parties, however, and a healthy system allows for an important measure of local political pluralism and autonomy. This chapter further illustrates, moreover, that most often decentralization is the result of major social and political factors, and it creates change in intergovernmental politics and party relationships; changes in parties do not typically bring about decentralization.

Building on this discussion, I define the local electoral and other conditions that constitute the minimum requirements for political decentralization. I ask a fundamental question: What are the institutions of local electoral democracy and how many of them need to be present (i.e., decentralized) to accord a local system sufficient political autonomy? In addressing this question, I make three assertions. First, relying on the work of Dahl and others, I put forward that one can identify a fairly objective set of conditions for systems that minimally define political decentralization. The five requirements are: (1) elected local officials; (2) free and fair local elections; (3) direct election of local officials; (4) local elected officials not removed arbitrarily; and (5) local associational autonomy.

Where these five conditions hold within a democratic national regime, the local system can be classified as politically decentralized. As such, local citizens have the generally unimpaired opportunity to present their preferences to local government, local government officials have a fundamental incentive to weigh those preferences, and the local constituency has the ability to hold those officials accountable for their decisions (see Dahl 1971, 1–3). As each country operates within its own complex institutions of intergovernmental interaction and control, political decentralization entails more than the act of voting. It requires according localities enough political autonomy to allow local government and its citizens to eventually move beyond the procedural and become habituated to the practice of democracy.

Second, through my definitional model, I posit that the achievement of local electoral democracy, or a process of local democratization, is tantamount to a minimum level of political decentralization. These five requirements, each treated with equal weight in terms of impact, provide for a fundamental level of political autonomy: together they allow for, but do not guarantee the presence of, the plural expression of local citizen interests and work to ensure that local elected officials respond to those interests. We also see that countries will institute a small group of secondary features, particularly the separation of national and local elections, in an effort to facilitate the emergence of local electoral democracy.

Third, my model allows a general assessment of the movement toward political decentralization in the developing world, and one would expect it to apply well. Indeed, the results allow for the development of a typology for the classification of systems according to the level of political autonomy found locally (see Table 3.7). Fifteen countries' municipal (or municipal-equivalent) systems, an illustrative sample selected across five geographic regions, are addressed here. Five countries—Bulgaria, Colombia, the Philippines, South Africa, and Ukraine—meet all five criteria and can be considered politically decentralized today.

Four of the countries have what one can consider "partially open" systems with cases that allow for a high degree of local pluralism and are nearly politically decentralized (meeting four of the five criteria). "Restricted autonomy" includes those countries with clear restrictions on

Table 3.7 A Typology of Progress Toward Local Electoral Democracy Based on the Fifteen Country Cases

Nonautonomous	Restricted Autonomy	Partially Open	Politically Decentralized
Jordan	Bolivia	Armenia	Bulgaria
	Cambodia	Benin	Colombia
	Indonesia	Costa Rica	Philippines
	Lebanon	Zambia	South Africa
	Morocco		Ukraine

the development of local electoral democracy (failing to meet two or more of the criteria), such as heavy political party or ministerial control, and considerable reform remains to be achieved. In the cases of Lebanon and Morocco, the absence of national democracy is a major limitation. Finally, Jordan, which also is not a national democracy and does not elect more than half of its local government representatives, is the sole representative of the "nonautonomous" category, which would include any country that does not elect its local officials and fails to meet most of the criteria. There is ample room for additional research along these lines in many other developing countries, which would allow further assessment of the value of such an institutional approach. One finding that requires additional investigation is the impact when the local electoral system is distinct from the national system, as seen to varying degrees in South Africa, Costa Rica, and Ukraine. Further research on the strength of the relationship between party nomination procedures and decentralization would also be helpful.

Because only five of the fifteen cases presented here are politically decentralized, this survey reflects the continuing legacy of centralized government in all parts of the developing world. Patches of progress can be found, and it bears noting that the group of four limited-open systems is close to achieving it. A surprising number of the country cases, however—more than half—do not protect their local elected officials from arbitrary removal from office. The absence of direct elections and the lack of local political parties or independents are also issues for consideration of reform.

Arguing for the adoption of prodemocratic features of a local system is not meant to suggest that such characteristics should be pursued immediately in all or even most institutional contexts. Indeed, if inappropriately or too quickly applied, these reforms could weaken central political authority and foster political instability, secessionist aspirations, or eventual authoritarian outcomes. Moreover, countries also need to consider, as Jonathan Hiskey points out in Chapter 2, the trade-offs between the twin complementary but sometimes conflicting objectives of democracy and development. If one believes that political and economic development go hand in hand, however, this model and the fifteen cases presented above indicate that countries will do better the sooner they are able to put in place local electoral democracy. Generally—with the exception of arbitrary removal of elected officials—the adoption of local electoral democracy should be a steady, gradual process to ensure acceptance and success. It must be noted, however, that institutional contexts vary widely and the opposite may be required: rapid adoption can prove essential to the achievement of political stability where the public demand for reform is strong. The secondary reform features mentioned above are likely to be less central or controversial.

Local electoral democracy is a local government system that is almost completely responsive to all local citizens. It requires faith in the superiority of consensus building over authoritarianism or open conflict as a means of resolving disagreement in local affairs. The local institutionalization of this process of compromise is achieved through agreement on the rules of the game, the application of those rules, and their continued operation over a long period of time.[28] In this sense, local electoral democracy is no different from its national counterpart. There is one strategic difference, however. The establishment of electoral democracy also requires the cession of real power to the local level by central decisionmakers[29]—be they aging dictators or reformist democrats. It is my contention in this chapter that, unless fairly specific local political–institutional features, including significant electoral reform, are put into operation, the local system that emerges will be less than democratic.

Notes

I thank the editors, as well as Mark Payne, Andrew Selee, Brian Wampler, and two anonymous reviewers for their helpful comments on this chapter.

1. For the purposes of this chapter, the terms "local" and "subnational" refer to any government below the national level and are used interchangeably.

2. See, for example, Kornblith and Levine (1995); International IDEA (2004); Hofman and Kaiser (2004); and Chaudhuri (2006).

3. Administrative and financial decentralization are also heavily influential on the autonomy of local officials and can easily be seen as equally "political." In this chapter, however, I focus on the political institutions alone—on political decentralization. Financial decentralization refers to the authority of local governments to generate their own revenue, the receipt of fiscal transfers, and the expenditure of those resources. Administrative decentralization refers to the assumption by local governments of public and social service functions.

4. Publications on elections, local democracy, and decentralization include Wunsch and Olowu (1996); Gervasoni (2006, 2008); Gibson (2005); Gibson and

Suarez-Cao (2006–2007); Hopkin (2003); International IDEA (2003, 2004); Montero and Samuels (2004); O'Neill (2005).

5. Only a few of the major works in the transitions and democratization literature address decentralization and local government, including Dahl (1971); Diamond (1999); Diamond et al. (1999).

6. However, this may not be terribly surprising given that, until a decade or so ago, empirical studies of the politics of intergovernmental reform or of decentralization within the context of democratic development (as opposed to fiscal federalism and public administration reform, for example) received little consideration in the scholarly community or international financial institutions.

7. See, for example, Dahl (1971, 226); Diamond (1999); Lijphart (1999).

8. See also Chhibber and Kollman (2004, 220).

9. Note that the "center" may not necessarily be considered the national government in large or federal countries with strong intermediate-level systems. In such cases, the state, region, or other intermediate government entity may be viewed as central.

10. See, for example, Poiré (2000).

11. The following discussion is drawn from Bland (2007b, 6–13).

12. Decentralization has been defined in a multitude of ways and definitional use tends to reflect the academic discipline of the author.

13. The eight conditions comprise the "expanded procedural minimum" definition of democracy (D. Collier and Levitsky 1997, 443) developed by Dahl (1971, 1982) and others (see Schmitter and Karl 1991, 81–82). They include government decisionmaking constitutionally vested in elected officials; free and fair elections; adult suffrage; freedom of adults to run for elective office; freedom of expression; free access to alternative information; freedom of association, including independent parties and interest groups; and effective power to govern.

14. Skepticism about relying too heavily on formal political institutions to understand democratic change is duly noted (e.g., Ostrom 2005; Mainwaring and Scully 2008; Roberts, forthcoming). Democratic outcomes are mediated by other factors that may never be fully considered, informality can counteract formal rules, and important socioeconomic factors may be missed. Electoral or party system rules do not alone provide the solution for local democratic change. As Sartori (1997, 27) points out, however, such rules do have important consequences: "If electoral systems were of little consequence why on earth would politicians fight so bitterly about them? And why would reformers fight so persistently to have them changed? Much ado about nothing?" Likewise, Gibson (2005, 128–129), in a rare comparative study of subnational democracy, concludes that a focus on institutional design is critical.

15. Bland (2007b). The framework is based on Dahl (1971, 1982). See also Molina and Hernández (1998); Nickson (1995).

16. Direct election can be seen in both majoritarian and proportional representation systems. In the former, for example, mayors are directly elected on a separate ballot or town councilors can be chosen in single-member districts. In the latter, open list voting for town council provides direct election, even if the council then selects the mayor. It is conceivable that in practice parties can be so weak that party labels become mere vehicles for individual candidates, even though direct election as defined here may not technically hold.

17. This is not to argue that individual representative accountability should be pursued at the expense of the cohesion of the party system.

18. This refers to electoral systems that provide locally based standards for the formation of local parties or independent candidacies. Or, if the system establishes standards based on national or other higher-level politicoadministrative units, the practical barriers to entry are so minimal that the formation of local parties is common.

19. Alan Wall, Indonesia country director, Democracy International, Jakarta, personal communication with the author, April 10, 2006; Alan Wall, Jakarta, interviewed by the author, May 29, 2006.

20. Steven Rood, country representative for the Philippines and Pacific Islands Nations, Asia Foundation, interviewed by the author, Manila, July 9, 2006.

21. Omar Touré, chief of party, RTI International, Benin Decentralization and Anti-Corruption Project, Cotonu, personal communication with the author, April 13, 2006.

22. Christian Arandel, deputy chief of party, RTI International, Morocco Local Governance Project, Rabat, interviewed by the author, July 20, 2006.

23. Political democracy requires that elected national government's hold a monopoly on the use of force. Only in 2005 did the Cedar Revolution lead to the removal of the Syrian military presence in Lebanon; Hezbollah continues to control the southern region of the country.

24. Paul Salem, director, Middle East Center, Carnegie Endowment for International Peace, Beirut, interviewed by the author, July 7, 2006.

25. This review of Armenia is also drawn from Sam Coxson, chief of party, RTI International, Local Government Project, Yerevan, interviewed by the author, June 27, 2006.

26. Hal Minis, technical manager, RTI International, Bulgaria Local Government Initiative, Research Triangle Park, North Carolina, interviewed by the author, April 15, 2006.

27. Bohdan Radejko, chief of party, Indiana University Parliamentary Development Project (IUPDP), Kiev, interviewed by the author, July 14, 2006; Robert Bodo, chief of party, RTI International, Municipal Budget Reform Project, Kiev, interviewed by the author, July 18, 2006; Edward Rakhimkulov, deputy field director, IUPDP, Kiev, interviewed by the author, July 24, 2006.

28. On democracy as consensus building, see Rustow (1970, 362–363).

29. In the federal systems, especially, the intermediate-level policymakers also must relinquish some authority to the municipal level.

4

Decentralization and Community Empowerment

Derick W. Brinkerhoff, with Omar Azfar

Decentralization is frequently recommended as a means to enact and deepen democratic governance and to improve administrative and service delivery effectiveness. While decentralization is often regarded as a top-down process driven by the unitary or federal state in which the center grants functions, authorities, and resources to subnational and local levels, impulses for decentralization can also originate from these lower levels. Closely associated with the bottom-up dynamic is community empowerment, whereby local actors, capacities, and resources are mobilized for collective action to achieve public purposes. Local governments (LGs) and jurisdictions constitute the institutional loci where these top-down and bottom-up drives meet. Thus, an important question for the successful achievement of decentralization's democratic and service delivery aims is whether and how community empowerment interacts with local governments to further these objectives.

At first glance, one might expect community empowerment to help whenever decentralization does because, if decentralization moves government closer to the people, community empowerment moves it closer still. However, precisely because decentralization concerns politics and power as well as technocratic efficiency and effectiveness, the assumption that empowerment automatically enhances democracy and service delivery merits investigation.

This chapter focuses on community empowerment and explores its relationship to democratic decentralized local government. Besides looking at community empowerment as a contributor to the extent to which decentralization can strengthen democracy and service delivery, the chapter also addresses how various degrees of decentralization influence opportunities for, and outcomes of, community empowerment. In the following section, we review the meaning of decentralization and the arguments for pursuing it, and discuss a set of expected outcomes to which decentralization contributes. In the next section, we define community empowerment and examine the range of mechanisms employed to empower communities in relation to local government. Next, we frame issues for community empowerment that emerge as decentralization moves from deconcentration to democratic devolution. We then address the question: how does community empowerment improve the ability of decentralization to deepen democracy and provide better public services? In the next section, we look in more depth at community empowerment and democratic local governance, and examine arguments that empowerment mechanisms may in some situations weaken, rather than support, democratic local governance. In the final section, we offer implications.

Decentralization

Definitions

"Decentralization" deals with the allocation between center and periphery of power, authority, and responsibility for political, fiscal, and administrative systems. The most common definitions of decentralization distinguish variants along a continuum where, at one end, the center maintains strong control with limited power and discretion at lower levels (deconcentration) to progressively decreasing central control and increasing local discretion at the other (devolution). The devolutionary end of the continuum is associated with more democratic governance.

In principle, accompanying the transfer of authority and responsibility and the expanded discretionary space to make decisions locally is a shift in accountability. Upward accountability to the center is supplemented with, or in the case of devolution largely superseded by, downward accountability. And indirect accountability, mediated by higher level authorities is augmented with direct accountability. The nature of decentralized accountability relationships are significant factors in creating options and avenues for community empowerment. An important question is whether or not decentralization choices, and the accountability structures and incentives they put in place for local government and local service delivery agencies, enfranchise communities (see Ribot 2004).

Table 4.1 summarizes the different types of decentralization, and identifies the features of local government under each type. The table presents stylized versions of local government's administrative, financial, and polit-

Table 4.1 Types of Decentralization and Impacts on Local Government

Administrative	Financial/Fiscal	Political
Deconcentration		
Local government (LG) follows central policies, plans according to central norms. Form and structure of LG centrally determined. LG staff are employees of central ministries, accountable to center. LG is service delivery arm of center, little or no discretion in service choice or mix and modes of provision. LG provides information upward to center.	LG is dependent on center for funds; sectoral ministries and Ministry of Finance provide spending priorities and budget envelope. LG has no independent revenue sources. LG reports to center on expenditure according to central formulas and norms. Center conducts LG audits.	No elected LG, officials appointed by center and serve central interests. Civil society and citizens rely on remote and weak links to central government for exercising accountability. for local civil society, central elites control politics.
Delegation		
LG follows central policies and norms, has some discretion to tailor to local needs and to modify form and structure. LG staff may be mix of central and LG employees, LG has authority on hiring and placement, center handles promotion and firing. LG provides service menu set by center, some discretion in mix to fit local needs and in modes of provision. LG provides most information upward to center and selected information to local officials, citizens.	LG is dependent on center for funds; LG has some discretion on spending priorities within budget envelope. Block grants and conditional transfers from center offer some autonomy. LG has no independent revenue sources. LG reports to center and local officials on expenditure according to central formulas and norms. Center and LG conduct LG audits.	LG may be a mix of elected and centrally appointed officials. Local officials often tied to national party platforms, little discretion. Some local accountability, but strong central orientation. Some political space for local civil society.

continues

ical dimensions under progressively more democratic decentralized governance systems. In reality, local governments are much more complex and nuanced blends of these characteristics. The table illustrates that, in general, democratic local governance offers both a greater range of decisions and more autonomous decision space within that range to local government actors. However, the specific contours of that democratic space will be strongly influenced by how authority is distributed at the local level. Strong mayor–weak council systems create narrower space than systems that balance authority more evenly between mayors and councils, and that

Table 4.1 continued

Administrative	Financial/Fiscal	Political
Devolution		
LG is subject to national norms, but sets local policies and priorities, plans autonomously in response to local preferences and needs. LG determines own form and structure. LG staff are employees of LG, which sets salaries, numbers, assignments, and handles hiring and firing. LG determines service mix, modes of provision, eligibility, and allocation. LG provides information to local officials, citizens.	LG sets spending priorities, plans how to meet service delivery obligations given resource availability. LG has mix of own-source revenues, revenue sharing, central transfers. LG may have some authority for debt financing, but is subject to a hard budget constraint. LG reports to local officials and citizens on expenditure according to central formulas and norms. LG is responsible for audits, reports results locally and to center.	Locally elected officials lead LG, may or may not be linked to national parties, platforms respond to constituent demands and needs. Strong local accountability; LG shapes budget priorities, investments, service mix to fit local preferences and needs. Broad political space for local civil society.

Sources: Derick W. Brinkerhoff and Charlotte Leighton, "Decentralization and Health System Reform: Issue in Brief" (Washington, DC: US Agency for International Development, 2002); Ronald Johnson, "Decentralization Strategy Design: Complementary Perspectives on a Common Theme" (Washington, DC: US Agency for International Development, 1995); World Bank, *World Development Report: Making Services Work for the Poor* (Washington, DC: World Bank, 2004).

provide for citizen input to council meetings. For example, in Latin America, LGs are characterized by a strong executive who has both policy and administrative roles. The executive wields considerable power, much more than the local legislature or council, both formally and informally. Mayors tend to fill several roles, for instance, as influential political party members and community leaders.

Expected Outcomes

Two broad categories of outcomes anticipated from decentralization are usually identified: (1) those related to deepening democracy and (2) those concerning improved service delivery. The distinction between these two categories is not hard and fast. There is overlap and positive feedback between the democracy and service delivery outcomes.

The concept of "democratic deepening" refers to processes of consolidation and institutionalization such that democracy becomes "the only game in town" (Diamond 1997, xvii). Democratic deepening concerns not simply the structures and procedures by which democratic governance is exercised, but its quality and substance (Gaventa 2005). For example, in principle, the existence of formal representative structures provides for political participation for all citizens. Yet in practice, if political parties and elections consistently exclude the interests of the poor, women, and minorities, then the quality of democracy is called into question. Deepening democracy requires the active engagement in public affairs of citizens from all socioeconomic strata (see Fung and Wright 2003a). Decentralization is recognized in the democracy literature as contributing importantly to democratic deepening, but with the caveat that elite capture is a danger requiring explicit countervailing measures to avoid (e.g., Bardhan and Mookherjee 2000; UNDP 2002).

Central-local relations play an important role in influencing whether decentralization achieves democratic outcomes (Manor 1999; Crook 2003; Crook and Sverrisson 1999). The multiple layers of government in decentralized democracies create a separation of powers that can provide checks on actions at various levels. Different levels of government can then discipline each other. As Monica Das Gupta, Helene Grandvoinnet, and Mattia Romani (2004) note, central governments can exercise their power over subnational levels to support the achievement of national objectives such as poverty reduction. In Indonesia, a recent study (Olken 2005) found that increasing the likelihood of audits by a central government agency reduces corruption in local governments.

Much of the decentralization literature focuses on the second outcome category, service delivery. Major analytic threads focus on how decentralization improves allocative efficiency through matching services with citizen preferences, increases service production efficiency and cost recovery, and affects intergovernmental fiscal relations (see, e.g., Azfar, Kahkonen, and Meagher 2001; Shah and Thompson 2004; Oates 1999; Tiebout 1956). Related threads explore decentralization's impacts on service providers' incentives for accountability, innovation, and equitable distribution (e.g., Dillinger 1994).

We select the following specific outcomes to explore—three decentralization outcomes that deepen democracy and three that contribute to improved service delivery:

Deepened Democracy

1. Improved accountability and responsiveness to a broad range of citizens.
2. Improved skills and capacity of citizens to participate effectively in public affairs.
3. New and expanded cadre of leaders with democratic skills that can transform the contestability of political markets.

Improved Service Delivery

1. Better matching of public services to citizens' needs and preferences.
2. Improved technical efficiency because of "a race to the top" as different jurisdictions compete with each other for taxpaying firms and residents by providing more attractive service mixes and incentives.
3. Increased innovation as problems are solved at the local level and as successes are disseminated.

Community Empowerment

Definitions

Conceptually, community empowerment is closely allied with citizen participation (see, e.g., Craig and Mayo 1995; Mansuri and Rao 2004). From its original meaning of to invest with decisionmaking power and authority, definitions of "empowerment" have expanded to include: having access to information and resources, having a range of choices beyond yes or no, exercise of "voice" and "exit," feeling a sense of efficacy, and mobilizing like-minded others for common goals. These latter elements reflect a perspective on empowerment that encompasses psychological capabilities, including belief in citizenship rights and aspirations to a better future (see Cornwall and Gaventa 2001; Diener and Biswas-Diener 2005; Appadurai 2004).

Combining community with empowerment emphasizes the essentiality of collective action. "Community empowerment" concerns how members of a group are able to act collectively in ways that enhance their influence on, or control over, decisions that affect their interests. Although a community is often defined generically as a group of people living in the same locality and under the same government, we employ a working definition that focuses on the collective action dimension: a "community" is a group that shares a sufficient commonality of interests such that its members are motivated to engage in collective action (see Olson 1965).

This definition does not mean that everyone agrees, or that there are no socioeconomic divisions or conflicts within a community. Particularly in countries with weak civil societies, or postconflict situations where societies exhibit deep socioethnic cleavages, collective action capacity is likely to be fragile and easily broken through internal distrust or external efforts by state actors to exert control.

Further, this definition does not assume that all community members engage equally. In practice empowerment is most likely to emerge first among a small group of motivated individuals, before expanding to a broader base though constituency building, education, and outreach. It is unrealistic to expect that large numbers of people will necessarily be interested ex ante in collective action. Rather, small numbers are likely to engage initially, acting on behalf of their communities.

We define community empowerment operationally in terms of four elements. Communities are empowered if they: (1) have access to information; (2) are included and participate in forums where issues are discussed and decisions are made; (3) can hold decisionmakers accountable for their choices and actions; and (4) have the capacity and resources to organize to aggregate and express their interests or to take on roles as partners with public service delivery agencies.

Mechanisms

We categorize mechanisms according to the four elements of our definition of community empowerment. However, we recognize that most of the mechanisms contribute to more than one of them. Further, we distinguish between: (a) mechanisms that result from decisions taken by state actors and where outcomes are determined in state-centered arenas (executive agencies, legislatures, courts); and (b) those mechanisms where the impetus comes from nonstate actors and outcomes are resolved in public arenas that, in many cases, are independent of the state. These two arenas are interconnected and, in some situations, overlapping, but this distinction highlights the importance of empowerment as a source of countervailing strength vis-à-vis the state. In a democracy, community empowerment is less something that state actors bestow on communities at their discretion than it is a right or a demand that communities exercise in their relations with the state. Table 4.2 provides a summary.

Access to information. Access to information is the basic foundation for empowerment; thus, core empowerment mechanisms that reside within the state's legal and institutional structures include laws and procedures that make information available and transparent. These include freedom of information acts (FOIAs), so-called sunshine laws that mandate government to disseminate budget and program documents, and procedural requirements for open hearings on matters of concern to communities. A donor-initiated mechanism is the public expenditure tracking survey (PETS), which documents resource flows between different levels of government regarding

Table 4.2 Community Empowerment Mechanisms

Information	Inclusion/ Participation	Accountability	Local Organizational Capacity
State-centered arena Access to information laws (FIOA) Sunshine laws Open hearings Public expenditure tracking surveys	Participatory budgeting Quotas for women and minorities Joint planning Laws on participation Question periods	Citizen review boards Local councils Elections Litigation	Parents' associations School committees Health committees Natural resources comanagement contracts
Society-centered arena Citizen report cards Media reporting Information/advocacy campaigns Civic education	Grassroots movements *Journées de réflexion*	Referendums Recalls Watchdog NGOs *Observatoires*	Civil society organizations/ nongovernmental organizations Social capital formation Church groups

Source: Adapted from Deepa Narayan, ed. *Empowerment and Poverty Reduction: A Sourcebook* (Washington, DC: World Bank, 2002).

funding for services such as health or education (see Reinikka and Svensson 2004). These surveys track leakage and time lag. The information they provide can be used by communities to hold service providers accountable, and to fight corruption.

Empowerment mechanisms in this category that emanate from nonstate actors include citizen report cards, media investigations, information or advocacy campaigns by civil society organizations (CSOs), and civic education programs. Citizen report cards have gained in popularity since their introduction in India by the Public Affairs Centre (PAC), a CSO established in 1994 in Bangalore. The World Bank and other international agencies have helped to spread report cards to other countries, and PAC now offers assistance to other organizations to conduct surveys.

An example of a civil society–initiated information campaign is the South Africa Women's Budget Initiative (WBI). Started in 1995 by the South African advocacy nongovernmental organization (NGO), Institute for Democracy in Africa (IDASA), the WBI has analyzed the impacts of the government budget on different groups. The initiative influenced policymakers as they prepared South Africa's budget (Budlender 1998). The WBI's members organized a number of conferences to foster an exchange of views and to generate consensus.

Civic education programs seek both to inform communities and to mobilize citizen action regarding democratic governance. For example, the

US Agency for International Development (USAID) supported numerous civic education programs in countries of the former Soviet Union, in South Africa, and more recently in Iraq (Blair 2003; Finkel 2003; Brinkerhoff and Mayfield 2005).

Inclusion and participation. Mechanisms to foster inclusion and community participation range from legally mandated measures such as Bolivia's law on participation and India's quotas for women and minorities in local legislatures (see Chattopadhyay and Duflo 2003), to procedural routines in public agencies such as joint planning with communities and service providers or question and notice periods for pending regulations and laws. Probably the most widely recognized procedural empowerment mechanism is participatory budgeting, initiated in the Brazilian municipality of Porto Alegre, whose experience has led to widespread dissemination of participatory budgeting in other Brazilian cities and other countries (see Baiocchi 2003; Heller 2001; Brautigam 2004; McNulty 2006).

Grassroots movements are an example of a community empowerment mechanism that originates outside of government structures. Landless peasant movements are an example such as the Movimiento dos Trabalhadores Rurais Sem-Terra, formed in 1984 in Brazil, which used techniques of peaceful land occupations to pressure state governments to change land policies (Wright and Wolford 2003). Grassroots movements highlight the political nature of empowerment mechanisms when they are used to challenge state power and the dominance of local elites such as, in the Brazilian example, large landholders.

Another society-centered example of an empowerment mechanism is civil society dialogue forums (*journées de réflexion*). These mechanisms were often used to facilitate citizen consultations as input to Poverty Reduction Strategy Papers (PRSPs). The case of Bolivia illustrates a situation where CSOs' negative experience with a government-initiated participatory process, the First National Dialogue in 1997, led to a second exercise in which civil society groups, under the umbrella of the Catholic Church, organized the dialogue (Coventry 1999).

Accountability. "Accountability" is defined as a relationship where one party has the obligation to answer questions regarding decisions or actions posed by another party, and the accountable party is subject to sanctions for failures or transgressions (see Schedler 1999). "Horizontal accountability" concerns the classic separation of powers, but also includes a variety of oversight entities such as audit offices, ombudsmen, courts of accounts, and electoral commissions. "Vertical accountability" refers to actors located outside the state that play a role in holding state actors accountable.

In democracies, the classic empowerment mechanism that addresses vertical accountability is voting. Whether or not elections actually serve to empower local communities to exercise accountability is debatable (see Schroeder 2003; Brinkerhoff 2005). Much depends on the rules in place that govern elections. For example, in Indonesia even though new laws establish direct voting for regional parliament members and mayors, the impact on local accountability is blunted by existing laws that preclude the possibility of independent regional candidates, which means that officials' loyalties are oriented to national political parties rather than to local citizens (DEMOS 2005).

Local councils are another community empowerment mechanism. As with elections, the extent to which councils empower communities depends heavily on the rules by which they operate. For example, the shift from a weak to a strong mayor system in Zimbabwean cities in the mid-1990s increased the accountability of local public officials to elected representatives of the municipalities (Olowu 2003). Uganda has a local council system with reserved places for women, youth, and persons with disabilities (Devas and Grant 2003). Uganda's local council system at the village level (LC1) has rules that forbid the use of lawyers in LC1 courts, which are presided over by a nine-person committee. These rules limit the influence of the rich and influential (who can afford lawyers) and reduced corruption because bribery is more difficult (Wunsch and Ottemoeller 2004). In postwar Iraq, for example, USAID assistance put in place local councils to introduce accountability for service delivery and responsiveness to community needs at the local level (Brinkerhoff and Mayfield 2005). Peru's recent reforms incorporated community groups into local and regional planning, but the success of these efforts is strongly influenced by the political will of regional governors and by communities' belief in the effectiveness of participatory planning (McNulty 2006).

Citizen review boards are another type of accountability-focused empowerment mechanism. For example, Bolivia's Popular Participation Law established oversight committees made up of elected community organization leaders to review local government investment plans for conformity with community priorities and municipal council decisions (Faguet 2001). A similar structure can be found in several francophone African countries; for example, Madagascar passed a law in 2001 to set up a Forest Sector Observatory to serve as an external oversight body for forest management and exploitation in response to problems of corruption. Such entities often straddle the border between horizontal and vertical accountability; they have formal legal standing, and are part of a state system of checks and balances, but they depend on nonstate actors for their functioning.

Related to observatories are NGO "watchdog" groups that take on a monitoring and reporting function. Their vertical accountability power comes from publicizing their findings, exposing failure to deliver services as mandated or malfeasance, mobilizing citizens to pressure decisionmakers for redress, and, in some situations, pursuing litigation.

In the Indian state of Gujarat, for example, a local NGO, Developing Initiatives for Social and Human Action (DISHA), decided to monitor the state's budget to determine whether funds allocated to provide services for the poor and tribal groups were actually spent on them. After a struggle to obtain the documents, DISHA issued its first budget analysis in 1993, revealing a large gap between stated and actual pro-poor expenditures. DISHA expanded to disseminate information and analysis on the budget and budgetary process to policymakers, members of the community, and the press. It also organized training programs to teach other NGOs about the state government budgetary process (Buhl 1997).

Local organizational capacity. There are numerous examples of organizational mechanisms that empower communities both to engage with public agencies in service partnerships and to undertake autonomous collective action. In the education sector, parents' associations and school committees incorporate the views and desires of communities into decisions related to their children's education. In some cases, these organizations give community members management and oversight authority. Such mechanisms become, in effect, learning laboratories for the participants, enhancing communities' organizational capabilities over time. Simon M. Fass and Gerrit M. Desloovere (2004), for example, recount how in Chad in the middle to late 1990s in the absence of central government capacity, parents' associations evolved to fulfill an expanded set of education management functions, including hiring and paying teachers, raising local revenues for school operations, and exercising performance oversight.

As another example, Madagascar has two community organizations in the education sector. The Fikambanan'ny Ray-Amandrenin'ny Mpianatra (FRAM) is the association of parents, and is supported by voluntary contributions. In communities whose schools do not have enough teachers, FRAMs have hired teachers, paying them with money, bags of rice, and donated agricultural labor and land. FRAM members also provide in-kind support to school operations and rehabilitation. FRAM leaders are elected by the community. The Farimbon'Asa Iambonana ho Fampandrosoana ny Sekoly (FAF), a government-community partnership organization for school development, was created by a ministerial decree in 2002, in response to the need for a formal organization to receive World Bank funds. Its partnership structure combines school directors with elected community members to manage a fund whose transactions are publicly posted to assure transparency (Brinkerhoff 2004).

Self-governing irrigation associations in Asia are another example. Elinor Ostrom (1990) and Shui Yan Tang (1992) analyzed how farmers organized to handle water distribution and canal maintenance, to devise and enforce rules, and to interact with public officials. They identified the importance of trust and communication, factors that play a role in the creation of social capital, a resource recognized in the literature on empowerment as important to local organizational capacity (see Narayan 2005).

Community Empowerment and Decentralization

Table 4.3 adds the community empowerment dimension to the previously developed picture of decentralized local government (see Table 4.1). It reveals several core points. First, the more decentralization moves toward democratic devolution, the greater: (a) the space for communities to exercise voice with local officials; and (b) the space for local officials to exercise discretion in response to citizen preferences. As noted above, the distribution of LG authorities has an impact on how this space can be exploited (see also Ostrom 1990). Without such space, though, community empowerment mechanisms will have difficulty functioning. Second, delegation and devolution call for higher levels of LG capacity, and thus capacity deficits may constrain the chances that LGs can respond to citizens' preferences. Third, increasingly democratic forms of decentralization do not necessarily reduce the incentives for poor and marginalized groups to seek clientelist relationships.

These findings confirm that, as the potential for positive synergies expands, so too does the need for LG capacity. The necessary capabilities involve skills that may not be strong among local officials. They will be called on to conduct town or neighborhood meetings, explain policies and options, mediate conflicts, and build consensus. Local government capacity alone cannot ensure that local discretion will result in choices that are citizen responsive or democratic. In some cases, the local penetration of the central state is so weak that strongmen can predominate with little outside interference (Migdal 1988). In others, political elites at the center, who maintain their power through hierarchical connections with local officials, act as a check on local discretion to respond to other interests such as the poor (Crook 2003). In still other situations, for example, Mexican municipalities, citizens petition for services from powerholders at the center when LG officials prove unresponsive (Grindle 2007). Hence, clien-

Table 4.3 Decentralization, Local Government, and Issues for Community Empowerment

Administrative	Financial/Fiscal	Political	Community Empowerment Issues
Deconcentration			
Local government (LG) follows central policies, plans according to central norms. Form and structure of LG centrally determined. LG staff are employees of central ministries, accountable to center. LG is service delivery arm of center, little or no discretion in service choice or mix and modes of provision. LG provides information upward to center.	LG is dependent on center for funds; sectoral ministries and Ministry of Finance provide spending priorities and budget envelope. LG has no independent revenue sources. LG reports to center on expenditure according to central formulas and norms. Center conducts LG audits.	No elected LG, officials appointed by center and serve central interests. Civil society and citizens rely on remote and weak links to central government for exercising accountability. Little political space for local civil society, central elites control politics.	LG has little capacity and few incentives to seek community input or be responsive to local needs. No incorporation of local preferences in service mix. Local communities and poor seek clientelist and patronage relationships with elites at center.
Delegation			
LG follows central policies and norms, has some discretion to tailor to local needs and to modify form and structure. LG staff may be mix of central and LG employees, LG has authority on hiring and placement, center handles promotion and firing. LG provides service menu set by center, some discretion in mix to fit local needs and in modes of provision. LG provides most information upward to center and selected information to local officials, citizens.	LG is dependent on center for funds; LG has some discretion on spending priorities within budget envelope. Block grants and conditional transfers from center offer some autonomy. LG has no independent revenue sources. LG reports to center and local officials on expenditure according to central formulas and norms. Center and LG conducts LG audits.	LG may be a mix of elected and centrally appointed officials. Local officials often tied to national party platforms, little discretion. Some local accountability, but strong central orientation. Some political space for local civil society.	Citizens have some local voice and accountability links, but center remains able to override local decisions. Some incorporation of local preferences. Blended center-local accountability offers some limited options for community empowerment. Local officials have relatively weak incentives to respond to citizen demands. Poor retain clientelist links to center for some services.

continues

Table 4.3 continued

Administrative	Financial/Fiscal	Political	Community Empowerment Issues
Devolution			
LG is subject to national norms, but sets local policies and priorities, plans autonomously in response to local preferences and needs. LG determines own form and structure. LG staff are employees of LG, which sets salaries, numbers, assignments, and handles hiring and firing. LG determines service mix, modes of provision, eligibility, and allocation. LG provides information to local officials, citizens.	LG sets spending priorities, plans how to meet service delivery obligations given resource availability. LG has mix of own-source revenues, revenue sharing, central transfers. LG may have some authority for debt financing, but is subject to a hard budget constraint. LG reports to local officials and citizens on expenditure according to central formulas and norms. LG is responsible for audits, reports results locally and to center.	Locally elected officials lead LG, may or may not be linked to national parties, platforms respond to constituent demands and needs. Strong local accountability, LG shapes budget priorities, investments, service mix to fit local preferences and needs. Broad political space for local civil society.	Civil society and citizens have strong links to LG for expressing voice, exercising accountability. Local officials have strong incentives and capacity to be responsive to citizen preferences and demands. Risk of local elite capture of LG. Poor develop clientelist and patronage relationships with local elites as well as maintain those with center.

Sources: Adapted from Derick W. Brinkerhoff and Arthur Goldsmith, "Good Governance, Clientelism and Patrimonialism: New Perspectives on Old Problems," *International Public Management Journal* 7 (2) (2004): 163–185; Derick W. Brinkerhoff and Charlotte Leighton, "Decentralization and Health System Reform: Issue in Brief" (Washington, DC: US Agency for International Development, 2002); Ronald Johnson, "Decentralization Strategy Design: Complementary Perspectives on a Common Theme" (Washington, DC: US Agency for International Development, 1995); World Bank, *World Development Report: Making Services Work for the Poor* (Washington, DC: World Bank, 2004).

telist relationships and patronage persist despite de jure democratic local governance (Brinkerhoff and Goldsmith 2004).

The interests and strategies of political parties, politicians, bureaucrats, and community activists will influence prospects for community empowerment. Some governments may pursue efforts to increase empowerment and decentralization because they believe that it is in their interest to do so, and that as a result they will be strengthened. Conversely, however, governments that perceive little gain from increased openness, transparency, and direct citizen involvement will be less likely to support empowerment. As with any reform, entrenched interests will resist changes. Dealing with resistance at the local level calls for political will and proactive intervention from the center.

However, the effectiveness of checks and balances exercised by higher levels of government depends upon the relationship between local and national elites (Crook 2003). Whether community empowerment at the LG level can achieve its potential is related to the existence of commitment at those higher levels to engaging local citizens. Among the best-known examples is participatory health service delivery in the Brazilian state of Ceará, where state health officials set and enforced the standards for hiring and performance of community health workers (which avoided clientelism in hiring) while establishing local structures and procedures that engaged local health service users as active participants in assessing health worker performance (Tendler 1997).

Community Empowerment's Contribution to Decentralization

We now turn to the question: how does community empowerment help in attaining the benefits that decentralized, democratic local government is conjectured to produce? We consider decentralization's expected outcomes, associated with deepening democracy and improving service delivery, and the role community empowerment may play in contributing to them.

Improved Accountability and Responsiveness

A core democratic outcome expected from decentralization is improved accountability and responsiveness to increased numbers of citizens through the creation of subnational jurisdictions. Local governments with delegated and devolved powers deal with issues and services of direct concern to their constituents and, through elections, referenda, and open governmental processes and procedures (e.g., town hall meetings, council hearings and committees, "one-stop shop" service centers, ombudsmen), face pressures to respond to citizens and to be accountable for decisions taken. In principal-agent terms, citizens or principals exercise voice through their agents, elected local officials, who then in their role as principals create service delivery compacts with service providers (agents) to furnish citizens with the public goods and services they need and want. These principal-agent links are nourished with information, which allows the principals to determine whether their agents are acting according to their wishes. Decentralization provides better information flows at the local level than at the national level due to proximity of principals to agents.

Regarding the extent to which this expected outcome of decentralization is found in practice in developing countries, much of the literature reveals negative or highly circumscribed findings. Crook (2003), for example, looking at African decentralization and responsiveness to local citizens for poverty reduction, found few traces of a relationship. In a comparative study of Uganda and the Philippines, Omar Azfar, Satu Kahkonen, and Patrick Meagher (2001) found little evidence of local election voting being driven by service delivery concerns. Further, this study reveals that citizens tended to obtain information on local government performance from community leaders rather than independent sources. As a result, their potential to hold officials accountable was constrained by an inability to form accurate judgments of the results of local officials' actions since community leaders showed a positive bias in the opinions they expressed about local governments.

How might community empowerment help increase the accountability and responsiveness of local governments? Information is a prerequisite for any effective exercise of accountability; thus, mechanisms to provide information—such as FOIAs, PETS, and citizen report cards—to the extent that they offer information on government intentions, plans, activities, and results, provide fundamental input to accountability and responsiveness. Community empowerment mechanisms that increase participation and inclusiveness, such as participatory budgeting, also improve information flows about government performance. In addition, they bring community members into the budgetary process itself, strengthening the responsiveness of government by influencing spending priorities. Other community empowerment mechanisms are explicitly designed to increase vertical accountability such as citizen review boards, local councils, and watchdog NGOs. Local organizations, such as school or health committees, can increase responsiveness through their membership of service users, which creates a structure where providers interact with users on a regular basis.

Some evidence points toward the effectiveness of community empowerment in vertical accountability and oversight, particularly in cases where service delivery is easily observable by communities. Benjamin Olken (2005), in a study of Indonesian municipalities, found that community participation in anticorruption monitoring was effective where residents had access to information and a direct interest in reducing theft such as in subsidies for food, health care, or education. Emmanuel Jimenez and Yasuyuki Sawada (1999) found that decentralized community-managed schools in El Salvador, where associations with locally elected leadership from parents were involved in hiring and monitoring teachers and in managing school supplies and facilities, had lower teacher and student absenteeism, and improved educational outcomes. Carol L. Dauda (2004) documented how parent-teacher associations partnered with local governments in Uganda to improve school performance and accountability. The case studies in Andrea Cornwall, Henry Lucas, and Kath Pasteur (2000) provide examples of village health committees and local health councils where communities played an integral role in accountability of public health service providers to community needs.

Numerous studies of these mechanisms reveal that their effectiveness in empowering the poor is mediated strongly by political power. Regarding FOIAs, for example, studies of six states in India document the struggles of local CSOs to use right-to-information provisions to obtain information on pro-poor state spending and corruption in the face of bureaucratic stonewalling and elite hostility, and this is in one of the most democratic nations in the developing world (Jenkins and Goetz 1999; Goetz and Jenkins 2001, 2004). PETS have had the benefit of support by the World Bank and the International Monetary Fund, which have employed them as analytic input to poverty-focused loan packages. Porto Alegre's experiment with participatory budgeting was launched in the wake of the electoral victory of the workers' party. Thus, without the motivation of politicians to create a base of political support, the acclaimed community empowerment results would not have been achieved, a factor that some enthusiasts for participatory budgeting have overlooked.

Regarding citizen committees, Vijayendra Rao and Ana M. Ibáñez's (2003) study of the Jamaica Social Investment Fund found that local elites, the better educated and better connected, dominated decisionmaking for the fund. Gavin Shatkin's (2000) study of empowerment in municipal government in Manila revealed that civil society organizations faced competition from powerful business interests in their often unsuccessful efforts to influence public officials to respond to their needs. A study in South Africa found that community members serving on hospital boards, ostensibly to increase responsiveness to community needs, were at a disadvantage in the face of the superior technical authority and political clout of the medical profession (NPPHCN 1998).

The evidence on community empowerment's role in enhancing democratic local government through increased vertical accountability is mixed. The effectiveness of empowerment mechanisms for accountability purposes is muted by existing distributions of social and political power, both nationally and at the local level. For example, in Uganda health service users hesitated to complain to local councilors about poor service or abuse because they felt that the social relationships among health workers and local politicians made complaining a waste of time or even risky (Golooba-Mutebi 2005).

Community participation in local government does not lead to more accountability absent: (1) local political support for such involvement; and (2) discipline imposed by higher levels of government. Regarding this latter point, Benjamin Olken (2005) found that community monitoring, while increasing local participation in oversight, had little effect on local government corruption in infrastructure spending; on the other hand, accountability to the national government, in the form of increased probability of an audit, proved more effective. Similarly, Merilee Grindle (2007) found in a number of Mexican municipalities that decentralization did not increase accountability. Deborah Brautigam (2004) echoes this view, noting that horizontal accountability institutions of central government are more effective in curbing local government corruption than community monitoring.

Improved Skills and Capacity to Participate Effectively in Public Affairs

Democratic decentralization that devolves decisionmaking authority, accompanied by resources to implement decisions (revenue-raising capacity and intergovernmental transfers), creates the conditions for local governments to become institutional arenas where citizens learn democratic skills and how to exercise their rights. Deepening democracy requires expanding the number of citizens who are able to participate effectively in public affairs, and democratic local government offers potential participatory possibilities to a large number of citizens. However, to take advantage of those participatory options, citizens need skills along with motivation. As John Gaventa says, "citizen participation does not just happen, even when the political space and opportunities emerge for it to do so. Developing effective citizenship and building democratic institutions take effort, skill, and attention" (1999, 50). This involves the experience of deliberating in public forums and voting on issues close to home such as education, streetlights, and garbage collection; making tax and budget choices; and monitoring the results can expand citizens' skills. Positive experiences with local government can lead to citizens who have a deeper faith in the democratic process, are more willing to participate in it, and are more willing to defend it. These experiences help citizens learn how government works, gain confidence in interacting with local officials, and understand how to protect and pursue their political and civil rights.

How does community empowerment help to build these skills among citizens? Community empowerment mechanisms like participatory budgeting, citizen oversight committees, service delivery report cards, information campaigns, notice and comment, and direct elections, referendums, and recalls all offer avenues for citizens to engage with local governments. When communities pursue these various options, their members have the potential to build democratic participation skills. Not all these mechanisms are equal in terms of such skills. Voting is often thought of as a relatively passive activity, without much skill involved. Yet when we think about voting as an act of voice that connects candidates for office with issues, policies, and outcomes, then the element of democratic skills becomes more evident.

Communities that understand these connections will be better able to vote in ways that help them advance their interests, subject to the constraints imposed by electoral rules (e.g., party-list systems). However, Azfar, Kahkonen, and Meagher (2001) found that local voters tended not to make choices based on issues, which lends a cautionary note to such interpretations. Patterns of personality-based politics are well recognized in developing countries. However, in societies where policy decisions are dominated by patronage, such voting behavior may in fact demonstrate savvy democratic skills (Brinkerhoff and Goldsmith 2004, 2005). As Grindle (2007) demonstrates in Mexico, communities are often well informed about the personal interests and backgrounds of elected and appointed officials, and are able to use that knowledge to extract benefits from the state.

The more active empowerment mechanisms are credited with skills development in areas such as joint planning and budgeting, monitoring government performance, preparing advocacy campaigns, and so on (see Narayan 2002, 2005). The DISHA case, mentioned above, illustrates how the budget analysis skills that the organization developed provided DISHA members with an analytic capacity that surpassed that of many legislators. DISHA employed that capacity to advocate for the rights of disempowered tribal groups. The Self-Employed Women's Association (SEWA), also from India, is a well-known example of how efforts to empower poor, marginalized women in the informal sector have led not just to economic benefits for women, but have built their leadership capacity, self-confidence, and ability to interact with government officials and policymakers (Blaxall 2004).

The literature on community-driven development and social capital notes that, among the outcomes of community empowerment, are skills and capacity for collective action (see Mansuri and Rao 2004). These skills are instrumental for citizens to mobilize to express their interests and advocate for their rights. Donor-supported programs, such as the World Bank's Kecamatan Development Program in Indonesia, engage communities in large-scale participatory planning and management schemes for local service delivery. Through involvement in implementation, villagers acquire skills and capacity for collective action that can enhance prospects for continued progress with democratic decentralization (Guggenheim et al. 2004). These capacities can extend democratic governance beyond the program sites through demonstration effects, constituency mobilization, and confidence building.

However, these gains are mediated by local and national power structures. As the study of the Jamaica Social Investment Fund showed, the better-off community members were the ones who gained (Rao and Ibáñez 2003). Das Gupta, Grandvoinnet, and Romani (2004) discuss cases where clientelist social relations limited communities' abilities to apply their new collective action skills. A sobering finding emerges from a study in Indonesia of participation in village-level government (Alatas, Pritchett, and Wetterberg 2002). Households with high involvement in village government organizations had greater capacity to access information, participate in decisionmaking, and obtain responsive services. These benefits were offset by their negative aggregate effect on less engaged households, resulting in reduced capacity to obtain information, exercise voice, and influence responsiveness.

New and Expanded Cadre of Leaders with Democratic Skills

The above discussion of citizenship skills for communities also applies to local leaders. Through the expanded political space afforded by devolutionary decentralization, local residents have opportunities to develop democratic leadership skills. In some cases, these individuals pursue local political office, and thus contribute to an expanded pool of local government leaders. In addition, there can be a trickle-up effect in cases where leaders who have gained democratic skills and experience in decentralized local government seek elected office at higher levels of government. This outcome of democratic decentralization has increased the contestability of political markets. Leaders of local governments build experience in managing public affairs and in running a campaign. Hence, they acquire skills and credibility that can assist when running for higher office. Mayors of small towns can run for provincial governor, and mayors of large cities and provinces can run for president. This expansion of the cadre of political leadership can have a significant impact on the contestability of political markets, and thus deepen democracy.

Decentralization also allows opposition leaders to remain in government at the local level. This feature can contribute to political stability in postconflict societies where the multiplication of arenas of political power avoids the zero-sum, winner-take-all dynamics that can destabilize a new government if control of the center is the sole arena for political contestation. Gary Bland (2007a) explores this dynamic in El Salvador, Colombia, and Guatemala, for example. Democratic decentralization can also provide a check on centralized, single-party dominance (and possibly increased authoritarianism) if opposition leaders are able to maintain a power base from where they can challenge the central government. In Latin America, where large capital cities contain a significant percentage of the population in most countries, the emergence of democratic local government in these cities has transformed the national political landscape by allowing increasingly credible challenges to incumbent leaders and their parties (Campbell 2003). Grindle (2007) notes that, in Mexico, democratic alternation started at the local level, then graduated to the state level, and finally took place at the national level.

How does community empowerment, when combined with democratic local government, help to build democratic leadership skills and increase the contestability of political markets? Community empowerment mechanisms such as participatory budgeting, open hearings, joint planning, and local councils all provide community leaders and elected officials with opportunities to build their skills and experience in public speaking and debate, managing public meetings, dealing with constituents' demands, mobilizing coalitions, and compromising to achieve results. These are all vital skills for election to both local and national positions. In addition, the visibility of these participatory processes helps leaders in their runs for local or national office. Other community empowerment mechanisms, such as citizen report cards, can give nationwide attention to well-run local governments and their leaders and help them jump into national politics. These mechanisms also accustom public officials to accountability and transparency in their dealings with citizens.

Community empowerment, through watchdog NGOs, grassroots movements, community associations, and advocacy campaigns, creates leaders who have the skills and motivation to confront public officials, demand accountability, and mount pressure to make them respond (e.g., Fass and Desloovere 2004). Several of the most striking examples of this outcome are from India. The advocacy NGOs involved in uncovering corruption in public works and in public distribution of basic foodstuffs and commodities built the leadership capacities of their staff through their programmatic activities. For example, the Action Committee for Rationing in Mumbai, through its investigation of the Public Distribution System, established vigilance committees and trained illiterate women to monitor distribution at ration shops, collected the data from the women, prepared reports, and organized their own hearings to disseminate results and pressure politicians for accountability (Goetz and Jenkins 2001). DISHA (www.disha-india.org), the Gujarat-based NGO mentioned above, is another example. The staff built on their successful skills and experience with budget analysis to launch a political movement to support the rights of tribal groups that has spread beyond Gujarat to other parts of the country.

Better Matching of Public Services to Citizen Needs and Preferences

A classic argument for decentralization is that it leads to better allocative efficiency by matching public services to demand. Local governments are conjectured to gain more access to information about the preferences of local citizens, greater political incentives to provide preferred services, and greater flexibility and imagination to do so than a central government (see Azfar 2006). Though the center may have some knowledge about differences in demands, in a democracy national governments are required to treat all their citizens relatively equally. Local governments, on the other hand, are free to decide what to provide to their citizens often within quite wide parameters. Hence, according to the argument, government is more flexible if decisions are decentralized.

In practice, this outcome cannot automatically be presumed. Azfar, Kahkonen, and Meagher (2001) found that public officials at the intermediate level (districts in Uganda and provinces in the Philippines) showed no evidence of having better knowledge of the preferences of local inhabitants, and local officials at lower levels of government (subcounties in Uganda and municipalities in the Philippines) have only weak knowledge of preferences. As James Manor (2006) states, there appears to be a lot of distance between local officials and citizens, and only imperfect knowledge transmission.

How does community empowerment help local governments improve allocative efficiency? Experience with participatory budgeting suggests that it may improve the match between what people want and what is provided. There are few rigorous evaluations of the impact of participatory budgeting or any other form of community empowerment on preference matching, although Barbara Pozzoni and Nalini Kumar (2005) note that the Porto Alegre case itself is an exception, having been extensively studied. The Jamaica study cited above is another example. Rao and Ibáñez (2003) found that the participatory processes introduced in Jamaica led to elite domination of decisions on the allocation of social fund investments, but also that the decisions taken by the elite were ex post popular. They call this phenomenon "benevolent capture": elites decide, and after the fact (perhaps because things turn out well) the decision is popular. The study highlights the importance of preference formation as well as elicitation. These outcomes may reflect much of what happens in a participatory process. Before the process begins, citizens may be scarcely aware of what budgets are, what can be achieved by various sums in various sectors, how important these achievements would be in terms of outcomes that ultimately mattered, and what everybody else wants. Thus, in some fundamental presumptive sense a participatory process is valuable—not only would public officials not know what people want in its absence, but people themselves may not know what they want. Further, the existence of the right and the opportunity to participate, even when not acted on, may incline citizens to be relatively more satisfied with the results.

Manor (2006) describes how the introduction of a demand-driven education program led public officials to realize that villages lacked schools. The chief minister and his aides started a program whereby local councils could ask for a school if they did not have one, expecting the scheme to be small but useful. They found there was a massive demand for the program because half the villages did not have schools. Absent the demand-led program, the officials would not have known that half the villages lacked schools.

Experience from the Kecamatan Development Program in Indonesia suggests that participation may have helped align supply with demand, though the data are impressionistic (Guggenheim et al. 2004). In the Indian state of Kerala, for instance, local governments instituted a participatory process that engaged service delivery departments with *panchayats* and their task forces in priority setting and project design. Examining the results, Patrick Heller states that, "the effect of autonomous local decision making is most evident in the shift in allocative priorities. There have thus been notable increases over the past in allocations for housing schemes, sanitation, and drinking water" (2001, 143).

The community empowerment mechanisms in the local organizational capacity category are well-recognized means to match service delivery to local needs and preferences. Parents' associations, health committees, and community-based natural resource contracts bring communities into partnership with public providers precisely for the purpose of assuring that services meet user needs. The literature on state-society synergies for service coproduction highlights this outcome as well as the benefits for efficiency and effectiveness (e.g., Evans 1996, World Bank 2005a). The empowerment aspect of these partnerships emerges most strongly when the information provision on needs and preferences is joined with oversight and accountability. For example, a development program in Pakistan's Northwest Frontier Province that linked village organizations with local government and sectoral departments established village-level conferences as an information exchange and coordination mechanism to engage local citizens with the government. Over time, however, "they evolved into a mechanism for village activists to hold line departments accountable for promises made and quality and timely implementation" (Brinkerhoff 2002, 103). Another example comes from the Philippines, where the government's National Irrigation Administration (NIA) reorganized irrigation associations to increase farmer participation to assume both responsibility and control over irrigation system maintenance in partnership with local NIA offices. The innovative program led to dramatic improvements in operations and maintenance as well as increases in farmer satisfaction with irrigation services (Bagadion 1997).

Citizen report cards can serve to generate information on what kinds of services communities want, and what quality levels they expect. These and the other empowerment mechanisms discussed in this chapter can often lead to valuable information flows to public officials about demands. Information alone, however, does not assure that local officials will use that information to provide more tailored or higher-quality services. Accountability and enforcement are needed.

Improved Technical Efficiency

Another outcome posited for decentralization is improved service delivery resulting from interjurisdictional competition and the race to the top (Tiebout 1956). Interjurisdictional competition may work by one of two mechanisms or their combination. First, governments may vie with each other for a tax base and compete to attract labor and capital to their jurisdiction. Second, governments may compete with their neighbors through yardstick competition by providing better services to get reelected—presuming that voters are more likely to reward governments that do better than their neighbors. Combinations of these two mechanisms may also work. For instance, government that can attract tax bases to their locality may then be able to provide better services than their neighbors, which in turn may get them reelected.

It is not clear in developing countries whether citizens are sufficiently mobile to achieve these gains, nor how strongly the possibility of mobility might motivate local governments to provide better services. Azfar, Kahkonen, and Meagher (2001) found that in Uganda and the Philippines mobility is rarely driven by concerns about service delivery. Conflict situations, however, demonstrate that concerns about basic security can indeed induce citizens to move from less secure to more secure localities, but in such cases local governments usually have limited ability to enhance security. Shatkin's (2000) study of Metro Manila in the Philippines suggests that municipal governments are likely to be more interested in responding to private sector interests than worried about citizens moving away because their needs were not met. Thus, in developing countries, and arguably also in some developed ones, the race to the top argument may apply more to competing to attract private investment than to providing services for citizens.

There are some examples, however, of competition among municipalities that create incentives for efficiency and improvement. A possible incentive is the provision of prizes to localities that do well. In Bulgaria, the Foundation for Local Government Reform (FLGR), a local NGO, promotes innovative practices with its Innovative Municipality Annual Award, which recognizes pathbreaking local governments' efforts to improve performance (Goldsmith and Brinkerhoff 2004).

How would community empowerment sharpen the incentives provided by interjurisdictional competition? Citizen report cards, or service satisfaction surveys, which measure and compare performance, can strengthen incentives by publicizing information on the relative performance of local governments. Especially if such information were disseminated prior to nationwide—or statewide—local elections, it could influence political incentives to provide better services or at least to promise them (Khemani 2006). The media are likely to publicize such information because of a general human interest in competitions—witness the vast amount of attention given to Transparency International's Corruption Perceptions Index by the media every year.

Several technical barriers exist to using service satisfaction surveys on a broad scale. First, information must be collected on a wide range of outcome variables, otherwise local governments may give inordinate amounts of attention to the variables being measured. Second, the outcome variables would have to be designed in such a way that they are difficult to manipulate. Third, a vast number of households would have to be surveyed, using sophisticated sampling techniques to ensure representativeness. Several hundred respondents would be needed in each locality. Thus, collecting data would require interviewing tens of thousands of households, and processing large amounts of information.

PETS and related analytic methodologies have demonstrated that such analyses can be undertaken and can yield useful results. However, these have been undertaken with support from the World Bank and as part of project preparation. The capacity and incentives to undertake the analyses are unlikely to exist absent the Bank's resources. To institutionalize such analytic exercises on a scale that would enable them to serve as a credible basis for competitive comparisons across local governments would stretch the capacities and budgets of local governments, ministries, and most survey firms even if the political will to conduct them were present.

In sum, community empowerment mechanisms that focus on the collection of information on the performance of local governments may sharpen the incentives to provide better services in the jurisdictions where those surveys have taken place, as PAC's report cards in Bangalore have shown (Paul and Sekhar 2000). The resource and technical challenges to expanding their application to where they would fulfill the Tieboutian function of spurring local government competition are immense and unlikely to be met. Local citizens tend to be more interested in the availability (or lack) of specific services than in abstract notions of government performance. Community empowerment mechanisms that connect performance information directly to accountability for service delivery are more likely to contribute to technical efficiency than information provision and reporting alone. The assumption that public officials lack information on what citizens want and what services are provided may not always be warranted; often what is lacking are incentives for them to respond and be accountable (Goetz and Jenkins 2001).

Increased Innovation

Decentralization is expected to improve service delivery through the opportunities it provides for greater local innovation, and through the demonstration effect, whereby other jurisdictions imitate the innovations and spread better practices to other localities. The concept of experimental federalism states that decentralization encourages a few municipalities to adopt reforms and then successful reforms are adopted by other localities (Oates 1999). The Welfare Reform Act in the United States, which was tried in some states before being widely adopted, is one example. As noted above, participatory budgeting is an innovation that originated in Porto Alegre and has subsequently been widely adopted by other municipalities.

Another example of innovation diffusion among municipalities comes from Bulgaria. There, one-stop shops (city licensing and service centers) have spread throughout the country. After witnessing these one-stop shops in the United States and Poland, five Bulgarian municipal mayors decided to replicate the idea at home. These early adopters formed a team that introduced one-stop shops to other municipalities, with support from the FLGR. The concept spread quickly, and currently more than seventy Bulgarian municipalities have set up one-stop shops, with a combination of USAID grants (provided through the FLGR) and their own funds (Goldsmith and Brinkerhoff 2004).

How does community empowerment help the process of innovation? In terms of helping bring fresh ideas into national government, empowerment mechanisms can make fresh ideas more likely, and also subject to critical public debate so they are more likely to be accepted at the central level and in other local jurisdictions. The story of participatory budgeting itself helps to tell this story. Participatory budgeting was introduced in Porto Alegre by the workers' party, and its success combined with the election victory of the party helped in disseminating participatory budgeting across Brazil and eventually to other countries. Many authors note that there is greater innovation at the local government level, especially when combined with empowered community participation (see Grindle 2007; Campbell and Fuhr 2004; Nelson 2006; Manor 2006).

Adoption of innovation requires dissemination, and information campaigns can help spread new ideas. To return to the Bulgaria example cited above, the FLGR organizes policy forums, training courses, and seminars, covering such topics as customer-friendly service delivery, citizens' participation, and municipal property management. Through its regular "innovative practices bulletins," the FLGR makes available case studies of resourceful new ideas from municipalities (Goldsmith and Brinkerhoff 2004).

Community participation may also make innovation more difficult. The processes may disproportionately empower groups that want to block reform, who are usually better organized than proponents. Turnout by the general public at a participatory meeting can be low and a sizable showing by organized opposition groups can dominate the discussion and block reform. Local officials may need to take proactive steps to assure attendance of the poor and marginalized at meetings. Procedures such as targeting excluded groups for invitation to meetings, and feeding or paying participants may encourage attendance and mitigate capture. In the decentralization reform in Peru, for example, one of the obstacles to improved local government–civil society relations was the lack of travel support for community organization representatives to attend meetings (McNulty 2006).

Considerations for Achieving Democratic Local Governance

Almost all analyses have signaled the political dimension of community empowerment. Politics clearly influences the potential for creating the anticipated synergies between community empowerment and democratic decentralization. Other important factors include the institutional dimension and, specifically, the balance between LG capacity to supply democratic governance and community capacity for demand. The political and institutional dimensions strongly mediate the prospects for elite capture.

Further, interpretation of whether such capture constitutes a failure of community empowerment depends upon the time horizon one is considering. This section explores these issues, and addresses critics of community empowerment approaches to democratic local governance.

A recurring theme in the literature is the potential for elite capture of local governments, empowerment mechanisms, and the benefits they produce (e.g., Reinikka and Svensson 2004). Assessment of community empowerment needs to be placed in the broader context of the politics of democracies in general. Mature democracies tend to produce outcomes that are very roughly representative of their citizens' preferences. We say very roughly because representative democracy can result in outcomes that may favor elites, the better organized, or simply those more likely to vote. Mancur Olson (1982), for example, describes how democracies become more prone to cooptation by organized interests with the passage of time. The issue of which groups in a society have the power to influence public officials to respond to their particular concerns, endemic to any governance system, plays out in democracies through the chains of vertical accountability that connect citizens to elected officials and to executive agencies.

We have identified a variety of analyses that highlight problems of elite capture of community empowerment mechanisms; for example, local committees where the better-off members dominate decisionmaking, or local elections where strongmen use patronage to buy the votes of the poor. Even mechanisms widely acknowledged as successfully empowering previously excluded groups, such as participatory budgeting, are imperfect in preventing already mobilized and advantaged communities from engaging and benefiting more than those not so positively endowed. Pozzoni and Kumar (2005) show that participatory budgeting, and more generally forms of community-driven development, are prone to such capture (see also Nylen 2002; Brautigam 2004; Nelson 2006).

Effective decentralization and community empowerment require attention to both the supply and demand sides of democratic governance. Regarding supply, appropriate public institutions and rules, and their attendant incentives, are needed to link citizens with the state, connect subnational governments to higher levels, and govern public officials' behaviors (e.g., Azfar, Kahkonen, and Meagher 2001; Crook and Manor 1998; Silverman 2004). Regarding demand, capacity building is needed for community groups to exploit the access that empowerment mechanisms create and inject their views into policymaking and service delivery. Disadvantaged or marginalized groups will not have greater access or command increased responsiveness solely as a function of decentralization's ability to bring them closer to government absent measures to counter co-optation by local elites and to make community empowerment politically advantageous for elected officials (Fung and Wright 2003a). Jerry Silverman (2004), for example, discusses the need for incentives that can create what he calls "mutual dependencies between the poor and the state" to support poverty reduction. An illustration of such an incentive comes from Rwanda, where a system of performance-based contracts between district mayors and the president's office mandates public commitment to service delivery and outcome targets that engage both service providers and users (Uwimana and Swerdlin 2007).

On occasion, lack of community capacity is assumed to be the culprit when expected results of empowered governance do not emerge. However, Peter Evans nuances this view in his study of the positive role of government-community interaction in service delivery, and argues that, "if synergy fails to occur, it is probably not because the relevant neighborhoods and communities were too fissiparous and mistrusting but because some other crucial ingredient was lacking. The most obvious candidate for the missing ingredient is a competent, engaging set of public institutions" (1996, 1125). Heller identifies the interplay between supply and demand in his analysis of Kerala, South Africa, and Porto Alegre, noting that the capacities of citizens to engage the state

> are constructed both from below—through particular patterns and trajectories of mobilization—and from above, in the artifactuality of group formation, that is, the ways in which states create and structure channels, opportunities, and incentives (or disincentives) for collective action. Citizen capacities are as such highly malleable and forged in and through state-society engagements. (2001, 148)

Heller's characterization of the emergent nature of empowerment capacity indicates the need to look beyond one-time assessments of experience with community empowerment. If elites capture the mechanisms and the benefits of community empowerment at a particular point in time, it does not necessarily mean that it will happen all the time. Citizens' empowerment experiences can generate positive spillover effects. Successful experience, and even failure as Albert O. Hirschman (1984) has documented, can provide the basis for the application of empowered democratic governance, including the social capital it can generate, from one time to another, and from one area to others. Empowering a community is a long-term process that takes years, building on the collective experience and skills of gradually expanding groups of citizens.

Another spillover is that, once the forces of community empowerment are set in motion, the broadened demand for transparency and accountability makes it more difficult for public officials to revert to former behaviors.

The Indian right-to-information movement is a good example, illustrating the tenacity of local groups in carving out empowered space and forcing a response from powerholders (Jenkins and Goetz 1999; Goetz and Jenkins 2001; Ackerman 2004). Further, community empowerment experience also increases the opportunities for citizens to develop new expectations of government, which can include expectations of respect for rights and equity, and inclusion of the interests of the poor relative to elites.

In situations where local governments have been captured by elites, and local public institutions and structures exclude poor and marginalized communities, empowerment mechanisms—largely supported by international donors—have been employed to establish alternative paths for citizen engagement to achieve service delivery responsiveness and poverty reduction. Hans P. Binswanger and Swaminathan S. Aiyar (2003), for example, present a sample of community-driven development projects that used decentralized participatory planning, citizen committees, service satisfaction surveys, and social funds to empower communities for pro-poor service delivery. Some observers express concern that these approaches to community empowerment may weaken democratic local governance (e.g., Manor 2004a, 2004b; Czajkowska et al. 2005).

Several arguments are advanced. First, social funds and decentralized sector service delivery programs inject resources at the local level that bypass local governments, thereby intruding on what are—or should be—classic LG functions (such as infrastructure provision), and weakening local authorities' effectiveness and legitimacy in the eyes of citizens. Second, the participatory planning processes and citizen committees put in place to implement community-driven development privilege a set of unelected community members, which may result in services that are not representative of majority preferences or which may usurp the role of local elected officials. Third, empowerment mechanisms that encourage citizens to engage in joint planning and municipal decisionmaking may limit their participation to lobbying and one-shot efforts to influence decisionmakers, which may come at the expense of fostering democratic accountability where citizens understand and demand their rights to good governance. Fourth, by virtue of their reliance on donor support, such empowerment approaches are inherently unsustainable unless their structures and procedures are incorporated into LGs as standard operating procedures; and because of the tendency to bypass LGs, this institutionalization is unlikely to take place.

Some of these critiques may be justified, but the empowerment strategies pursued are undertaken precisely to address the elite capture plus the demand and supply deficits discussed previously. In some cases, the problems identified with empowerment strategies and mechanisms are artifacts of deficiencies in the design and implementation of decentralization and local democracy. For example, social funds can end up substituting for the lack of LG resources to fund service provision that decentralization policies mandate. Many local governments have extremely limited revenue-raising capacity and are highly dependent on transfers from higher levels of government. Efforts to shift service delivery responsibility to local governments can create equity problems and reduce access by the poor. In the health sector, for example, community-based health financing organizations can help to fill these gaps while also contributing to community empowerment (e.g., Franco, Mbengue, and Atim 2004). Citizen committees and participatory planning may compensate for failures of representativeness in local elected bodies. Harry Blair (2000), for instance, discusses how Indian women, elected to *panchayats* following passage of a law authorizing set-asides for women and minorities, voted according to their husbands' and tribal elders' wishes, and thus did not fulfill the democratic intent of their reserved council seats.

The concern that empowerment mechanisms may orient communities to focus on extracting resources from local government rather than on demanding broader accountability from public officials strikes us as something that has more to do with the stage of a country's economic development than with "defective" empowerment mechanisms. The kinds of machine politics and patronage that democracy promoters worry about characterized governance in the United States for an extended period of history (Brinkerhoff and Goldsmith 2005). The shift to citizen concern for accountability and good governance occurred with the emergence of a strong middle class. The Indian right-to-information examples cited above offer encouragement that such transitions are possible in developing countries.

The sustainability question, raised by critics of community empowerment strategies, is an enduring one for any reform effort. Donor resources and programs can help with empowerment, but cannot substitute for home-grown collective action that translates into political clout. Efforts to "move the state," as Heller (2001) calls it, depend on a mix of motivation and political muscle, along with supportive institutions, that engage citizens and public officials in a long-term renegotiation of state-society relations. From the standpoint of a donor's particular project, the sustainability issue looms large, but seen against the backdrop of this extended time frame, what matters is not necessarily that one individual community empowerment mechanism, such as a school or health committee, outlasts its external funding, but whether the community's and the local government's experience gained through participation in that committee contributes at some later time to reinforcing the building blocks of democratic local governance.

Implications

As this discussion of community empowerment and decentralization reveals, the literatures on these topics are vast, and our review has been necessarily selective. Nonetheless, we identify some lessons and implications.

1. This chapter reveals the key role of central government in supporting decentralization and local community empowerment. First, centrally devolved responsibilities must be accompanied by sufficient authority and resources to carry them out. Second, central authorities can provide incentives and sanctions that will encourage lower levels of government to be responsive and accountable to local needs and preferences, particularly when those needs and preferences serve to accomplish national socioeconomic goals such as poverty reduction and pro-poor service delivery. Third, central authorities can potentially sidestep local special interests in support of marginalized and disadvantaged communities (e.g., Das Gupta, Grandvoinnet, and Romani 2004), and can be a counterbalance for the poor and minorities to local elite domination of local government (see Bardhan 2002).

2. While it is clear that the potential for community empowerment to contribute to democratization and service delivery effectiveness at the local level depends on the extent to which a country's governance structure tends toward the devolutionary end of the decentralization continuum, the existence of a legal and institutional framework, in and of itself, is insufficient. In a substantial number of countries, existing decentralization laws, institutions, and procedures are incompletely and often weakly implemented, creating an institutional "limbo" where decentralized local government suffers from incoherence, hazy accountability, and poor performance (e.g., McNulty 2006; Crook 2003). The limited benefit of top-down decentralization in Ghana is an example (Ayee 2004). The gap between what exists "on paper" and in practice can be wide, with deleterious effects on community empowerment. Donor efforts to circumvent weak local governments by empowering project-based user committees can exacerbate this limbo, thus impeding prospects for full implementation of decentralization and for more formalized community empowerment (Manor 2004b).

3. In light of this gap, both the implementation and the effectiveness of the community empowerment mechanisms presented in the upper row of Table 4.2, those that are state centered, may be limited. They may exist, but communities may be unaware of them or insufficiently organized to take advantage of them. The implication is that a strong civil society, mobilizing the mechanisms in the lower, society-centered row of the table,

is needed to fully exploit the other mechanisms. Among the clearest examples of this dynamic is the fierce campaign of Indian CSOs to obtain public budget and expenditure data using right-to-information laws in six states, which later culminated in the passage of a national FOIA (Goetz and Jenkins 2004). In countries where civil society is weak, and where certain social groups have been marginalized over extended periods of time, their ability to engage in effective collective action is likely to be highly circumscribed and fragile.

4. An important driver of the effectiveness of community empowerment lies with community members themselves. Communities need the capacities and resources to engage in collective action, including belief in their own agency, for empowerment mechanisms to achieve their intended effects (Narayan 2002, 2005; Kakarala 2004). These capacities take time to develop, and evolve from learning from both success and failure. The role of incentives for citizens to engage with the state is critical. Donor expectations regarding community interest in better governance are often out of touch with citizens' desires to get the state to provide resources and services through recourse to clientelist connections if necessary (Brinkerhoff and Goldsmith 2004, 2005; Grindle 2007). Democratic decentralization depends on sufficient discretion of local authorities and on space for communities to organize for interest aggregation and voice; and better-off and better-endowed community members will have an advantage in exploiting that space. Rather than ignoring the differential power and access realities, it may be best to pay the price of a bit of elite capture in order to provide opportunities and incentives for less well-resourced community members to become engaged while seeking to assure that a supportive legal and institutional framework for democratic local governance is in place or can be built.

5. Building on the previous implication, besides the legal and institutional framework and the nature of central-local relationships, this chapter highlights the mediating impacts of social relations, especially elites of various types (social, political, economic, ethnic), on community empowerment's potential contribution to both democratic and service delivery outcomes. Both decentralization and empowerment concern at their core redistributions of power and access, which in any country are challenges to someone's vested interests (e.g., Nijenhuis 2003). Some donor-funded initiatives that seek to use community empowerment mechanisms (e.g., school committees or natural resource management associations) are on occasion able, because of their financial clout and convening authority, to bypass or temporarily mitigate the influence of politics and elites. However, such approaches are not sustainable; often the local organizations wither away with the termination of donor funding, or they are co-opted as

outreach arms of public service providers, tasked with responsibilities but not given any rights (Ribot 2004). Such approaches may also inadvertently do damage to existing democratic structures; for example, when donor-funded participatory efforts ignore locally elected councils, an issue raised regarding the PRSP process in many countries (McGee 2000) and social fund management (Manor 2004a, 2004b). Sustainability of community empowerment, however, needs to be considered within a longer time frame than a single-donor project, with attention to cumulative gains in capacity and learning over time.

6. Wishing politics away is not a viable strategy for enabling community empowerment or democratic decentralization. What is required are policies, structures, and mechanisms that reduce or neutralize the advantages and dominance of powerful actors, rather than seek to avoid or eliminate elite domination or capture (see Fung and Wright 2003a; Pozzoni and Kumar 2005). This means bringing politics into community empowerment. Archon Fung and Eric O. Wright (2003b) suggest that there are two ways to do this: (1) top-down adversarial strategies and (2) participatory collaboration. Support for community empowerment in the context of decentralization will arise from stakeholders who view it as good politics and a means to build political support and legitimacy. What Ann Marie Goetz and Rob Jenkins (2004) call the "new accountability agenda" is a manifestation of bringing politics and community empowerment together in ways that can reinforce political incentives.

5

Decentralization, Authority, and Local Democracy

Jesse C. Ribot, Ashwini Chhatre, and Tomila Lankina

When does the mix of institutions being created and supported in the name of decentralization contribute to the formation and consolidation of democratic local government? The studies synthesized in this chapter examine the effects of institutional choices by central governments, international development agencies, and large nongovernmental organizations (NGOs) on three dimensions of local democracy: representation, citizenship, and the public domain. In some decentralizations, elected local governments are receiving support. In most, they are avoided in favor of a plethora of parallel institutions. Is this multiplication of local institutions and the cultivation of identity- and interest-based forms of inclusion over residency-based citizenship fragmenting the local arena into competing and conflicting identity and interest groups? Is the public domain—which we define as the material resources and decisions under public control—being enclosed, diminished, and desecularized via various forms of privatization?[1] Is citizenship—the right and ability of people to be politically engaged and shape the fate of their polity—being undermined as a result of these processes? This chapter explores the origins and effects of the emerging local institutional mix on local democratization.

Since the mid-1980s, the majority of developing countries have legislated decentralization reforms (Crook and Manor 1998; World Bank

---

An earlier version of this chapter appeared as "The Politics of Choice and Recognition in Democratic Decentralization," *Conservation and Society* 6 (1) (2008).

2000a; Ndegwa 2002). Most claim that they are undergoing democratic decentralization (Ndegwa 2002). The stated aim of these reforms is to establish and democratize local government for purposes of democratization itself and for improving service delivery, local development, and resource management. While adequately justified on the basis that democracy is a good in itself, political and development theorists also emphasize the material benefits of local representation. These reforms—whether administrative or democratic—are believed by many theorists and practitioners to improve efficiency and equity (Mawhood 1983; Crook and Manor 1998).[2] Local decisionmakers are expected to be better able to decipher and respond to local needs because they are physically close to the people and are mandated to work on behalf of the whole local population (as in administrative decentralizations), or are systematically accountable[3] to the population (as in democratic decentralizations). The general logic of decentralization is inclusive and public. It is predicated on proximity and democratic processes reducing transaction costs, producing better accountability of decisionmakers to the population, enabling them to better integrate across local needs and to match decisions and resources to local needs and aspirations (Agrawal and Ribot 1999).

In the name of decentralization, central governments, international development agencies and international NGOs are transferring power to local private bodies, customary authorities, and NGOs. Transfers to these bodies, however, are better labeled as privatization, participatory, or empowerment approaches, NGO and civil society support, social funds, or community-driven development (Ribot 2003; Pritchett and Woolcock 2004). Each approach empowers different kinds of local institutions or authorities, with potentially different democratic and distributional outcomes. Because of support for and proliferation of local institutional forms, fledgling democratic local governments often receive few public resources or powers and must compete with a plethora of new local institutions (Ribot 1999; Namara and Nsabagasani 2003; Manor 2004b; Poteete 2007, 16). Democratic local government is rarely given the means—discretionary authority, technical support, equipment, or finances—to represent or to engage local people in public affairs (Crook and Manor 1998; Ribot 2003). The case studies[4] synthesized in this chapter illustrate how local government has been fettered in this manner (Bandiaky 2008; Hara 2008; Spierenburg, Steenkamp, and Wels 2008; Toni 2007; see also Xiaoyi 2007) as well as how government or external actors have successfully—even if not wholeheartedly—promoted local representation (Chhatre 2008; Larson 2008; Lankina 2008; Ito 2007).

This chapter explores the reasons behind local institutional choices and the effects of choosing or recognizing different kinds of local authorities on local democracy. In what are called "decentralization reforms," central actors are choosing powers to transfer and local institutions to transfer them to. These reforms may be motivated by internal political or public dynamics or by external pressures by donors or social movements. The chapter focuses on how these choices shape local authority. Institutional choice refers to the choice of the locus of authority. We use the term "choice" to attribute agency and, therefore, responsibility to government and international organizations for their decisions. Governments and international organizations choose local authorities by transferring powers to them, conducting joint activities, or soliciting their input. Through their choices, they are transforming the local institutional landscape. The term "recognition," as defined by Charles Taylor (1994), evokes the political philosophy literature on identity politics and multiculturalism.[5] We use the concept of recognition to better understand these choices and to explore the effects that the chosen mix of local authorities has on representation, citizenship, and the public domain. Different forms of local authority imply different development and equity outcomes. Understanding the link between forms of authority and outcomes is critical for motivating and for redesigning decentralization reforms.

The authors of the case studies on which this chapter is based (Chhatre 2008; Bandiaky 2008; Lankina 2008; Larson 2008; Hara 2008; Ito 2007; Mongbo 2008; Spierenburg, Steenkamp, and Wels 2008; Toni 2007) were asked to examine (1) which kinds of local authorities are being chosen and why, and then to focus on (2) the effects of these choices, that is, the "effects of recognition," on democracy and development in their case studies. The public justifications for the choices are varied, including pro-poor agendas, virtues of civil society, superiority of community-based or indigenous systems, and advantages of direct participation. Behind the public justifications are private interests such as donor pressure, fear of loss of power and authority, fiscal crises, maintaining privilege, or cultivating political constituencies. Understanding choice helps to separate the public justifications from the complex of political and private interests driving them, potentially illuminating ways to influence decentralization policy processes. Understanding the effects helps us to identify approaches most likely to foster dynamic and articulated local democracy.[6]

Most of the cases focus on decentralizations involving natural resources. Natural resources are a powerful lens on decentralization because they are important to a multitude of public and private actors. They are a source of subsistence and income for the rural world and of income and wealth for central governments and national elites. Transfer of natural resource powers from central to local authorities mobilizes a wide range of interested parties.

This chapter proceeds as follows. Having outlined in this introduction the institutional choice and recognition framework (Ribot 2006) for analyzing the prospects for a consolidation of local democracy in the context of decentralization reforms, in the following section we outline our focus on authority. We then develop the basic concepts of choice and recognition while laying out criteria with which to examine their effects. In the next section, we draw out key findings of the case studies. In the final section, we provide a concluding discussion.

Recognizing Authority

Taylor's "politics of recognition" (1994) describes a set of tenets for redressing identity-based inequities. For Taylor, recognition redresses inequities by privileging cultures and identity groups that have been marginalized. The politics of recognition identifies marginality as a product of misrecognition or prejudices against cultures and cultural forms. Taylor argues that misrecognized cultures must be recognized—promoted, protected, and empowered—so as to enable individual members to develop a positive image of themselves and to fulfill their potential as individuals within the broader society. Recognition, for Taylor, is an act of enfranchisement. We observe that states and international institutions are always engaged in recognizing new authorities around the world—strengthening some and weakening others. In the process, they are strengthening and weakening different forms of authority and those authorities' reign over their constituent populations. This article shifts the focus from the recognition of *culture* and *identities* to the recognition of *authority*.[7] In doing so, we are also promoting a shift in much of the economics, common property, and development literature from a focus on property and tenure to a focus on authority. While property is an enforceable claim (MacPherson 1978), too much attention is trained on the rules of the game rather than the origins and construction of the authorities enforcing the rules. We find that critiques of Taylor's concept of recognition by Nancy Fraser (2000), James Tully (2000), Patchen Markell (2000), and Elizabeth A. Povinelli (2002) shed light on the enfranchising and disenfranchising effects of recognizing different kinds of authorities. As such, the recognition literature provides the conceptual tools for analyzing the production of democratic local authority.

Recognition of representative authorities can provide for representation of diverse interests. Recognition of nonrepresentative authorities subjects individuals to the cultural or ideological vagaries of those authorities. As Tully argues, struggles over recognition and distribution are not ends in themselves, but must to be subject to "democratic disagreement, dispute, negotiation, amendment, implementation, review, and further disagreement" (2000, 477). To remain democratic, these struggles need to be under democratic authority. "A free and democratic society will be legitimate even though its rules of recognition harbor elements of injustice and non-consensus if the citizens are always free to enter into processes of contestation and negotiation of the rules of recognition" (2000, 477). But rules are not easily contestable when chosen authorities are nondemocratic and the choice of those authorities is imposed by inaccessible higher authorities. The central irony of recognizing cultural authorities—chiefs, indigenous or ethnic leaders—in the name of freedom or democracy is that this recognition can constrain the very contestation that makes a society free and democratic.

Fraser argues that Taylor's recognition of specific misrecognized groups, "insofar as it reifies group identities, . . . risks sanctioning violations of human rights and freezing the very antagonisms it purports to mediate" (2000, 108). By reifying culture, Fraser suggests, the politics of recognition places "moral pressure on individual members to conform to a given group culture. Cultural dissonance and experimentation are accordingly discouraged, when they are not simply equated with disloyalty. So too is cultural criticism, including efforts to explore intragroup divisions, such as those of gender, sexuality and class" (2000, 112). Fraser also argues that privileging culture and identity diverts attention from material and social bases of distribution, potentially reinforcing material injustices (2000, 108–111). Recognizing identity- and interest-based authorities imposes their notions of culture and their interest on those under their rule—similarly suppressing intragroup difference (see Mamdani 1996). Indeed, by reifying group identity, recognition obscures internal cultural differences and subordinates the "struggles within the group for the authority—and the power—to represent it" (Fraser 2000, 112; see also Povinelli 2002, 6–13).

These critiques are not limited to instances where culture-based injustices are redressed through strengthening of cultural identities or privileging of one cultural form over another. By focusing on the role of recognition in the construction of local authority, the politics of choice and recognition framework extends these critiques to analysis of any reforms where powers are transferred to local authorities. Recognition is not merely an act of acknowledging an existing identity or authority; recognition creates or enforces that authority (Markell 2000, 496–497), and therefore must be analyzed as a political act with profound consequences for democracy.

The desire to privilege misrecognized cultures often drives international development interventions. Across sub-Saharan Africa, Southeast

Asia, and Latin America, for example, indigenous, customary, and traditional authorities are making a political comeback (Geschiere and Boone, 2003; Benda-Beckmann et al. 2003; Larson 2008). This reemergence is at least partly cultivated from above—a result of government, donors, and international NGOs recognizing the authority of chiefs and headmen. The reemergence of customary authority is so widespread and takes so many forms that it must also be attributed to particular local histories reshaped by global changes that give new life to traditional forms of belonging and identity (Engelbert 2002). Important blind spots, however, are evident in development approaches that favor indigeneity. First, political analysis and judgment of indigenous governance systems are rarely featured in the new approaches (a new kind of "antipolitics," as defined by Ferguson 1994). Second, custom and customary authority are conflated such that customary authorities are favored rather than custom itself (see also Moore 1986; Chanock 1991).

But, not everything indigenous is good. Many of the indigenous governance systems, when analyzed as *political systems* rather than being viewed as *cultural forms*, would be labeled totalitarian, despotic, oppressive, patriarchal, gender-biased, or gerontocratic. Some indigenous cultures condone and continue forms of servitude and slavery. But when we call them indigenous, it is as if suddenly the nature of authority and governance is obscured behind a fog of cultural relativism. Those who favor other cultures and indigenous peoples do not want to judge them. The confusion is deepened since many cultural or indigenous authorities are substantively democratic and do indeed work on behalf of their people (Larson 2008; Spierenburg, Steenkamp, and Wels 2008; Spierenburg 1995; Olowu and Wunsch 2004) while elected local governments often marginalize the poor, women, indigenous peoples, and lower castes (Agrawal and Gupta 2005; Crook and Manor 1998; Crook and Sverrisson 2001). Where communities are already highly stratified along the lines of power, income, wealth, and social status, recognizing local governments can have the effect of obscuring internal differences within the village, thereby further marginalizing lower castes (Agrawal and Gupta 2005).

Clearly, authority should not be legitimized just because it is labeled democratic, customary, or indigenous, nor should authority over the public domain be transferred uncritically to NGOs or private bodies. While elected local government is often scrutinized, the terms "culture," "private," or "NGO" should not provide protection from political analysis—even if these authorities are locally legitimate or considered authentic (see Ntsebeza 2005). To avoid double standards, cultural and political authorities as well as community and private leaders should be viewed in the same critical light. This critical equity provides a starting point for a dialogue among cultural and political stances. All local authorities need to be evaluated for how they represent people, encourage citizenship, and produce an engaging public domain.

The Politics of Choice and Recognition

This section outlines an analytic framework for evaluating the enfranchising potential of forms of local authority.

The Politics of Choice: Policy Processes in the Establishment of Local Authorities

Decentralizations can provide the infrastructure for popular engagement and expression (Ribot 2003; Heller, Harilal, and Chaudhuri 2007, 628). They can open spaces for new kinds of local agency to initiate active citizen engagement (Gaventa 2002; Eckert 2006). But, as *policy reforms* they are top-down affairs—designed and implemented by central actors. How do policymakers and development professionals choose local institutions in democratic decentralization or local development interventions? Do their institutional choices reflect the aggregate aspirations of individuals maximizing their own good (Ostrom 1990)? Do they select authorities and institutions to meet their own narrow economic and political interests (see Bates 1981; see also Frye 1997)? Do local institutions choose themselves and impose themselves on emerging opportunities and decisionmaking processes (Eckert 2006; Boone 2003; Benda Beckmann and Benda-Beckmann 2006; Gaventa 2002)? Clearly all of these processes are in play. Studies by Ashwini Chhatre (2008), Mafaniso Hara (2008), Takeshi Ito (2007), and Fabiano Toni (2007) address the politics of choice. They describe how policies and decisions of higher-level authorities, with or without influence of local citizens, result in the creation, selection, or appointment of specific authorities and/or enable local actors to engage or capture new opportunities.

Institutions—whether rules or authorities—are not merely organically emerging solutions to collective action problems. Rather, they are created or cultivated by powerful interests. We start with Robert Bates's (1981) notion of institutional choice to bring attention to the motives and actions of the central authorities crafting decentralizations, and, in the process, shaping the local institutional landscape. Complementing this concept with Taylor's (1994) politics of recognition focuses attention on the struggle of social actors to redress historical wrongs in order to force the state to recognize marginalized groups. Combining choice and recognition enables an integration of both choices from above and pressure from below in understanding institutional choices while the critique of recognition helps to illuminate potential effects of these choices.

The Effects of Recognition

Governments and international organizations usually emphasize development and environmental outcomes when promoting "natural resource" decentralization, and most also give high billing to participation and democracy outcomes. But the results of their institutional choices on development, the environment, or on the emergence and consolidation of local democracy often differ from stated objectives or expected outcomes.[8] The studies drawn on for this chapter focus on the democracy effects of institutional choice. Is the mix of recognized institutions helping to establish, strengthen, or consolidate local democracy?

The politics of choice and recognition framework extends the discussion of recognition to institutions. Like the recognition of culture or individuals, the recognition of local institutions or authorities confers power and legitimacy, and cultivates identities and forms of belonging. The choice of local authorities or organizations by government or international agencies is a form of recognition. Following Markell, "'recognition' is something used to refer not to the successful cognition of an already-existing thing, but to the constructive act through which recognition's very object is shaped or brought into being." (2000, 496). This recognition takes place through the transfer of powers, partnering in projects, engagement through contracts, or via participation in dialogue and decisionmaking. Recognition strengthens the chosen authorities and organizations with resources and backing, reinforcing the forms of belonging these local institutions engender and the identities of their members. In doing so, recognition shapes three key aspects of democracy discussed below: representation, citizenship, and public domain.

Representation. In decentralization and other local development interventions, outside authorities choose to work with, and therefore recognize, local authorities. In doing so, they cultivate these authorities, strengthening and legitimating them. But, how representative are the chosen institutions? In current decentralizations—even those called democratic—governments and international donors are largely choosing to avoid elected local government in favor of other institutions (see Hara 2008; Bandiaky 2008; Toni 2007; Romeo 1996; Agrawal and Ribot 1999; Manor 2004b; for exceptions, see Lankina 2008; Lankina and Getachew 2006). This choice is critical in that it deprives local elected authorities of the powers transferred to the local arena while empowering alternative or so-called parallel authorities. Empowering local line ministry offices, NGOs, customary chiefs, and private corporations can delegitimate elected local authorities while legitimating parallel bodies. Elected local government is forced to compete and struggle with other local institutions for the legitimacy that follows from control of public decisions and service delivery.

Representative local authorities can be strengthened through recognition (Lankina 2008). They may be weakened, however, (1) if they receive too little power to be effective (see Bandiaky 2008; Hara 2008; Larson 2008; Spierenburg, Steenkamp, and Wels 2008; Toni 2007); or (2) if parallel institutions overshadow or preempt their ability to serve public interest (as described by Hara 2008; Bandiaky 2008; Toni 2007). James Manor (2004b) describes democracy effects of underfunded local governments with a mandate to manage natural resources operating in an arena with overfunded environment committees. Transferring public powers to parallel authorities in the local arena can take powers away from, and produce competition with, democratic local government. That competition can be divisive (see Toni 2007), or it may lead to more efficiency and better representation all around (see Chhatre 2008; Ito 2007). It can undermine the legitimacy of local democratic authorities while producing conditions for elite capture, or it may produce a pluralism of competition and cooperation that helps establish and thicken civil society and articulation between society and government (Chhatre 2008; Lankina 2008).[9]

Citizenship. Recognition of different kinds of authorities and organizations entails different forms of belonging (see Lankina 2008; Larson 2008; Bandiaky 2008; Toni 2007). Under democratic authorities, belonging is inclusive of those who reside in a jurisdiction—residency-based citizenship. In liberal democracies, citizenship is usually associated with entitlement to certain civil, social, and political rights irrespective of one's identity and interests (Sparke 2004). But "rather than merely focusing on citizenship as legal rights," Engin F. Isin and Bryan S. Turner argue that "there is now agreement that citizenship must also be defined as a social process through which individual and social groups engaged in claiming, expanding or losing rights" (2002, 4). Citizenship has come to be a process of being politically engaged and of shaping the fate of the polity in which one is involved (Isin and Turner 2002).

Power transfers authorize. Empowering an authority gives it a role and resources, making it worth engaging, giving people a reason to belong and exert influence. Authorities that are open to influence foster citizenship while those that impose their will are less inviting of engagement.[10] Different authorities also authorize different forms of belonging. Residency-based citizenship is inclusive and democratic authorities are ostensibly more open to influence by the population. In private groups and NGOs, belonging is more narrow, based on interest—often class or objective driven. Membership can also be based on identity such as professional or any other entry criteria the members establish. In customary and religious institutions, membership is often based on identity such as ethnicity, place of origin, language, or religion. Self-appointed or hereditary private and customary leaders may be less systematically accountable to their members.

Different kinds of authorities confer different rights and recourse—they are accountable to the population to different degrees. Under some authorities, people are citizens—with rights and recourse—under others, they are reduced to subjects (Mamdani 1996). Citizenship emerges where there are empowered and downwardly accountable authorities—worth engaging and open to engagement. Choosing the locus of authority establishes, strengthens, or weakens citizenship. Where public resources are channeled into private bodies or autocratic authorities, the scope for citizen engagement is diminished.

Public domain. Without powers, no authorities are worth influencing—even if they are accountable. A "domain" is that which is dominated by an authority. The public domain consists of the powers (resources and decisions) held, or citizen rights defended by, a public authority. It is the set of political powers vis-à-vis which citizens are able and entitled to influence public authorities. Retaining powers in the public domain maintains and reinforces public belonging in, and citizen identification with, the public authorities and with other citizens in the polity. Conversely, privatizing public resources and powers to individuals, corporations, customary authorities, or NGOs diminishes the public domain. Such enclosure shrinks the integrative space of democratic public interaction. Without public powers, there is no space of democracy—there is no public domain for citizens to engage in.

In decentralizations, the choice to allocate public powers among multiple interest and identity groups may enclose the public domain and fragment society into interest- and identity-based forms of belonging. The privatization of public powers to NGOs and other private bodies is a form of enclosure. When actors receiving these powers are customary or religious authorities, this enclosure constitutes a desecularization of powers. These acts diminish the domain of integrative public action, undermining residency-based belonging and citizenship. A public domain is a necessary part of representation and of the production of citizenship. It is the space of integrative collective action that constitutes democracy. For decentralizations to produce benefits in equity, efficiency, and democratization, retaining substantial public powers in the public domain is essential.

Case Study Findings

In this section, we discuss the key findings generated from research conducted from 2004 to 2007 by a group of researchers in the World Resources Institute's comparative research program entitled "Institutional Choice and Recognition in Natural Resource Decentralization." These researchers used the conceptual framework outlined above to interrogate the democracy effects of recognition of local institutions and authorities (including elected local government, pluralism, privatization, NGOism, support for customary chiefs). By examining the effects of choosing these different institutions in decentralizations, researchers can examine the propositions that: (1) the support given to local authorities privileges and strengthens them—whether their constituencies are residency, identity, or interest based; and (2) when governments and international agencies empower local authorities, they are enforcing upon the members of the groups the particular forms of comportment, accountability relations, belonging, and beliefs of the chosen authorities.

Chhatre's (2008) case study details the process of democratic consolidation in Himachal Pradesh, India. Here, legislators chose *panchayats* as local interlocutors because local people chose to use them as a channel of influence. Local people chose *panchayats* due to their political connections and their emerging powers under decentralization reforms. Chhatre describes this political "virtuous circle" linking people to *panchayats* and *panchayats* to legislators as "political articulation;" defining "an articulated democratic system" as one that "will enable local communities to influence local institutions" (2008, 13). In a disarticulated political system, elected representatives are alienated from their constituents and lack incentive or ability to respond to demands from below. The key to Himachal Pradesh's local government success was that it created "spaces for engagement of citizens and civil society with state agents"generated by political articulation (2008, 14). Chhatre's articulation approach enables a dynamic multilayered analysis of emerging local democracy in which power and accountability are relational and not located in a single authority. Here higher-level competition explains the choices by parties that helped make lower-level authorities locally accountable (see Schumpeter 1943). Recognition of the *panchayat* by parties and via decentralization explains their consolidation as a local political force and locus of engagement.

Toni (2007) shows how in the state of Para, Brazil, the national ruling party, local government authorities, donors, and national bureaucrats marginalize elected local government. In Brazil, the ruling party is supported by a union-based social movement while local government authorities are dominated by an opposition party. In Para, the ruling party is allied with an NGO Foundation representing some 100 grassroots movements. The lack of political overlap between the foundation-supported ruling party and opposition-supported local government—most mayors being of the opposition—has institutionalized local government marginality. Further, donors sideline the few elected pro-poor ruling party mayors or councilors due to mistrust of local authorities and choose to work instead through the NGO Foundation which, despite its pro-poor stance, does not appear to represent the grassroots. Toni describes the NGO Foundation as a government-paid service sector accountable to the higher bodies and provides examples of the marginalization of women within the movement. In Brazil's Amazon, rather than fostering broad-based citizen engagement, the current politics of choice institutionalizes social divisions between the traditional elite and the newly empowered social movement. Such choices fragment the local public domain, and prevent the consolidation of local democracy.

Ito (2007) describes a dynamic decentralization in the Bandung District of Java, Indonesia, under which powers and resources are transferred to popularly elected district governments, opening new opportunities to influence policy and its implementation at the district level. The district mayor (*bupati*), however, chose to collaborate with interest groups of village elites. The new elite-based civil society approach to decentralization gives village heads significant influence. Other parties now compete for the attention of the village heads, who no longer need to show loyalty to the ruling party. There is a clear opening of space for political competition in which the village heads have gained a significant role in higher-level electoral politics (see also Chhatre 2008). Despite the advances of decentralization, Ito shows that a civil society approach to local democracy is systematically excluding marginal populations from democratic decisionmaking. Indonesia's central government chose democratic decentralization to the elected district *bupati* while, in Bandung, the *bupati* systematically chose to partner with local rural elite associations tethered to the state in a web of patronage. These associations do not represent a broad cross-section of civil society working with local government in a voluntary and broad-based manner. The resulting articulation (see Chhatre 2008) is starkly class based—it is between government and elite while the poor remain disarticulated and unrepresented. The alignment of district government with village elite associations—whose interests are antagonistic to those of the poor—is hemming in the public domain by effectively reserving public decisions for village heads and the narrow elite to which they belong.

Tomila Lankina (2008) shows that promotion of a local sense of citizenship, belonging, and representation transcends the national state. Karelia, a region on the Finnish border of Russia, boasts relatively autonomous local government compared to other Russian regions. Western involvement accounts for Karelia's postcommunist institutional development: the European Union (EU) works with local governments while also urging their cooperation with NGOs. In the 1990s, Karelia adopted the Nordic neighbors' local government models. In 2003 the federal government, however, embarked on recentralization, including in forestry management, using the pro-Kremlin regional governor as an ally in undermining local government autonomy. Lankina suggests that local citizens and authorities resist being hemmed in by seeking to emulate Nordic and EU practices across the border. By working with local government and by providing an alternative vision of local democracy, external donors in Karelia inspire citizen engagement and struggles for democratic local government. The sense of discrepancy between what people see at home and abroad fosters a productive kind of fragmented belonging that motivates people to emulate their Western neighbors. Lankina shows that this fragmentation translates into local institutional choices. The regional capital city councilors have successfully resisted the Kremlin's local government reforms. They attempt to expand citizenship and belonging in their polity by making appeals to democratic norms and the authority of the EU and the Council of Europe. The result is local governments that are more representative and downwardly accountable than in many other Russian regions.

Anne Larson (2008) argues that poor and excluded indigenous people "need organizations and collective action, allies, interlocutors and sympathetic, or at least open, government officials" if they are to be heard. In Guatemala, a long history of integrationist policies has shaped indigenous people's healthy mistrust of government and, consequently, their ability to take advantage of new local government institutions. While the government of Guatemala has chosen to work through local government, many local people have chosen to exercise agency through a mix of parallel institutions and individuals—in one of her cases through their indigenous leaders. These leaders helped translate local concerns into policy by defending indigenous peoples' rights to be included in political decisions. Larson shows that empowering indigenous leaders can enable communities to influence public policies in their favor, bringing into question whether liberal democracy is the only means for people to achieve representation. The empowerment of customary chiefs with discretionary authority over public decisions carries the risk, flagged by Mahmood Mamdani (1996), of encapsulating individuals in a customary system they cannot influence—for example, indigenous chiefs—depriving them of rights while diminishing the public domain for those who are not indigenous. Larson confronts this conundrum of liberal democracy showing that justice may still be better served for the most-marginalized populations when indigenous leaders can speak and negotiate for their constituents. Larson (2008) suggests that local democracy can be supported through state-created spaces for contestation in which indigenous authorities can play a representative role.

Roch Mongbo (2008) compares the disengagement of elected local government in the forests of Toui-Kilibo and Lokoly in Benin. In Toui-Kilibo the Forest Service, under a participatory forestry project, chose to set up forest management committees—pushing elected local government to the sidelines (see Bandiaky 2008; Manor 2004b). These elected local committees carry out project-determined activities, acting as local administrative branches of the central state. The committees implemented activities against the interests of local people. When the local government tried to intervene, the project committee members depicted them as agitators and the local government was intimidated into remaining marginal. By contrast, Lokoly Forest is regulated by a customary chief and priest. The local government has limited knowledge of its own stakes in the forest or its management and takes no action to intervene. The head of the Arrondissement, the next-higher level of government, tried to assert authority over the forests by calling a meeting between the population and environmental NGOs. The NGOs suggested tourism as a viable activity—discouraging other income-generating forest activities in favor of conservation. Villagers and customary authorities asked for infrastructure to help them market forest products. Seeing conflict, the local government was too timid to engage. In Benin, as in Senegal (Bandiaky 2008), the local public domain is diminished by the failure of local elected governments to exercise their legal powers.

Solange Bandiaky (2008) shows how donors' and Forest Service's ostensibly gender-neutral institutional choices deepen existing gender, class, political, and ethnic hierarchies in the World Bank–funded Malidino Biodiversity Community Reserve project in Senegal. Decentralization and forestry laws in Senegal give elected local government (rural councils) the right to manage natural resources. The project, however, circumvented the rural councils, creating village committees led by village chiefs, imams, and village elite "wise men" to manage the reserve. The project addressed gender by assigning elite women to administrative committee positions, such as treasurer, and by giving fictitious paper positions to elite family women. In turn, these elite women allocated project positions and resources to women in their families and ethnic groups. Male committee leaders, mostly from the ruling Socialist Party (PS), excluded opposition party members from reserve benefits. The Forest Service appointed an elected PS rural councilor as reserve president who allocated project food assistance to his extended kin and PS members. The reserve presidency allowed a private individual to use public powers to further his political agenda (see Bates 1981). The project enclosed the reserve from the larger citizenry in the service of one political party and associated families. Bandiaky (2008) shows that, by failing to confront underlying power relations, ostensibly gender-sensitive arrangements continued to reinforce gender hierarchies. She also shows how women are "dragged into male political rivalries" (2008, 70), dividing women along these same political lines and fragmenting gender solidarity.

In Mangochi District, Malawi, Hara (2008) shows how the parliament, the Fisheries Department and the international donors structured two levels of local institutions to represent local people in fisheries management: Beach Village Committees (BVCs) and District Assemblies. Headmen in the villages traditionally played a mediating role in fisheries decisions. The Fisheries Department with donor support, however, opted for elected committees representing the whole population of each fishing village in order to balance the vested interests of fishers. Subsequent to the creation of BVCs, Malawi's decentralization laws created District Assemblies with the power to manage fisheries. The new laws would transfer supervision over BVCs from the Fisheries Department to the District Assemblies. However, this shift was prevented by concerted opposition from members of parliament, threatened by the creation of District Assemblies. Conflict of interest and mistrust shaped choices by the Fisheries Department, donors, and the parliament. The Fisheries Department did not trust the BVCs enough to give them significant powers. Central government had no interest in empowering the District Assemblies enough to allow sectoral committees—fisheries in this case—to be transferred out of centrally controlled line ministries. Parliament had no interest in allowing District Assemblies to even come into being. Donors did not trust local communities enough to allow their elected representatives to control the BVCs. The result was a weak BVC functioning outside of the legal framework of a decentralization that never took place.

In 1969, the Makuleke people were evicted from South Africa's Kruger National Park. Marja Spierenburg, Conrad Steenkamp, and Harry Wels (2008) describe how, in the 1990s, the Makuleke used existing law to reclaim their land from the South African National Parks authority (SANParks). To reduce tensions between the Makuleke and SANParks, Germany's international development agency (GTZ) introduced a multi-stakeholder platform so the Makuleke could bargain with SANParks. But the South Africa Land Claims Commission rejected the stakeholder approach and introduced an advocacy-based approach emphasizing the differences in interests between the Makuleke and SANParks. In lieu of negotiating a compromise, the commission helped the Makuleke articulate and defend their position. The Makuleke chose the land commission's adversarial approach and brokered a solution with SANParks. The Makuleke established a Communal Property Association (CPA) to collectively manage their land—including the entire Makuleke community and an elected leadership. They elected their traditional chief as chairperson. SANParks, however, attenuated the Makuleke's gains with long-term use restrictions. In addition, the CPA signed a ninety-nine-year lease with a private hunting concession, further restricting their land use options in exchange for a potential future benefit stream. In this process, a global commons shifted from an ostensibly national South African public under the control of SANParks to the control and management of a private communal land association (the CPA) that represents a local identity-based, and perhaps residency-based, public (the Makuleke), to a private firm. As control over resources and lucrative opportunities changed hands, the public domain was simultaneously expanded and shrunken at different scales.

Conclusion

The governments of India, Brazil, Indonesia, Russia, Guatemala, Benin, Senegal, Malawi, and South Africa have launched processes ostensibly designed to enable local people to govern their own affairs. In all of the cases under study, central government, donors, or development professionals proclaimed a belief in democratic local government. This belief seems to have driven choices in India, Indonesia, Russia, and Guatemala. In Brazil, Guatemala, and Malawi, mistrust of local government, however, compelled politicians, government agencies, and donors to choose alternative local authorities. Mobilization of a union social movement in Brazil and an indigenous social movement in Guatemala; instrumental management objectives in Malawi, Benin, and Senegal; belief in civil society in Brazil, Indonesia, and Senegal; and a line ministry's support for group rights in South Africa drove the choice toward parallel local authorities. The outcomes of these choices were mixed. Recognition of local government in India, Indonesia, Russia, and Guatemala helped local governments to become relevant and more representative. In Brazil, Malawi, Benin, and Senegal, the circumvention of elected local government channeled resources into deconcentrated project committees and other private civil society organizations. In South Africa, recognition of collective private rights produced a democratically chosen ethnic leader.

The empowerment of local government in India and Indonesia illustrates how democratic competition shapes the political articulation of citizens with the state (see Chhatre 2008; Ito 2007). While in India citizen engagement is broad based, in Indonesia engagement is between the state and a narrow elite. This narrow engagement followed from a selective civil society approach to local democracy in which policymakers choose or cultivate an elite state–allied civil society. While the Indonesia case shows the limits of a civil society approach to local democracy and development, increasing competition to influence decentralized public office could over time generate incentives for the elite to expand social inclusion, providing opportunities for poor villagers to influence policy (Ito 2007). As Chhatre (2008) argues, competitive elections at multiple levels over time and several electoral cycles are needed for articulation to trickle down to the most marginalized sections of society. Lankina (2008) also shows how the struggle for local power in Russia has engaged deputies with the population in a more articulated political struggle. The governor, aligned with the Kremlin, is at odds with municipal deputies who are actively cultivating a local citizenry and appealing to European donors and governance standards as part of their struggle to consolidate their locality's political power and autonomy.

The selective civil society approach was also used in project implementation by the Forestry and Fisheries Departments in Senegal, Malawi, and Benin where projects produced civil society committees composed of hand-picked local actors allied with project objectives. In these and the Indonesia case, civil society approaches are used to selectively empower class, party, ethnic, and gendered allies, reproducing and entrenching existing social stratification. This civil society approach is not enabling all groups within society to influence governance on an equal basis. In Brazil, however, the state chose an arguably pro-poor local union movement as its institutional ally and in Guatemala the self-selected indigenous leaders did effectively protect the interests of their marginalized population. Where civil society emerged from social movements, it appears that a civil society approach was effective at broad-based representation and serving interests of the poor. Similarly, in the India case, a locally constituted social movement against a forestry project articulated broad-based representation through local government—the *panchayat*.

Democratic deepening is shaped by the way "unequal social relations and uneven institutional environments impinge upon the exercise of citizenship" (Heller, Harilal, and Chaudhuri 2007, 627). In most of the case studies, transferred powers—whether discretionary or merely the implementation of mandates—follow the contours of existing divisions and inequalities shaping national and local politics. The powers took on the contours of a balanced political competition in Himachal Pradesh, India. They divided along party lines in Para, Brazil. They articulated via class divisions in Bandung, Indonesia. They fractured along indigenous and settler integrationist lines in Guatemala. Where few discretionary powers are transferred, as in Benin and Senegal, project funds and interventions still flow along lines of traditional ethnic and gender hierarchies. Arun Agrawal and Krishna Gupta (2005) argue that decentralization can exacerbate existing socioeconomic inequality unless decentralization programs are specifically biased toward disadvantaged groups, rather than being formally neutral in their design and implementation. Bandiaky (2008) also shows that gender biases are not addressed by gender-neutral projects and argues for skewing recognition toward women and other marginalized groups.

The case studies show that distributive aspects of recognition are not solely local. Mechanisms are needed to ensure that marginal populations can engage in their own governance. Local and central government play roles in assuring both inclusion and empowerment of marginal groups. In the Indonesia case, the choice of elite civil society is biasing distribution by channeling investments toward elite interests. In Guatemala and South Africa, however, it appears that marginal populations are being served by their own local institutions while in South Africa that success came with the support of the central government's land commission. When does local authority or local democracy serve the poor? Are Richard Crook and Alan Sverrisson (2001) right that local democracy does not serve the poor without central mandate to do so? How significant is Andrew D. Foster and Mark R. Rosenzweig's (2004) research showing that democratic local governments in India are more pro-poor than autocratic local authorities or Patrick Heller, K. N. Harilal, and Shubham Chaudhuri's (2007) findings that all categories of respondents—including farmers, unions, scheduled castes, and women—found improved service delivery following democratic decentralization reforms? Clearly, democratic decentralization can serve the poor, but targeting women, low castes, and underprivileged groups with focused attention on biased hierarchy is probably a needed complement to any local authority if local democracy is to redress entrenched inequity (see also Mansuri and Rao, 2003, 11–14; Heller, Harilal, and Chaudhuri 2007, 629).

More than progressive targeting of the poor, of women, and of marginalized castes and ethnicities is required. Criteria are needed to judge the likely human rights and material equity effects of choosing particular authorities. Fraser (2000, 115) does so by proposing the ideal of participatory parity, by which all citizens and citizen groups, regardless of identity, must have equal opportunity to participate in democratic institutions. In the institutions chosen by governments and international organizations, inclusive parity is not always evident. Chosen authorities are enabled to recognize other actors as authentic, or to discipline those they consider inauthentic. They are able to determine who belongs and who does not. In the cases we have explored, chosen actors are shaping who belongs and benefits—they are choosing by gender, migrant status, indigenousness, ethnicity, and interest. Recognition is enabling cultural and noncultural authorities who can in turn shape the boundaries of inclusion and determine what resources and decisions are made by a broad public and which are to serve individual and collective private ends. To produce and maintain the opportunity for equal inclusion will require built-in bias in favor of poor and marginal groups.

Notes

We thank Lisa Peattie for her inspiring presence and for providing the wonderfully funky venue in which this chapter was hammered out. We extend sincere thanks to Daniel Brockington, Jonathan Fox, Amanda Hammar, Fidelx Pious Kulipossa, Amy Poteete, Thomas Sikor, Jacob Trane Ibsen, and Wang Xiaoyi for their constructive comments on drafts of this chapter. Ribot gives special thanks to Keebet and Franz von Benda-Beckmann for their detailed comments and encouragement and for providing a supportive venue for writing up the initial synthesis of this research at the Max Planck Institute for Social Anthropology. Finance for the research program was generously furnished by the Royal Dutch Embassy in Senegal, World Bank Program on Forestry (PROFOR), and USAID's Bureau for Economic Growth, Agriculture and Trade.

1. In contrast to Habermas's (1991) focus on the discursive domain of public interaction, we emphasize the material basis of authority; that is, the powers (resources and domains of decisionmaking) over which citizens can interact and attempt to influence public decisions.

2. For counterarguments, see (Treisman 2007; Rubin 2005; Lankina 2004).

3. Accountability is counterpower (Agrawal and Ribot 1999) or the ability to sanction (see Manin, Przeworski, and Stokes 1999).

4. The research for this article was conducted under a World Resources Institute (WRI) research program entitled "Institutional Choice and Recognition: Effects on the Formation and Consolidation of Local Democracy." Most of these case studies are published in *Conservation and Society* 6 (1) (2008). All of the case studies are available in the WRI Representation, Equity and Environment Working Paper Series, available at http://pdf.wri.org.

5. See also Kymlicka (2002) and Fraser (2000).

6. On political articulation, see Chhatre (2008).

7. This includes instances where the authorities being recognized are created by those recognizing them.

8. Despite the extreme difficulty in establishing links between institutional arrangements and development or ecological outcomes, a body of data is emerging

(World Bank 2000a; Conyers 2002; Mansuri and Rao 2003; Foster and Rosenzweig 2004; Heller, Harilal, and Chaudhuri 2007).

9. This is not to deny the importance of competition between public and private agencies, or local governments, for efficient provision of public services (see Lankina, Hudalla, and Wollmann 2008).

10. Engagement does not have to be invited. Resistance is also a form of engagement that is used to confront imposed authority.

6

Decentralization and Internal Conflict

Joseph Siegle and Patrick O'Mahony

We live in a golden era of decentralization. Enthusiasm for shifting power to local tiers of government has never been higher. Moreover, decentralization is regularly put forward as a solution to nearly every governance challenge encountered. This perspective is grounded in the belief that decentralization will enhance government responsiveness and accountability to citizens, flexibility to address the diverse needs of often highly heterogeneous populations, transparency through enhanced oversight, and the dispersal of power from what have often been highly monopolized political structures, among other attributes. In the process, it is argued, decentralization will augment political legitimacy while strengthening a sense of citizen ownership of their government.

Greater popular participation at the local level is also commonly felt to foster political stability. If citizens believe government is concerned about and responsive to their needs, then there is little impetus for armed struggle. Similarly, if decentralization fosters more space to exercise local customs and religious beliefs without fear of persecution, the risk of intergroup strife in ethnically diverse societies can be minimized.

Skeptics contend, on the other hand, that decentralization increases the risks of ethnic and civil strife. Loosening central control triggers a sequence of ever greater demands for autonomy, ratcheting up the centrifugal pressures on the state. Rather than building a stronger sense of ownership and affinity with the nation as a whole, decentralized authority accentuates differences between regions, fosters citizen identification with ethnic or geographic groups rather than the state, and emboldens demands for particularized services by minority groups. By weakening incentives to consider national interests, decentralization encourages local politicians to stake out hard-line positions in defense of local priorities, deepening political polarization.

The heightened attention on decentralization is an outgrowth of the ongoing global democratization movement. Over the past two decades, more than 100 countries have taken discernible steps toward democracy—80 percent of which are in the developing world. This has resulted in a sea change of global governance norms. This, in turn, has dramatically expanded opportunities to pursue decentralization. It is also a reminder that most decentralization experiences take place in countries undergoing macrolevel political and economic transitions.

The policy implications stemming from understanding the relationship between decentralization and intrastate conflict are considerable. If decentralization raises the risk of conflict, the current enthusiasm for this governance reform could have destabilizing effects. If, on the other hand, decentralization has a mitigating effect on conflict, it represents an underappreciated peacemaking tool to be deployed more vigorously.

Empirically grounded answers to these questions remain elusive. This chapter attempts to sift through what is known about this relationship to help guide policymakers and practitioners contemplating decentralization initiatives.

Decentralization and Post–Cold War Intrastate Conflict

Continuing a pattern seen since the late 1950s, intrastate conflict accounts for the vast majority of episodes of armed violence in the twenty-first century. At the same time—and contrary to popular perception—the frequency and intensity of armed intrastate conflict has, in fact, declined by 60 percent since the early 1990s (Marshall and Gurr 2005). Thirty-six countries were faced with major armed conflict in 1991. By 2009, there were twenty-one.[1] Rather than ushering in an era of instability and ethnic violence that many predicted, the end of the superpower rivalry has given way to a period of comparative historic calm (Marshall 2002). The powerful effect that the Cold War had on fomenting and sustaining internal conflicts in the developing world raises an important intertemporal cautionary flag to the study of contemporary conflict. Cross-national analysis drawing heavily on the pre-1990 time period is subject to misinterpretation—and misapplication in the twenty-first-century context.

In addition to epochal considerations, income level is another powerful influence on internal conflict. Poor countries have consistently been more prone to intrastate conflict than relatively better-off countries. Specifically, countries with per capita incomes below $2,000 have been nearly fourteen times as likely to engage in intrastate conflict in the post–Cold War period as countries with per capita incomes above $4,000. The issue of how decentralization affects conflict, therefore, is most meaningful for a developing country context. While the close link between poverty and conflict is well accepted, the reasons for this are less clear. The legacy of the Cold War and the spate of long conflicts in the developing world that this generated, the tendency for these conflicts to persist once started, competition for limited resources, weak institutions of power sharing and peacebuilding, a history of autocratic political structures and use of repression, the relative ease with which small bands of rebels can destabilize weak states, and spillover from conflict in neighboring countries, among other explanations, all contribute to this outcome.

The fact that the dramatic decline in armed conflict occurred concurrently to the period of unprecedented democratic expansion is highly relevant to this discussion of decentralization. The logic underlying the democratic peace—the phenomenon that democracies rarely fight each other—appears also to have bearing on internal conflicts. Established democracies are several times less likely to give rise to violent civil conflict than are nondemocratic systems (Gurr 2000; Oneal and Russett 2001; Hegre et al. 2001). Moreover, the risk of conflict in low-income democratizers is declining more rapidly in the post–Cold War period than in low-income autocracies (Halperin, Siegle, and Weinstein 2010).

The remainder of this section reviews the theory and empirics surrounding decentralization vis-à-vis two broad drivers of internal conflict—intercommunal divisions and political polarization—that account for 80 percent of all contemporary intrastate conflicts (Marshall and Gurr 2005).

Intercommunal Divisions

The conflict-mitigating rationale for decentralization in ethnically diverse societies is that, by ensuring minority group representation, it provides political channels through which differences can be reconciled. The prospect of attaining power within the national structure, furthermore, represents an incentive for minority group cooperation with the central state. Greater local control over issues that affect the vast majority of citizens' daily routines, moreover, provides assurances to minority groups that their priority concerns will be considered. In this way, decentralization is seen as a flexible institutional mechanism to accommodate the varied priorities of diverse populations within a single state. Similarly, by providing more layers of government, decentralized systems diffuse competition (and fears) away from a single, winner-take-all prize. This reflects the view of many supporters of decentralization in ethnically diverse societies that the state, rather than another ethnic group, poses the greatest potential security threat to a given group (Rummel 1994; Horowitz 1985; Saideman et al. 2002). Devolving state power is a mechanism to reduce this threat. Federal and unitary states differ significantly in how they approach decentralization in ethnically diverse populations. In unitary states, governments tend to use decentralization as a tool for eroding ethnic identity and solidarity. Federal states, in contrast, are more inclined to recognize the rights of ethnic groups in the belief that accommodation augments stability and unity (Schou and Haug 2005).

The principal concerns over decentralization in ethnically diverse societies are that it encourages ethnic identification, accentuates intergroup differences, and opens the door to local elite capture and discrimination against local minorities—all increasing the likelihood of intercommunal strife. It is also argued that decentralization in ethnically diverse societies with weak central governments encourages intergroup competition and collapsed states (Posen 1993). Moreover, the process of decentralization increases the probability that the dominant ethnic group or political party affiliation at local levels will differ from those at the national level. This potentially antagonistic equation can amplify central-subnational tensions, particularly during elections (Schou and Haug 2005). Decentralization is also believed to increase vulnerability to external influences by opening up cleavages that outside actors can exploit. Of particular risk are contexts in which an ethnic group engaged in sectarian conflict has a strong base of support just across the border. Indeed, under such circumstances, secession is more likely (Lake and Rothchild 2005).

Some research does find a positive relationship between degree of ethnic diversity and probability of conflict (Easterly and Levine 1997). However, other analysis finds a parabolic pattern—countries with highly diverse or homogeneous populations are remarkably stable (Collier and Hoeffler 2000). In the latter, no threat from a competing group is felt; in the former, no one group is large enough to impose its will on the others and the mutual recognition of this reality leads to greater interethnic assimilation. The greatest threat of ethnic conflict comes from societies where there is a dominant group comprising between 45 and 90 percent of the population. In these cases, minority groups fear they will be permanently excluded from politics and are inherently vulnerable to discrimination. At the same time, they are large enough to assert their priorities and be perceived as a threat to the majority. This is consistent with studies showing that societies with more geographically concentrated minority populations are more susceptible to ethnic conflict (Saideman and Ayres 2000; Gurr 1993). The potential for intercommunal conflict is accentuated when regional parties dominate the political system. Regional parties are more likely to precipitate intergroup conflict and the drive to secession by mobilizing constituencies on ethnic or geographic grounds. Regional parties may also produce legislation that threatens other groups in a country or block legislation that can alleviate tensions already present in a society (Brancati 2006).

Empirical study of twenty-eight ethnofederal states finds that federalism reduces the threat of secession (the extreme outcome of self-determination) and violent partition *with the notable exception of federal states that contain a "core ethnic region,"* defined as a region with an outright majority of the population or a population that exceeds the second largest group by 20 percent or more. Seven of fourteen such cases ultimately collapsed. Examples include Czechoslovakia in 1990–1992, the Mali Federation in 1960, the Soviet Union in 1990–1991, and Pakistan in 1970–1971 (Hale 2004). A broader sample of countries also finds multinational federations to be highly vulnerable with additional failures in Kenya, Uganda, Tanganyika, Nigeria, Ethiopia, Indochina, and Burma (Schou and Haug 2005). Important qualifications emerge, however. Imposed federalist systems in particular have a poor track record. Every federalist country that split apart or turned toward unitarism in the twentieth century was imposed by an outside power (Bermeo 2002). Ethnofederal states lacking a core ethnic region proved very resistant to secessionism and collapse. Of the thirteen cases that were so categorized between World War II and 1999, not a single one collapsed (Hale 2004). The bad track record of multinational federations, accordingly, owes as much to the fact that (1) they were forced together and were autocratically governed (e.g., the Soviet Union and Yugoslavia); (2) they did not genuinely accommodate national minorities; (3) they were dominated by certain ethnic groups; and (4) the extreme ethnonational diversity in the communist federations made them particularly unstable (McGarry and O'Leary 2002; Schou and Haug 2005).

Decentralization is more likely to be observed in countries that started out as federations or were the result of merging distinct ethnic and religious groups. It is less likely to be observed in countries that started out with highly centralized political systems or where there were large inflows of migrant populations who become territorially integrated and demand some peripheral autonomy and more resources (Sambanis 2002; Fearon and Laitin 2001). Comparative studies show that decentralization contributes to enhanced popular participation (Crook and Manor 1998), though the depth of this participation may be limited (Blair 2000).

Area specialists tend to come to significantly different conclusions about the stabilization effects of decentralization (Bermeo 2005). Those skeptical of federalism's conflict-mitigating function base their arguments largely on the Eastern European experience where decentralization policies generated conflict and promoted secession or partition and greater intolerance toward minority groups left behind (Roeder 1991; Snyder 2000). Proponents of federalism, on the other hand, tend to cite successful examples from Asia, Africa, or Latin America to show how political decentralization reduces intercommunal conflict.

Democracies that use proportional representation are found to be particularly effective at reducing ethnic tensions, even in societies with significant minority ethnic group concentrations (Saideman et al. 2002). A related finding is that ethnic diversity appears to be more problematic in autocratic states. Specifically, economic growth in ethnically diverse societies with autocratic governments is three percentage points lower than the norm. In contrast, ethnic diversity is associated with no adverse effects in democratic states (Collier 2001). This is explained by the fact that autocratic governments have a narrow base of core supporters, which in ethnically diverse societies often breaks down along ethnic lines. Typically, the party in power and the military are dominated by one ethnic group, frequently a minority.

In a thoughtful review of the literature, A. Schou and M. Haug (2005) conclude that decentralization fulfills a conflict-mitigating role when it (1) broadens popular participation, including minority groups; (2) brings subnational groups into a bargaining process with the government; (3) increases state legitimation through broadened local popular participation; (4) establishes state outreach and control in remote areas; (5) builds trust between groups that participate in local governance institutions; and (6) redistributes resources between regions.

Decentralization risks raising conflict potential when it increases competition between local and national powerholders. This may entail subnational actors using decentralized resources for political mobilization, including the capacity of groups to break away. In response, central governments may attempt to undermine devolved powers to regain authority. Decentralization also risks increasing interregional conflict when, for example, the reallocation of resources between regions precipitates demands in resource-rich regions for separation.

A shortcoming of this literature is the limited number of large-N cross-national studies of developing countries (Schou and Haug 2005). This has led to an overreliance on anecdotal findings. The highly varied perspectives on the relationship between decentralization and ethnic conflict, therefore, should not be surprising.

Political Polarization

While ethnic factionalism is a major vulnerability of autocratic systems given their limited ability to accommodate diverse interests, political factionalism—the polarization of distinct political or social groups—is a risk predominantly faced by young democracies because they rely on cooperation and compromise (Marshall and Gurr 2005).[2] Decentralization may accentuate this risk because incentives under decentralized structures may reward uncompromising political platforms, advance parochial interests, and create a contentious atmosphere in which negotiated solutions to policy differences are difficult to achieve (Marshall and Gurr 2005). In other words, subnational political leaders in decentralized systems may find it expedient not to seek compromise with the central government. In a system where local leaders are accountable to only their local constituents, competitive politics will almost necessarily reward taking ever more hard-line positions in defense of the region or group. Replicating this dynamic across subnational regions throughout a country, it is easy to envision scenarios where there is little middle ground in which to govern in the national interest.

Decentralization is also considered a vulnerability in transitioning political systems because local structures often lack accountability mechanisms, making them particularly prone to local elite capture. Local elite capture tends to be linked to a lack of local democratic practices based on uneven political participation and competition, lack of information available to citizens, lack of central government oversight, and lack of independent media.

> In the traditional discussion of decentralization and federalism, the focus is on checks and balances, on how to restrain the central government's power, whereas in many situations in developing countries the poor and the minorities, oppressed by the local power groups, may be looking to the central state for protection and relief. . . . [Accordingly] decentralization by itself is unlikely to be a panacea for problems of accountability. (Bardhan 2004)

Proponents counter that decentralization helps mitigate civil conflict by facilitating the dispersal of power from the center to the periphery—compensating for historically highly centralized power structures established under autocratic governments. Decentralization thus builds additional checks and balances into a political structure while attempting to establish a more stable political equilibrium between the center and periphery. Spreading power among a wider array of actors, furthermore, provides them greater incentives to participate and cooperate, helping to reduce grievances, moderate extremist or violent positions, and incorporate them into the political process. In this way, decentralization can build a national dialogue, cohesion, and state legitimation.

Decentralization in postconflict environments is made more difficult in that the requisite levels of trust and reciprocity required for this system to work effectively are particularly lacking. Tensions between national and subnational governments are likely to be especially acute given the weak fiscal position of most governments in postconflict contexts. Minority representation in local police forces, on the other hand, is an important stabilizing element of negotiated post–civil war settlements as this increases confidence and effective monitoring of violations of the peace (Sambanis 2002).

Decentralization in conflict-affected situations is further complicated by the fact that certain regions may be armed. Pursuing decentralization in these contexts is tantamount to ceding the central government's monopoly over the legitimate use of coercion. Indeed, many observers believe this was an outcome of Colombia's decentralization push of the mid-1980s and early 1990s (Eaton 2006b). Since greater autonomy also increases the risk of secession, it is an option central authorities will likely pursue only as a last resort (Sambanis 2002). According to David Lake and Ronald Rothchild (2005), there are highly restricted contexts in which political decentralization after civil war has been successful: multiple groups compete for political influence at the national level, none can dominate the state, each is led by moderates tolerant of the desire for autonomy of the others, and democracy is robust. Perhaps it is unsurprising, therefore, that of the fifty-five civil wars that have reached a successful settlement since 1945, none had territorial decentralization included as part of the settlement. The more observable tendency is toward more centralization after civil war, seen for example in Argentina, Nigeria, Pakistan, and Venezuela (Lake and Rothchild 2005).

Data for Quantitative Analysis

Decentralization Data

Decentralization is rarely implemented in pure form. Instead, it often entails a combination of political, fiscal, and administrative responsibilities being shifted to local levels of government—across hybrid forms of decentralization (i.e., devolution, deconcentration, and delegation). This reality confounds efforts to measure, much less assess, the impacts of decentralization.[3] Reliable cross-national analysis on decentralization is also seriously constrained by the shortage of comparable measures across a sufficiently large sample of countries to enable meaningful generalizations. An exception is a decentralization dataset of 166 countries covering the mid-1990s created by UCLA political science professor, Daniel Treisman (2002). Treisman defines and constructs a dozen variables on six facets of decentralization—vertical, decisionmaking, appointment, electoral, fiscal, and personnel—from some 130 constitutions and more than 200 publications on the structure of local governments. Following are the most relevant of these variables for this analysis.

- Number of tiers of government—the number of administrative levels at which a political executive was (1) funded from the public budget; (2) had authority to administer a range of public services; and (3) had territorial jurisdiction.
- Electoral decentralization—the proportion of tiers at which elections are held to pick executives (or the legislatures who then choose an executive).
- Two measures of fiscal decentralization:[4] (1) revenue decentralization—the share of total tax revenues that subnational tiers receive; and (2) expenditure decentralization—the share of total public expenditures funded from subnational budgets.
- Personnel decentralization—the share of total government personnel employed at subnational tiers.
- Two indicators of decisionmaking decentralization: (1) "residual authority," if the constitution assigns to a subnational legislature the exclusive right to legislate on issues that the constitution does not specifically assign to one level of government; or (2) when a constitution reserves decisionmaking on a specific set of questions explicitly to the subnational legislature, which we label "stipulated autonomy."
- Federal—a dichotomous classification of countries identified to have federal systems as determined independently by D. Elazar (1994) and S. Saideman et al. (2002).

Table 6.1 illustrates the median values of some of these decentralization measures by geographic region—reflecting considerable variance. Scores for Western Europe, by and large, reflect more decentralized governance structures than other regions. Africa and the Middle East are typically among the least decentralized.[5] This is not merely a function of income level. Middle-income South Asian and former Soviet states also score in the top end of many of these measures (the latter no doubt a reflection of their communist governance legacies).

Political decentralization, as reflected in the percentage of subnational tiers with elected representatives, reveals a trimodal distribution. At the high end are Eastern Europe, Western Europe, and Latin America with between 62 and 83 percent of subnational tiers holding elections. These figures reflect the speed with which Eastern European countries moved to adopt electorally decentralized systems after the end of the Cold War. This

Table 6.1 Median Levels of Decentralization Measures by Geographic Region, 1995 (percentage)

Decentralization Measure	Number of Observations	Sub-Saharan Africa	East Asia	South Asia	Latin America	Middle East	Eastern Europe	Former Soviet Union	Western Europe
Number of tiers	164	4	4	4	3	3.5	3	4	3
Percent elected	155	33.3	35.4	33.3	62.5	0.0	83.3	33.3	69.0
Subnational share of public expenditure	67	4.7	10.8	37.6	9.6	8.4	16.9	27.6	24.1
Subnational share of total tax revenue	53	4.0	6.5	N/A	6.7	6.3	7.3	24.2	13.4
Subnational share of public employment	90	23.1	41.0	50.0	20.8	35.8	26.4	35.4	48.4
Stipulated autonomy	133	6.9	11.8	20.0	23.5	0.0	8.3	15.4	33.0
Residual authority	133	3.8	5.9	20.0	22.2	0.0	16.7	7.7	23.8
Federal	164	4.8	5.2	28.6	14.8	5.3	9.1	7.1	23.8

Sources: Daniel Treisman, *Defining and Measuring Decentralization: A Global Perspective* (Los Angeles: University of California, 2002); D. Elazar, *Federal Systems of the World: A Handbook of Federal, Confederal and Autonomy Arrangements*, 2nd ed. (London: Longman, 1994); S. Saideman, D. Lanoue, M. Campenni, and S. Stanton, "Democratization, Political Institutions, and Ethnic Conflict: A Pooled Time-Series Analysis, 1985–1998," *Comparative Political Studies* 35 (1) (2002): 103–129.

is particularly noteworthy compared to the experience of the countries of the former Soviet Union where only 33 percent of subnational executives were elected. In addition to the former Soviet states, the second cluster in the elected tiers distribution comprises sub-Saharan Africa, East Asia, and South Asia. Finally, there were few elected subnational leaders in the Middle East during the mid-1990s resulting in a regional median of zero. It bears noting that this de jure measure of political decentralization does not distinguish genuinely competitive elections, leaving open the possibility that in some cases it is capturing the pro forma machinations of pseudo-democratizers. Indeed, the correlation between percent of elected subnational executives and the Polity IV measure of democracy was only 0.54, suggesting considerable superficial local representation.

While there is relatively little variance between regions in the median number of government tiers with an executive administrator (3–4), there is a modest correlation between numbers of governmental tiers and population size (corr. = 0.25), as one would expect. This relationship does not hold for countries above the median number of tiers, however, suggesting that the rationale for adopting more tiers of government has not primarily been based on increasing citizen access. Consistent with this interpretation, the correlation between total number of governmental tiers and level of democracy is –0.31. More tiers of government do not necessarily mean more authentic representation. Paradoxically, controlling for income, number of governmental tiers is also the decentralization measure most strongly linked with higher rates of infant mortality suggesting that more tiers also do not necessarily translate into more effective government.

The measures of fiscal decentralization revealed significant variance between regions. South Asia, the former Soviet Union, and Western Europe demonstrated the highest levels of subnational public expenditures, ranging from 24 to 38 percent. In contrast, Africa, the Middle East, and Latin America exhibited levels of subnational public expenditures of between 5 and 10 percent. Generally similar patterns hold for subnational employment with an estimated 40–50 percent of public jobs in South Asia, East Asia, and Western Europe being held at the subnational level. This is roughly double the levels seen in Latin America and Africa (21–23 percent). Interestingly, the regional breakdown in the subnational share of taxes does not directly coincide with the patterns of subnational expenditure and employment. For this category, subnational jurisdictions in the former Soviet Union received far and away the highest share of tax revenue—24 percent. This was roughly double that of the median in Western Europe—13 percent, which was in turn double that seen in the other regions. As a result, the former Soviet states had the lowest "efficiency" ratio of subnational expenditures relative to taxes, followed by Africa and the Middle East. By comparison,

Western Europe, Eastern Europe, and East Asia were the regions with the highest levels of subnational expenditure relative to subnational share of taxes. While comparable indicators from other datasets are difficult to find, Treisman's measure of expenditure decentralization obtains a 0.97 correlation with the World Bank's estimate of subnational share of expenditures for fifty-one countries over the same time period.

The measure of federalism closely parallels the measure of residual authority (corr. = 0.90). Western Europe and South Asia have a relatively greater share of federal systems, followed by Latin America. Federal systems that were also categorized as having residual authority for subnational authorities include Australia, Germany, Mexico, Pakistan, Russia, the United States, and Yugoslavia. By contrast, formal federal systems are substantially less linked with Treisman's more constrained category of "stipulated autonomy" (corr. = 0.50). This is intuitively reasonable since these systems have only certain prescribed powers relative to the default authorities attributed to the residual systems. In this way, the stipulated autonomy category reflects something of a hybrid or incremental form of federalism. Another cross-national measure relevant to this category of decentralization is a variable of "centralization of state authority" generated by the Polity III regime type and political authority index (Jaggers and Gurr 1995). Covering 147 countries, Polity's measure of "centralization" is based on the degree of geographic concentration of decisionmaking authority. States are scored as unitary, intermediate, or federal. Correlations between centralization and federalism were strong –0.74. Centralization also mirrored federalism's links to residual authority –0.72, though somewhat less strongly to the stipulated autonomy classification –0.49.

There are a number of limitations to the Treisman (2002) data that bear keeping in mind. As indicated above, decentralization is a process, usually evolving over a period of time, rather than a single event. Assigning a quantitative score to a facet of this process accordingly overlooks considerable nuance that characterizes these phenomena. The scoring process is also subject to subjectivity that may introduce unaccounted for skews to the data. Treisman attempts to control for this by relying on observable institutional qualities when assigning scores. However, this makes the data vulnerable to an overreliance on de jure rather than de facto characterizations of institutional functionality. Similarly, some of the source information for the dataset is derived from often unreliable national government statistics. The fact that this dataset covers only one time period (i.e., the mid-1990s) is another drawback of its applicability. Ideally, we could draw on panel data that would expand the opportunities for longitudinal analysis that would better capture the dynamic and sequential dimensions of the decentralization process. This is particularly true for countries that have undergone substantial regime and governance (including decentralization) reforms since the mid-1990s. Annual data compilation would also significantly contribute to data reliability and minimization of missing entries. Nonetheless, having access to data from the mid-1990s is particularly meaningful for this review since this period marked the apex of intrastate conflict. It thus provides a useful benchmark against which to assess links with subsequent conflict through 2005. The challenges of quantifying what are ultimately qualitative processes (e.g., democracy, governance, corruption), moreover, are typical of those faced in cross-national analysis throughout the social sciences. In sum, while imperfect, the Treisman decentralization dataset is the most complete cross-national dataset of various aspects of decentralization, notably including the developing world, of which we are aware. As such, it provides a useful baseline from which to explore patterns of conflict associated with differing facets of decentralization until which time more advanced decentralization datasets may emerge and corroborate or redefine the findings generated.

Conflict Data

Conflict data are drawn from the Major Episodes of Political Violence 1946–2008 dataset compiled by the Center for Systemic Peace (2009), data used extensively by leading conflict scholars, including the US government-sponsored Political Instability Task Force. This dataset provides annualized information of 316 conflict episodes representing all occurrences of major political violence since 1946. Conflicts are delineated as episodes of organized and sustained collective violence resulting in at least 500 battle-related deaths, at a rate in excess of 100 per year. Table 6.2 lists all civil and intercommunal conflicts initiated since 1995 as well as those that were ongoing as of 2005. Civil conflicts are defined as major episodes of armed conflict involving rival political groups. Intercommunal conflicts are armed conflicts between ethnic, religious, or sectarian groups or conflicts involving a distinct ethnic group and the state. In addition to identifying episodes of armed conflict, this dataset assesses the magnitude of societal impact from the conflict. This is based on a comparative scale of 1 (*smallest*) to 10 (*greatest*). To illustrate the range, a conflict magnitude of 1 reflects sporadic political violence; a score of 4 represents substantial and prolonged conflict (such as Liberia from 1990 to 1997 or Angola from 1961 to 1975); and a magnitude of 10 captures cases of extermination and annihilation (e.g., the Holocaust or nuclear war). Contemporary contexts do not exceed a magnitude of 7, pervasive conflict, such as that seen in

Table 6.2 Intercommunal and Civil Conflicts Initiated Post-1995 or Ongoing

Country	Conflict Type	Years	Conflict Magnitude (0–10)	Polity IV Democracy, 2008 (0–10)	Freedom House, Freedom Index, 2008 (2–14)	Federal System
Albania	Civil (pyramid schemes)	1997	2	9	10	Not federal
Angola	Civil war (UNITA)	1975–2002	6	2	5	Not federal
Burma	Ethnic (Karen, Shan, et al.)	1948–2005+	4	0	2	Not federal
Burundi	Ethnic (Hutus vs. Tutsis)	1993–2005	4	7	8	Not federal
Central African Republic	Civil (attacks by Bozize loyalists; coup)	2001–2003	1	1	7	Not federal
Colombia	Civil (FARC; drug lords)	1984–2005+	4	7	9	Not federal
Republic of Congo	Civil war	1997–1999	3	0	5	Not federal
	Civil (Ninja militants in Pool)	2002–2003	1			Not federal
Côte d'Ivoire	Civil (north, south, and west)	2000–2005+	2	0	5	Not federal
Democratic Republic of Congo	Civil (ouster of Mobutu and aftermath)	1996–2005+	5	6	4	Not federal
Ethiopia	Ethnic (Oromo separatists)	1999–2000	1	3	6	Not federal
Georgia	Ethnic (Abkhazia)	1998	1	7	10	Not federal
Guinea	Civil (Parrot's Beak clashes)	2000–2001	1	1	4	Not federal
Guinea-Bissau	Civil (coup attempt)	1998–1999	2	6	8	Not federal
Haiti	Civil (Unrest following ouster of Aristide)	2004–2005+	1	6	7	Not federal
India	Ethnic (Kashmiris)	1990–2005+	3	9	11	Federal
	Civil (Maoist insurgency)	2001–2005+	1			Federal
Indonesia	Ethnic Aceh; GAM militants	1997–2005	1	8	11	Not federal
	Civil (ouster of Suharto)	1998	2			Not federal
	Civil (East Timor)	1999	2			Not federal
	Ethnic (Moluccas; Muslim-Christian)	1999–2002	1			Not federal
	Ethnic Dayaks/Madurese immigrants	2001	1			Not federal
Iraq	Ethnic (Kurds)	1996–1998	1	Transitional	4	Not federal
Israel	Ethnic (Arab Palestinians/PLO)	1965–2005+	2	10	13	Not federal
Lesotho	Civil (May elections)	1998	1	8	11	Not federal
Liberia	Civil (LURD, ouster of Charles Taylor)	2000–2003	1	7	9	Not federal

continues

Table 6.2 continued

Country	Conflict Type	Years	Conflict Magnitude (0–10)	Polity IV Democracy, 2008 (0–10)	Freedom House, Freedom Index, 2008 (2–14)	Federal System
Nepal	Civil (UPF "People's War")	1996–2005+	2	7	8	Not federal
Nigeria	Ethnic (Delta Province; Ijaw, Itsekeri, et al.)	1997–2005+	1	4	7	Federal
	Ethnic (Christian-Muslim; Plateau, Kano)	2001–2004	3			Federal
Pakistan	Ethnic (Pashtuns in South Waziristan and NW Frontier)	2004–2005+	1	5	7	Federal
	Ethnic (Sunnis, Shiites, Ahmadis)	2001–2005+	1			Federal
Philippines	Ethnic (Moros)	1972–2005+	3	8	10	Not federal
Russia	Ethnic (Chechnya)	1999–2005+	4	5	5	Federal
Rwanda	Ethnic (Hutu guerrillas)	2001	1	0	5	Not federal
Saudi Arabia	Civil (Islamic militants)	2003–2005+	1	0	3	Not federal
Solomon Islands	Ethnic (Malaita/Isatabu islanders)	1998–2003	1	9	9	Not federal
Somalia	Civil war	1988–2005+	5	Transitional	2	Not federal
Sudan	Ethnic (Darfur)	2003–2005+	4	0	3	Not federal
Thailand	Civil (antidrug trafficking)	2003	1	5	7	Not federal
	Ethnic (Malay-Muslims in southern region)	2004–2005+	1			Not federal
Turkey	Ethnic (Kurds in southeast)	2004–2005+	1	8	10	Not federal
Uganda	Ethnic (Langi and Acholi)	1986–2005+	2	1	7	Not federal
Yemen	Civil (followers of al-Huthi in Sadaa)	2004–2005+	1	1	6	Not federal
Yugoslavia/Serbia	Ethnic war (Kosovar Albanians)	1998–1999	4	9	11	Federal

Sources: Center for Systemic Peace, *State Fragility and Warfare in the Global System 2009* (Severn, MD: Center for Systemic Peace, 2009), available at http://www.systemicpeace.org/warlist.htm; S. Saideman, D. Lanoue, M. Campenni, and S. Stanton, "Democratization, Political Institutions, and Ethnic Conflict: A Pooled Time-series Analysis, 1985–1998," *Comparative Political Studies* 35 (1) (2002): 103–129; D. Elazar, *Federal Systems of the World: A Handbook of Federal, Confederal, and Autonomy Arrangements,* 2nd ed. (London: Longman, 1994); Freedom House, *Freedom in the World: Annual Survey of Political Rights and Civil Liberties, 2009* (New York: Freedom House, 2009); M. Marshall and K. Jaggers, *Polity IV Project Codebook* (College Park: Center for International Development and Conflict Management, University of Maryland, 2000), available at http://www.systemicpeace.org/polity/polity4.htm.

Notes: UNITA, Union for the Total Independence of Angola; FLEC; Front for the Liberation of the Enclave of Cabinda; FARC, Revolutionary Armed Forces of Colombia; GAM, Gerakan Aceh Merdeka; PLO, Palestine Liberation Organization; LURD, Liberians United for Reconciliation and Democracy; UPF, United People's Front.

Rwanda in 1994 or Afghanistan from 1978 to the present. Magnitude scores reflect an aggregate assessment of state capabilities, scope of death and destruction, population displacement, and episode duration. In short, the magnitude measure is an acknowledgment that not all conflicts are equally devastating. What may be a major destabilizing event in Liberia may register as a relatively small episode in China or India.

Political and Economic Data

Democracy is measured using the Polity IV dataset on regime characteristics. This dataset assigns component and composite scores for democracy and autocracy for every country in the world (with populations above 500,000) from 1800 to the present. The (0–10) democracy score is based on institutional features of a state's political system, notably checks on the chief executive, regularized and competitive mechanisms for the selection of the chief executive, and institutional protections for popular participation in the political process (Jaggers and Gurr 1995; Marshall and Jaggers 2000). The Polity IV dataset is widely used in the conflict, governance, and economic literatures. Based on institutional features of governance, it is at times subject to discrepancies between the de jure and de facto realities of a context, particularly with regard to qualitative features of civil liberties.

Freedom House's Annual Index of Political Freedom (2009) is also used to measure democratic progress. Freedom House produces annual scores of a country's political rights and civil liberties, based on a systematic assessment process involving twenty-three questions. Each measure is assigned a score from 1 to 7 and the combined total is used in an aggregate categorization of countries into Free, Partly Free, and Not Free groupings. Every country, covering the years from 1972 to the present, is included. Its emphasis on liberties makes the Freedom House index a valuable complement to and point of comparison with the Polity IV democracy measure.

Socioeconomic data is drawn from the World Bank's (2007) well-known World Development Indicators 2007 dataset. This provides annualized data on some 700 economic, social, and institutional measures from 1960 through 2005 for all countries in the world. Corruption is represented on a 0–6 (*worst—best*) scale by the private firm Political Risk Services' International Country Risk Guide (2006). This variable measures corruption within the political system that distorts the economic and financial environment. It has a 0.87 correlation with Transparency International's well-known Corruption Perceptions Index (2006).

Methodology

The existing literature presents many equally compelling—and contradicting—perspectives on the links between decentralization and intrastate conflict. Accordingly, the aim of this analysis is to assess, using a comprehensive decentralization dataset, whether there is a discernible statistical pattern linking decentralization to subsequent civil or intercommunal conflict (or conflict mitigation) and, if so, to identify which dimensions of decentralization are most susceptible or beneficial. We test these questions using two cross-national analytic tools.[6]

Logit Regressions

Our dependent variables are the onset of intercommunal or civil conflict, respectively, since 1995 (the base year of our decentralization data). The two types of internal conflict are assessed separately since the theorized impact of decentralization on each differs. Employing a lagged dependent variable in this cross-sectional analysis provides greater insights into the potential causal effects of the independent variables. It also reduces possible bias from the endogenous effects of conflict on decentralization or governance and vice versa. The principal independent variable is decentralization (as operationalized sequentially via the seven different forms of decentralization described above).

Controls for other common explanatory factors to conflict are employed to isolate the distinct effects decentralization may have on intercommunal or civil conflict. These include conflict history,[7] per capita income, infant mortality rates, population size,[8] trade, ethnolinguistic differentiation, fuel exports, mineral exports, rates of inflation, and geographic region. Because low-income countries face a considerably higher risk of intrastate conflict than middle- or upper-income countries, this analysis limits its focus to countries with per capita incomes below $4,000.[9]

Ordinary Least Squares Regressions

A second round of multivariate regressions, using ordinary least squares (OLS), is then employed to assess decentralization's effect on the magnitude of intercommunal and civil conflict, respectively. Doing so allows us to assess whether decentralization contributes to the severity of a conflict's impact on society. It also introduces a linear dependent variable that serves as a check on any possible anomalies generated from the dichotomous nature of the logit analysis. The dependent variable is the magnitude of post-1995 intercommunal and civil conflicts, respectively, five and ten years out (i.e., in 2000 and 2005).

Results

Results from the multivariate analysis indicate three broad findings. First, factors other than decentralization were most powerful in predicting contemporary intrastate conflict. Second, the effects of decentralization on conflict were most apparent in relation to intercommunal conflict. In fact, none of the decentralization variables considered was consistently statistically significant in explaining the occurrence of post-1995 political conflict. Third, effects from decentralization on intercommunal conflict initiated since 1995 were highly varied. Certain characteristics of decentralization (i.e., higher percentages of elected subnational tiers, expenditures, and employment) are significantly linked to lower levels of intercommunal conflict. In contrast, formally established federal structures and subnational legislatures with residual governing authority are significantly associated with greater probabilities of intercommunal conflict.

Not surprisingly, context matters greatly. Previous intercommunal conflict (i.e., in 1990) and population size were consistently significant in predicting new cases of intercommunal conflict post-1995. The observed persistence of ethnic conflict is well known (Collier et al. 2003). Once a country has fallen into conflict, it is difficult to climb out of the trap of exacerbating conditions that prolong these tragedies. Notably, degree of ethnic fractionalization was not found to increase the propensity of intercommunal conflict since 1995. Likewise, a regional control for sub-Saharan Africa was not significant indicating that factors other than regional distinctiveness explain Africa's higher frequency of intercommunal conflict. Finally, level of democracy, while consistently negatively associated with new cases of intercommunal conflict, was typically not significant, or only marginally significant, in these estimates. This is, in part, attributed to the exclusion of cases of ongoing intercommunal conflict (often autocratically governed) so as to minimize possible endogeneity. Lest this result be misinterpreted, it is commonly recognized that greater levels of political legitimacy are associated with lower levels of armed internal conflict (Esty et al. 1999; Oneal and Russett 2001; Marshall and Gurr 2005).

We now turn to some of the details underlying these findings.[10] Table 6.3 summarizes the results of those decentralization indicators that demonstrate mitigating effects on intercommunal conflict. In Model 1, the term reflecting percentage of elected leaders at the subnational level is nega-

Table 6.3 Logit Estimates of Decentralization Measures with Mitigative Effects on Post-1995 Intercommunal Conflict

Variable	Model 1	Model 2	Model 3
Percent elected tiers	–0.025*		
	(–1.80)		
Subnational expenditures (% of total)		–0.099*	
		(–2.01)	
Subnational employment (% of total)			–0.057*
			(–1.78)
Democracy		–0.168	–0.210*
		(–1.23)	(–1.60)
Intercommunal conflict in 1990	1.333*	1.625**	1.493*
	(1.63)	(1.88)	(1.78)
Log population	0.499**	0.955***	0.882***
	(2.22)	(2.72)	(2.69)
Log infant mortality rate	–0.478	–0.537	–0.576
	(–0.95)	(–0.84)	(–0.93)
Constant	–8.074	–14.30	–12.10
	(–1.94)	(–2.19)	(–2.14)
Pseudo R^2	0.21	0.30	0.28
N	110	67	109

Notes: Sample limited to countries with less than $4,000 in per capita income. The estimates represented in Models 2 and 3 are for populations larger than 500,000.

z-values in parentheses.

* Statistically significant at 90 percent confidence interval.

** Statistically significant at 95 percent confidence interval.

*** Statistically significant at 99 percent confidence interval.

tively linked to subsequent incidences of intercommunal conflict. Greater political representation at the subnational level is linked to lower levels of intergroup strife (significant at the 90 percent confidence level). While modest, the significance of this variable is robust—holding across varying configurations. This includes the exclusion of the democracy term (not shown), indicating that the decentralization measure is picking up characteristics aside from its democratic value. Models 2 and 3 demonstrate similar patterns for other measures of decentralization. Low-income countries with higher levels of subnational expenditures and subnational employment in the mid-1990s were less likely to experience intercommunal conflict in the subsequent decade. These results were also significant at the 90 percent confidence level. The ability of elected subnational leaders to direct human and financial resources to identified priorities has an apparent mitigating effect on intergroup conflict. The subnational expenditures result is particularly relevant since fiscal decentralization—the shifting of greater shares of funds to the subnational level—is considered by many to be the most authentic indicator of national government commitment to decentralization.

Meanwhile, the results suggest a higher risk of intercommunal conflict in countries with certain types of formalized federal structures. Central governments that provide subnational legislatures "residual authority" to write legislation in areas not explicitly addressed in the national constitution have been far more prone to intercommunal conflict than other low-income countries. Model 1 of Table 6.4 shows this relationship is quite strong (significant at the 99 percent confidence level)—a result that is robust to various configurations and samples. The residual authority pattern is closely paralleled by the robust relationship seen between formally designated federal structures and intercommunal conflict (Model 2 of Table 6.4). This relationship is significant at the 95 percent confidence level, controlling for a host of other explanatory factors. In other words, controlling for democracy, countries with formal federal structures in 1995 were significantly more likely to experience intercommunal conflict in 2000 and 2005 than nonfederal systems. Nigeria, Pakistan, Russia, and

Table 6.4 Logit Estimates of Decentralization Measures Predicting Post-1995 Intercommunal Conflict

Variable	Model 1	Model 2	Model 3
Residual authority	3.013***		
	(2.87)		
Federal system		2.004**	
		(1.99)	
Centralization of authority			1.071*
			(1.80)
Democracy	–0.148	–0.148	–0.273*
	(–1.24)	(–1.28)	(–1.84)
Intercommunal conflict in 1990	1.714**	1.456*	0.812
	(1.93)	(1.63)	(0.86)
Log population	0.237	0.380*	0.494*
	(1.02)	(1.63)	(1.77)
Log infant mortality rate	–0.056	–0.310	–0.641
	(–0.10)	(–0.58)	(–0.95)
Constant	–5.833	–7.122	–7.904
	(–1.26)	(–1.51)	(–1.33)
Pseudo R^2	0.29	0.28	0.28
N	126	126	101

Notes: Sample limited to countries with less than $4,000 in per capita income. z-values in parentheses.

* Statistically significant at 90 percent confidence interval.

** Statistically significant at 95 percent confidence interval.

*** Statistically significant at 99 percent confidence interval.

Yugoslavia—all of which suffered new incidents of intercommunal conflict post-1995—contribute to this result. Notably, when the sample is further limited to the ninety-one countries with per capita incomes below $2,000 (not shown), the significance of the federal term grows stronger—equaling the 99 percent levels seen for the residual authority variable. This pattern is further corroborated by the result in Model 3, which includes the centralization of state authority variable generated by Polity III. The less geographically concentrated the decisionmaking authority, the greater the likelihood that it was associated with intercommunal conflict. These results remained significant for a full sample of countries (rather than just the lower-income category on which we have focused). In short, three independent measures assessing the legal autonomy of subnational structures all consistently find that such arrangements were more prone to intercommunal conflict post-1995 than countries without such structures. The consistency and robustness of these results point to a distinct phenomenon rather than anomalies in the data. Notably, the other (more narrow and specific) measure of subnational decisionmaking authority assessed in these models—"stipulated autonomy"—was not significant in explaining intercommunal conflict (not shown). These results suggest that incremental or hybrid forms of federalism, where the central government retains significant formal authority, avoid some of the vulnerability to intercommunal conflict experienced by formal federal systems. The divergence in results generated from these two measures of decisionmaking authority imply that the type of subnational authority matters to conflict outcomes.

The second stage of the multivariate analysis examines patterns between the various measures of decentralization with magnitude of intercommunal conflict lagged five and ten years out using OLS regressions. The results from the OLS analysis largely corroborate the patterns observed in the logit analysis. All of the decentralization terms found to be positively linked to intercommunal conflict in the logit analysis were also significant here.[11] Those that were negatively associated with intercommunal conflict previously were likewise negative, though not significant in the linear estimates.

One noteworthy difference observed from the OLS analysis was the significance of level of subnational revenues with magnitude of subsequent intercommunal conflict. Low-income countries in which subnational jurisdictions received a relatively higher share of tax revenues in the mid-1990s were significantly more likely to experience more intense intercommunal conflict ten years on (see Model 1 of Table 6.5). (Subnational revenues were consistently positive though not significant in the logit estimates.) We thus find a divergence in conflict outcomes between the two fiscal measures of decentralization: share of revenues local governments receive versus

Table 6.5 Ordinary Least Squares (OLS) Estimates of Decentralization on Magnitude of Intercommunal Conflict Lagged by 10 Years

Variable	Model 1	Model 2	Model 3	Model 4
Subnational tax revenues	0.047*** (5.24)			
Residual authority		0.521*** (2.65)		
Federal systems			0.507*** (2.76)	
Centralization of authority				0.195** (1.91)
Democracy	–0.023* (–1.71)	–0.013 (–0.86)	–0.014 (–1.00)	–0.020 (–1.13)
Intercommunal conflict in 1990	0.422*** (3.31)	0.284** (2.03)	0.287** (2.08)	0.255 (1.37)
Corruption controls	–0.116** (–2.02)	–0.086 (–1.39)	–0.102* (–1.65)	–0.159** (–1.97)
Log population	0.015 (0.87)	0.037 (1.21)	0.018 (0.98)	0.066 (1.44)
Log infant mortality rate	–0.105* (–1.62)	–0.094 (–1.39)	–0.106 (–1.58)	–0.166* (–1.86)
Constant	0.324 (0.73)	0.170 (0.25)	0.579 (1.24)	0.070 (0.07)
Adjusted R^2	0.24	0.13	0.12	0.13
N	53	126	126	101

Notes: Sample limited to countries with less than $4,000 in per capita income. Intercommunal conflict in Model 1 is lagged five years; Models 2 and 3 are lagged ten years. z-values in parentheses.

* Statistically significant at 90 percent confidence interval.

** Statistically significant at 95 percent confidence interval.

*** Statistically significant at 99 percent confidence interval.

share of total expenditures controlled by local governments. While data limitations prevent us from examining these difference by province within countries, this finding suggests that higher shares of revenues are not necessarily equivalent to greater local expenditures. Indeed, regions with higher ratios of subnational taxes relative to expenditures (e.g., the former Soviet Union and Africa) tend to be more conflict prone, potentially pointing to the destabilizing effects of local elite rent seeking.

Models 2–4 of Table 6.5 show the significant relationship (at the 95–99 percent level of confidence) of the three proxies of federalism/legal regional autonomy with magnitude of conflict. All three were strongly significant at both the 2000 and 2005 intervals, which when coupled with the patterns seen under the logit analysis, represent a robust relationship. Notably, four of the eleven countries that experienced intercommunal conflict in 2005 were considered federal systems—Russia, India, Pakistan, and Nigeria.

The OLS analysis also highlighted the importance of contextual factors. Intercommunal conflict in 1990 was the strongest predictor of magnitude of post-1995 intercommunal conflicts ongoing in 2005. This variable is significant at the 95–99 percent confidence level for Models 1–3. As with the logit estimates, levels of democracy in 1995 were consistently (though typically not significantly) negatively associated with magnitude of intercommunal conflict over the next decade. Meanwhile, low-income countries that scored strongly for their controls on corruption in the mid-1990s were also consistently less likely to experience intense intercommunal conflict in 2000 and 2005. For Models 1 and 4, this significance attained the 95 percent level of confidence.

A somewhat surprising result generated from the magnitude of new onset intercommunal conflict estimates is that infant mortality rates were negatively significant within this low-income sample. That is, lower levels of infant mortality, which are closely associated with higher per capita incomes, were linked to with higher intensity intercommunal conflicts in 2000 and 2005, controlling for other factors. In Model 1 of Table 6.5, for example, the log of infant mortality rate indicator is significant at the 90 percent confidence level. This finding runs contrary to the well-established relationship between poverty and conflict. On closer inspection, this finding reflects the relatively intense intercommunal conflicts experienced in comparatively better-off Russia, Turkey, Sri Lanka, and the Philippines during this period. This result is a reminder that there are different categories of conflict susceptibility. While most intercommunal conflict may occur among poor countries with autocratic governments, there is a notable group of lower-middle-income exceptions. Intercommunal conflict in these contexts is driven by factors that transcend income level.

Analysis

The results from this study show that the relationship between decentralization and intrastate conflict is not easily generalizable. Rather than confirming that decentralization is always a stabilizing or exacerbating factor to internal conflict, the results from this research show notable divergences depending on types of decentralization, conflict, and context.

Most notably, the effects of decentralization on conflict outcomes were far more apparent for intercommunal than civil conflict. While there are cases of overlap between intercommunal and political conflict, the underlying grievances and motivations of the two conflict types differ, a point recognized in the theoretical literature. Concerns over decentralization exacerbating intercommunal tensions include overlapping jurisdictional and group divisions creating incentives for local politicians to pursue local priorities at the expense of national interests, deepening political polarization and propelling demands for autonomy or secession, and creating local sectarian majorities facing few institutional checks on policies that exclude or repress local minorities and lead to destabilizing grievances. Similarly, perceptions of low levels of legitimacy, poor service delivery, and corruption, especially if differentiated among an ethnically diverse population, could be a trigger for intergroup tensions.

The effects of the various decentralization indicators on intercommunal conflict were highly differentiated, however, demonstrating both beneficial and deleterious effects. Relatively greater levels of subnational expenditures, employment, and percentage of elected subnational tiers were statistically linked to lower levels of new intercommunal conflict since 1995. In other words, decentralization that was marked by greater degrees of legitimacy, control over expenditures, and capacity seemed to have mitigative effects on intercommunal conflict. These findings support arguments that when local leaders are answerable to the general public, have the discretion to pursue identified local priorities, and are empowered with a base level of financial resources and staffing, the results will be more responsive government, better service delivery, and greater stability.

Conversely, formal measures of subnational autonomy were linked to higher levels of post-1995 intercommunal conflict. This was the most consistent finding of this analysis. Specifically, three measures of decentralized legal authority—Treisman's residual authority, independent indices of federalism, and Polity III's centralization of state authority—all showed higher levels of intergroup conflict. The consistency of this finding points to a tangible pattern of instability emerging from these forms of decentralization. This result supports the thesis that unrestricted subnational self-determination opens the door to local elite capture. This, in turn, may translate into selective enforcement of antidiscrimination legislation, the opportunistic polarization of ethnicity to mobilize support for a leader's agenda, and rent seeking, which may entail institutionalizing privileges for the local ethnic majority. The legitimacy of these leaders in the eyes of the local minority understandably declines rapidly under such circumstances, providing a justification for armed struggle as means of group protection. This finding also points out the risks inherent in explicitly highlighting ethnic differences—as federal structures tend to do—as compared to the emphasis on assimilation seen in unitary states (Schou and Haug 2005).

Another explanation for this finding is the often nebulous nature of local government authority, even in a constitutionally mandated federal structure (e.g., Nigeria, Pakistan, Indonesia, and Russia). Some of these federal systems are federal in name only, with political—and often financial and administrative—authority clearly resting with the center. Under these circumstances, local preferences may be frustrated, fostering restiveness. The ambiguity created by the divergence between de facto versus de jure authority also opens the door to political miscalculation and conflict. Emboldened by their autonomous designation, provincial leaders may attempt to assert more authority than they actually have—such as institutionalizing preferences to a local ethnic or religious majority. This sparks fear and resentment among the local minority. The ensuing agitation may ultimately compel the central government to intervene with force. These conflicts may be encouraged by external actors when an ethnic majority spills over into a bordering state. Alternately, if after raising expectations local authorities lack the resources and capacity to act on the priorities they have promoted, then ambiguous federal structures are likely to be a source of frustration and perceived grievance among local majorities, ultimately boiling over into intercommunal conflict. Indeed, the finding that a fourth measure of more limited, though explicit, local government decisionmaking authority (stipulated autonomy) was not linked to more frequent or serious intercommunal conflict may point to the value of decentralizing authority for specific functional issues while retaining national accountability and incentives for local and central government officials to work together.

More extensive local government expenditures were also linked to a lower propensity of post-1995 intercommunal conflict. This pattern suggests that it is local government control over expenditures and capacity to deliver services, more than the share of revenues, which improves government responsiveness to local citizen priorities. Increased control of expenditures provides more options to address the respective priorities of multiple groups in a local area and by so doing defuse social tensions in ethnically divided societies. Local control over expenditures can also enhance the legitimacy of local leaders and augment sentiments of government responsiveness to public concerns. In short, decentralization reforms that enhance the legitimacy, spending discretion, and capacity of local authorities have a stronger track record of avoiding intercommunal conflict than ambiguous de jure legal structures of provincial autonomy.

Political conflict has few reliable explanatory factors pertaining to decentralization—suggesting a greater degree of case specificity. Civil conflicts did more closely mirror income levels, consistent with the well-established poverty-conflict nexus. Relatively poorer countries were more subject to the onset of civil conflict, even within the limited low-income samples used in this analysis (i.e., below $4,000 and below $2,000 per capita incomes). The flip side of this is that intercommunal conflict posed a relatively greater risk to lower-middle-income countries than civil conflict in the post-1995 period (e.g., Indonesia, Russia, Serbia, Thailand, and Turkey). These results suggest that income was relatively less of a motivating factor for intercommunal conflicts. Accordingly, the risk of intercommunal conflict may persist even for countries making good progress developmentally.

In sum, the relationship between decentralization and intrastate conflict does not fit neatly into any single summary classification. Rather, the important distinction seems to have more to do with the manner in which decentralization is approached, with a value placed on enhancing local government service delivery capacity—resources and personnel—coupled with legitimately elected local leaders. Local governments with these qualities are apparently better able to address the priority needs of their respective constituencies and, by so doing, contribute to greater stability.

At the least, the results generated in this analysis force us to recognize that decentralization is not an unmitigated good. Under certain circumstances, decentralization can be a contributing factor to higher rates of intercommunal conflict. This requires that we consider circumstances under which decentralization may heighten the risks of conflict.

Analysis of potential patterns between decentralization and conflict also need to be contextualized in the reality that two-thirds of intercommunal and civil conflict is occurring in autocratic political environments. Accordingly, it is integral to distinguish between decentralization occurring in democratizing versus closed settings. The augmented legitimacy, accountability, and local government responsiveness that apparently contribute to lower levels of intercommunal conflict through political and fiscal decentralization cannot be assumed to materialize in autocratic settings. Promoting decentralization as a conflict-mitigating tool irregardless of context, accordingly, is imprudent. On its own, decentralization is unlikely to overcome the conflict-augmenting effects of an inhospitable environment. Worse, it could have a detrimental impact.

It is also important to keep in mind that decentralization is a dynamic process that often unfolds over a period of years. The cross-sectional nature of the quantitative analysis undertaken is not suited to capturing changes over the period in which decentralization takes place. This reality begs follow-up research. Consistent with the finding of the relative conflict mitigating benefits of limited federalism, qualitative analysis from decentralization experiences in postconflict Ghana and Uganda suggests that there are stabilization advantages to devolving power in a slow, incremental manner (Siegle and O'Mahony 2006; Asante 2004; Golola 2001). This fosters the gradual assumption of responsibilities at the local level, the buildup of capacity, and a shared appreciation of the complementary roles that local and central authorities play in effective governance. Policies guarding against the politicization of intercommunal cleavages, cultivating national pride and identity, ensuring adequate protections for minority groups, and redistributing resources to marginalized areas, among other possibilities, are all initiatives in which the central government will continue to play an indispensable role.

Policy Implications

The nuanced relationship between decentralization and conflict seen in this analysis precludes overarching generalizations. Additional comparative research, supported by more complete decentralization data, is needed. This should be complemented by longitudinal studies that help sort out features of decentralization that contribute to or undercut stabilization as well as identify the most appropriate timing and approaches for attaining them. Be that as it may, this analysis indicates that, on the whole, decentralization within low-income countries is not subject to higher rates of civil or intercommunal conflict than more centralized systems. In fact, this analysis shows that relatively higher levels of subnational expenditure and employment as well as authentic political decentralization are linked to a lower probability of intercommunal conflict. Nonetheless, real risks exist, particularly in weak federal systems or cases where the authority of provinces is ambiguously defined. Based on these patterns, several priority implications emerge.

Conflict Risk Assessments

Rather than assuming that decentralization is a solution for societies facing intergroup tensions, it should be recognized that decentralization initiatives may carry risks. As a result, conducting a systematic conflict risk assessment should become standard practice prior to undertaking decentralization initiatives. Focus should be given to factors influencing the two broad drivers of internal armed conflict—intercommunal divisions and political polarization—with an emphasis on the former. This analysis would be used to inform policymakers about the initial decision whether to support decentralization and, if so, how best to minimize potential vulnerabilities.

Clarify Authority of Autonomous Regions

Federal systems have been comparatively more likely to experience new outbreaks of intercommunal conflict in the post-1995 period. The factors underlying these conflicts are varied and complex.[12] This analysis suggests that the ambiguity of authority often associated with federal-type systems in practice may exacerbate tensions and miscalculations. Promoting regional autonomy, therefore, appears to be a high-risk strategy for accommodating ethnic or geographic differences. To the extent autonomous regions exist or are created, this process should be pursued incrementally with clearly defined roles and authorities for the local government relative to the center. Maintaining incentives for ongoing collaboration between subnational and national entities should be a priority.

Strengthen the Capacity and Control of Local Government

While there is much debate on the relative merits of various facets of decentralization, this analysis indicates that it is the combination of political, administrative, and fiscal strengthening at the local level that is linked to lower levels of conflict. A greater share of elected officials, subnational employment, and control of local expenditures—reflecting stronger local capacity and legitimacy—were shown to mitigate intercommunal conflict. A singular focus on fiscal transfers in the absence of these capacity-building and accountability-enhancing efforts can heighten societal divisions and fan secessionist aspirations, particularly if ethnic group demarcations coincide with geographic jurisdictions or disproportionate natural resource allocations.

Need for Multitiered Decentralization Strategy

An important observation highlighted by this analysis is that the threat of intercommunal conflict is present even in well-established and relatively better-off countries such as Sri Lanka and the Philippines. This is somewhat counterintuitive to the strong relationship observed between conflict and low-income countries and points to the fact that there are different classes of countries at risk of internal conflict. Conflating them obscures important differences to the causes and challenges that each faces. Recognizing these differentiated risks can facilitate a more customized approach to decentralization. Decentralization plans in countries with a history of intercommunal violence, even if middle income, demand special attention to creating protections for minorities, checks on local majorities, and incentives for strengthened ties with the center. Similarly, relatively greater effort will be required to create institutional and human capacity in low-income democratizing countries contemplating decentralization. External actors should be sensitive to these differences and careful not to rush these processes prematurely.

Central Government Control over the Security Sector

Transferring financial resources and administrative and political authority to provinces where the central government is not in control of the security sector is a recipe for disaster. Such a sequence can lead to central government resources effectively funding insurgent activities as happened in Colombia. Accordingly, a central government monopoly over the use of force should precede revenue decentralization. This guidance may lend itself to asymmetric decentralization in contexts where control of the security sector varies. Similarly, a focus on security sector reform—enhancing the democratic legitimacy of the armed forces that can facilitate central government control—may be needed before significant decentralization can be considered.

Decentralization That Strengthens Ties with the Center

Too often debates over decentralization are cast in a decentralization versus centralization framework. In fact, decentralization is not a zero-sum gain. Effective decentralization is closely tied to a capable, supportive central authority committed to the process. It is not a matter of either-or, but the appropriate distribution of responsibilities and resources among the various levels of government. In the case of mitigating conflict risk, this necessarily entails an important role for central authorities. Indeed, a risk of decentralization is that it can create a momentum toward wholly independent provinces with little affinity or compelling rationale to remain connected to the larger state. To mitigate these centrifugal effects, decentralization initiatives should simultaneously incorporate unifying initiatives into their strategies as a means of strengthening the connectedness of the subnational regions and respective group identities to the whole. Maintaining relatively high minimum thresholds for political party representation in the national legislature and requiring that national candidates garner a minimum share of the vote from multiple provinces can encourage cross-group and cross-regional partnerships. National economic development strategies that systematically facilitate interregional infrastructural cooperation (e.g., transportation, communications, water, energy, media) including leveraged financing for regions that undertake such projects could be other useful tactics in this effort.

Ensure Multidirectional Accountability

The vertical accountability created by the direct election of local leaders by constituents establishes a powerful incentive for improving the responsiveness of local government to citizen concerns. At the same time, political decentralization that leaves local politicians unaccountable to other tiers and regions of the state is prone to local elite capture, minority repression, and fragmentation. Accordingly, decentralization strategies should simultaneously seek to ensure there are multiple mechanisms of accountability for local leaders to reinforce good performance and curb abuses. Some examples include:

- Regularized federal audits and transparent reporting of all subregional financial operations.
- Legal authority of national government to intervene to prosecute local officials for misuse of public monies, links to organized crime, trafficking of illicit materials, or other illegal activity (perhaps conditioned on a federal court or grand jury–type approval so as to mitigate targeting of political opponents).
- Operate from the default position that (assuming adequate transparency and oversight procedures are in place) the central government is the primary entity responsible for collecting natural resource and customs revenues. Local jurisdictions, in turn, should have primary control of expenditures allotted for their province or municipality from the collection of these revenues. Moreover, local governments can benefit from the taxes and fees on the indirect economic activity generated. Taking this approach can reduce the fragmenting pressures and atomized views of entitlement that rentier economies produce.
- Focus decentralization efforts at the municipal rather than provincial level. This is where most service delivery occurs anyway and municipalities are far less likely to make autonomy claims.[13]
- Limit local jurisdictions' role in the security sector to the maintenance of a municipal police force while ensuring adequate minority representation on this force.
- Pursue ongoing "national unity" campaigns that strengthen social cohesion and national pride through broad representation in the national military and cultural, sports, and youth exchange activities.

In conclusion, decentralization offers numerous advantages to developing countries. Yet decentralization is not a risk-free endeavor. Unconditional support for decentralization can easily play into dynamics of intensified group identification and political polarization that are major contributors to internal conflict in weak states. Accordingly, despite its many potential benefits, decentralization initiatives should proceed only with constraints—recognizing the context, conflict risks, and need for concurrent efforts to strengthen ties between subnational and national political structures.

Notes

This chapter is a synthesis of a paper "Assessing the Merits of Decentralization as a Conflict-Mitigating Strategy," prepared for the *Decentralization and Democratic Local Governance Programming Handbook* of the US Agency for International Development's Office of Democracy and Governance. The authors thank Harry Blair, Monty Marshall, and Anthony Levitas for technical contributions; Christy Ferguson and Ashley Grable for research support; and Ed Connerley, Krishna Kumar, Lawrence Robertson, Tjip Walker, Andrew Green, Davin O'Regan, and two anonymous reviewers for comments on earlier drafts.

1. As tabulated from data compiled by the Center for Systemic Peace, Severn, Maryland.

2. Together, the two forms of factionalism predict 80 percent of the cases of instability in newly independent African countries.

3. A survey of the decentralization experience in Africa is illustrative of the challenge. While nearly all African countries claim to have pursued decentralization since the democratization wave swept the continent in the early 1990s, objective assessments reveal only a third exhibit functioning decentralized structures. Local governments control less than 5 percent of national public expenditure in two-thirds of African countries (Ndegwa 2002).

4. Notably, there are fewer data points for the fiscal decentralization measures than the others. Accordingly more caution is required in interpreting any results generated, even though these measures rely on comparatively more objective sources of information.

5. The relatively high level of subnational employment for the Middle East should be considered in light of overall low levels of subnational expenditures.

6. Case studies of the decentralization experiences in Colombia, Ghana, the Philippines, and Uganda were developed in a companion version of this chapter to provide some qualitative intranational insights of how the dynamics of decentralization may have influenced the conflict outcomes experienced in these individual contexts (Siegle and O'Mahony 2006).

7. Defined as the existence of intercommunal or civil conflict, respectively, in 1990.

8. Standardized measures (natural logs) of per capita income and population size are used in every estimate as a means of controlling for these effects and limiting the possible over- or underweighting of extremely large or small nominal figures. Population size is an important control for both decentralization and conflict. Infant mortality rates are commonly used as a proxy for income as it is known to be a reliable aggregate measure of service delivery and societal well-being. It has also been shown as a significant predictor of state failure (Esty et al. 1999).

9. In constant US$, with 2000 as the base year, derived from the World Bank's World Development Indicators 2007.

10. Coefficients generated by logit estimates are not subject to direct interpretation. Accordingly, this discussion focuses on the relative significance of the decentralization measures considered.

11. This was true for the 2000 and 2005 estimates, though only the latter are shown in Table 6.5. Similarly, estimates were run for all ongoing ethnic conflicts in 2000 and 2005 (rather than only those initiated post-1995). The results from these estimates did not alter the key findings. Rather, by and large, the factors

found significant in models of new ethnic conflicts were the same as those for ongoing conflicts.

12. Hale (2004), for example, finds ethnofederal structures to be particularly unstable.

13. The authors thank Anthony Levitas for this suggestion.

7

Measuring Decentralization

Kent Eaton and Larry Schroeder

One of the most important developments in the expanding literature on decentralization is the greater interest in and more precise specification of its multidimensional quality. More than is perhaps the case with the two other governance trends that define the age—democratization and economic liberalization—decentralization is a concept that covers a remarkably broad set of changes. Defined in the simplest terms as the transfer of power from national to subnational realms, decentralization can take on a daunting variety of forms.[1]

For example, shifting from the appointment of subnational officials to their direct election certainly counts as a decentralizing change, but so can the less formalized shift in power within parties toward local party brokers. Transferring built schools and hospitals to local governments is an obvious and increasingly widespread form of decentralization, but just as significant are the less visible changes in civil service codes that relax centralized control over the employees who work in these schools and hospitals. Letting subnational governments collect their own taxes or giving them a bigger stake in centrally collected revenues are important forms of decentralization, but so too are more discrete rule changes that allow them to spend (or borrow) revenues without the prior approval of higher authorities or that raise the threshold above which local actors need such approval. Thus, getting a handle on what decentralization actually means for the countries that have adopted it may involve the study of such disparate phenomena as ballot structure, the directorship of provincial banks, procedures for the appeal of lower court decisions, subnational borrowing requirements, the timing of national and local elections, the creation of governors' leagues, and the updating of local property registries. Stated more formally, decentralization requires scholars to master a number of distinct policy arenas (e.g., fiscal policies, social policies, internal security policies) and the behavior of many different institutional actors (e.g., executive and legislative branches, the judiciary, public sector enterprises, bureaucratic agencies).[2]

While decentralization takes on a number of different forms, it has also unfolded in a number of different contexts. Like democratization and economic liberalization, decentralization programs have been put in place in scores of countries that otherwise have very different cultural traditions, state-society relations, and institutional arrangements. The tremendous diversity of contexts in which decentralizing measures have been adopted speaks to the importance of arriving at some agreement about indicators that can help us determine a country's level of decentralization or, as Pranham Bardhan and Dilip Mookherjee (2006b) note, the possibility of cyclical changes in the levels of decentralization.[3] Deriving clear indicators of decentralization that can be used across disparate national contexts is particularly important because, as we discuss in greater detail later in this chapter, national politicians cannot always be taken at their word when they announce that they have decentralized.

The growing awareness that decentralization is not a unidimensional concept, and that we need a disaggregated set of indicators to determine the level of decentralization in its various dimensions, is very welcome (Schneider 2003; Smoke 2003; Treisman 2000). Naturally, different disciplinary bases have tended to encourage scholars to focus on particular dimensions of decentralization. As Paul Smoke argues, "economists focus on fiscal and economic development, political scientists focus on intergovernmental relations, local elections and accountability mechanisms, and public administration experts work on institutional structures, processes and procedures" (2003, 8). Among other things, this disaggregated approach to the study of decentralization has made it possible for experts in each of these three dimensions to identify what the most appropriate indicators are in the area they know best. Based on a review of this literature, we bring together in the first part of this chapter a set of indicators specific to three different dimensions of decentralization that analysts can use to help determine where a particular country sits on the continuum between centralization and decentralization.

But this disaggregated and disciplinary approach has also created certain problems in that it has come at the expense of a more integrated approach to decentralization. Appreciating the systemic quality of decentralization becomes all but impossible if indicators of different types of decentralizing changes are not integrated to form "the bigger picture." In order to deliver on the full promise of decentralization, subnational officials simultaneously need political, administrative, and fiscal independence, and not just independence in one or two of these areas. In the coming years, rather than design better indicators of political, administrative, or fiscal decentralization, the major challenge will be to effectively integrate these different indicators in order to produce a more comprehensive view of decentralization.[4] This more integrated approach will enable us to better assess how decentralization is working as a system, and where and when advocates of decentralization should intervene to support further decentralizing changes. Toward this end, the second part of the chapter illustrates the importance of a more integrated approach to indicators of decentralization.

Disaggregating Indicators of Decentralization Along Three Dimensions

Despite some important exceptions, most scholars have conceptualized decentralization as change along three main dimensions that are related to each other, but analytically distinct: political, fiscal, and administrative.[5] Before turning to each of these dimensions, it is important to note that the relative weight of these dimensions may differ depending on the overarching goal that has motivated the adoption of decentralization. For example, where democratization is the chief goal, establishing electoral mechanisms for the selection of subnational officials is likely to loom large. When national politicians decentralize in the attempt to better harness resources for developmental ends, fiscal decentralization may take the lead. In contrast, decentralization as a security-enhancing reform often puts a premium on changes that give subnational governments greater administrative authority over educational policy—particularly in societies with substantial linguistic, religious, and cultural diversity.

Political Decentralization

To this day, the literature on political decentralization remains much smaller than the literatures on its administrative and fiscal dimensions. This is due in large part to the fact that it was only in the 1990s that a consensus emerged on the need for decentralization to devolve political authority and not "simply" revenue and expenditure if it is to fully empower subnational actors. Despite its being a newer and smaller literature, we now know much more about the changes that either further or hinder political decentralization. The holding of free and fair elections at the subnational level—for both executive and legislative positions—has come to enjoy widespread use as the single most appropriate indicator of political decentralization. James

Manor's work has been most influential in this regard, with his widely quoted argument that, in the absence of subnational elections, it is hard to claim that subnational officials "are largely or wholly independent of higher levels of government" (1999, 6).

Other research, however, suggests that subnational elections should be thought of as a necessary, but not sufficient, condition for political decentralization.[6] Though critical, subnational elections are inadequate as a sole indicator of the political independence of subnational officials. Beyond the "mere" holding of subnational elections, analysts have an additional set of indicators they can use to determine the extent of political decentralization.[7] These indicators come in two main forms: the first are features of electoral rules and the second are internal characteristics of political parties.[8] With respect to electoral rules, the fusion or separation of elections for executive and representative offices, the use of proportional representation or plurality rules, the size of electoral districts, the timing of national and subnational elections, and the structure of ballots have all been emphasized by scholars.[9] Though there are differences of opinion, most of this literature would support the following judgments.[10]

- The separate (rather than fused) election of subnational executives and representatives multiplies the institutional spaces in which constituents can advance local interests (Shugart and Carey 1992).[11]
- If decentralization is meant to "bring government closer to the people," then use of the plurality rule in single-member districts probably does a better job creating closer identifications between individual representatives and their constituents (Hutchcroft 2001).[12]
- Where proportional representation is in use, smaller electoral districts increase the likelihood that voters will know who their local representatives are, and this information should help hold these officials accountable (Hutchcroft 2001).
- The nonconcurrent holding of national and subnational elections reduces the "nationalization" of subnational electoral contests, and increases the probability that subnational issues and performance dominate subnational elections (Jones 1997; Samuels 2000; Shugart and Carey 1992).[13]
- Ballots that enable voters to split their votes and support different candidates and parties at the national and subnational levels encourage subnational officials and candidates to localize their appeals and to differentiate themselves from their national counterparts (Eaton 2004a).
- Once elected, subnational decisionmakers cannot be overruled by higher-level government officials and have access to independent

judicial mechanisms to resolve disputes about the extent of jurisdiction.[14]

Shifting from electoral rules to the partisan dimension, attention to the internal characteristics of political parties can also give us better insight into whether the introduction of subnational elections is likely to produce genuine political decentralization. Political parties are especially critical in examining the link between political and civil society at the subnational level. Parties are the basic building blocks of all representative democracies, and this is no less true at the subnational level simply because governments at that level are physically closer to the people. In the struggle for democratic decentralization, political parties that are strong at the subnational level are easily as important as organized civil societies. At the same time, when partisan actors at the subnational level are insufficiently independent from copartisans at the national level, this lack of independence can operate as a significant drag on decentralization. From William Riker (1964) on, students of decentralization and federalism have underscored the extent to which national party discipline can counter the ability of subnational units to act autonomously. On the other hand, the lack of national party discipline and the fragmentation of national parties into their subnational constituent parts can seriously compromise governability at the national level. Positioning a country on the continuum between excessive and insufficient autonomy for subnational party leaders can be difficult and highly subjective.

Of great importance is the extent to which subnational officials, now elected in their own right, are nevertheless subordinate to the national leaders of the parties to which they belong (Bland, Chapter 3). Though what happens within parties is perhaps of even greater importance than the electoral rules discussed above, getting effective indicators of this degree of subordination is not a straightforward task. The degree of control that national party leaders exercise over candidate selection in subnational races is undoubtedly the fact that has received the most attention in the literature (Willis, Garman, and Haggard 1999; Heller 2001). Collecting information about internal party dynamics is difficult, but the following can be used as indicators of a greater degree of political decentralization: (1) subnational rather than national party officials decide which individuals get to use the party label in subnational races and determine candidates' placement on party lists, if applicable; and (2) political parties regularly hold subnational primaries to determine who their candidates will be in subnational electoral contests.

In addition to their internal characteristics, parties matter for decentralization in another way. In many countries, the transition to representative democracy at the national level in the 1980s and 1990s exposed the weakness of political parties, which too often failed to adequately and consistently reflect societal preferences (Mainwaring and Scully 1995). The gulf between political parties and civil society led many to support decentralization in the expectation that it could create opportunities for the emergence of new and more responsive parties at the subnational level. According to advocates of decentralization, because the costs of entry into politics are lower at the local level relative to increasingly expensive national races, new parties may be able to emerge only in the context of regularly held subnational electoral contests. In general, when existing parties rather than new parties come to dominate the subnational elections that are introduced by the national government, we would expect these existing parties to push less aggressively for decentralization. This suggests the following indicator of political decentralization: in the wake of decentralization, new parties have emerged and won subnational offices (so that these offices are not merely captured by established political parties).

The indicators presented above can be used to evaluate the extent of political independence enjoyed by subnational governments. Where new parties have emerged to contest subnational elections and where parties are structured internally to give voice to subnational actors, this is positive for political decentralization. But they do not work as indicators of how decentralized political power is within subnational governments. In practice, decentralization often replicates at the subnational level the same concentration of power at the national level that we see in executive (as opposed to legislative) branches.

In new democracies, a number of factors have conspired to keep subnational elected representatives from playing the critical roles they perform in successfully decentralized polities. When power is devolved to subnational governments, although these governments have both executive and legislative components, the absence of strong institutions tends to favor subnational chief executives over subnational representatives.[15] Due to the pervasive weakness and volatility of institutions in many new democracies, individual mayors and governors have an easier time making use of newly devolved powers than do the individual councilors and legislators who are elected to representative institutions.[16] As at the national level, subnational chief executives are often able to act more quickly and decisively than subnational representatives. Unfortunately, in most new democracies, the same challenges that make it difficult for national legislators to participate in the policy process on an equal footing with presidents and prime ministers are replicated at the subnational level.[17] This is reflected in the reality that, to date, the vast majority of the "local heroes" in the decentralization story are subnational chief executives and not subnational representatives (Angell, Lowden, and Thorp 2001; Campbell 2003; Stoner-Weiss 1997).[18]

Furthermore, if low levels of institutionalization disadvantage subnational representatives relative to executives, these representatives are also put somewhat at a disadvantage by the tremendous enthusiasm that has emerged in recent years for subnational civil society (Ribot 1999, 2002a, 51). The attempt to cultivate civil society groups is one of the most distinctive characteristics not only of the recent wave of decentralization, but of the interventions that bilateral and multilateral organizations have sponsored in support of decentralization—and for good reason. The organization of previously marginalized individuals into groups that can represent their interests is one of the chief tools in the struggle against subnational authoritarianism. At the same time, civil society organizations are not elected, questions have emerged about their representativeness (Armony 2004; Blair 2000, 2001), and no matter how representative these organizations are, they simply cannot replace elected subnational representatives.[19] These representatives have critical roles to play in making policy and responding to constituent demands, but in practice they can be easily overcome by dynamic mayors and civil society organizations. Summarizing this discussion, the following indicators can be used to assess the strength of subnational representative institutions in a given country.

- Subnational representatives can alter line items in the budget proposed by the subnational chief executive.
- Subnational representatives can override executive vetoes with simple rather than special majorities.
- Subnational representatives can set their own agenda and meeting times and have some minimal staff.
- Subnational executives cannot act unilaterally (e.g., they do not have formal decree powers).
- Subnational rather than national party leaders write the party lists on which subnational representatives campaign. Voters can indicate a preference for particular candidates on these lists (e.g., preferential or open list voting).

Administrative Decentralization

In the administrative dimension of decentralization, much has been written on the critical distinction between deconcentration, delegation, and devolution (Rondinelli 1989; Schneider 2003). This distinction is relevant for decentralization programmers because, while certain administrative changes truly empower subnational authorities (e.g., devolution), others may actually reinforce the control of the central state (e.g., deconcentration). Whereas deconcentration refers to the reassignment of responsibilities to the field offices of national bureaucracies and delegation refers to the transfer of responsibilities to subnational actors who remain accountable to national authorities, only devolution involves the expansion of administrative responsibilities by autonomous subnational authorities who are not beholden to national policymakers.

In any country, when national authorities announce that they have decentralized service delivery, it may not be easy for actors who wish to support decentralization to determine whether deconcentration, delegation, or devolution best characterizes what it is exactly that the government has done. For this reason, the sole use of one of the most widely available indicators of administrative decentralization, which is simply the level of the government with official responsibility for providing the service in question, can be misleading. It is not enough simply to identify which level of government has formal responsibility for the range of services that government provides, though the change in these formal responsibilities is an important part of the puzzle. It is a mistake to think that we can "read off" the level of administrative decentralization from the legislation that formally divides authority.[20] If subnational authorities are given responsibility for providing services, but must provide the service by using public sector employees whom they do not control, subnational autonomy and the scope for variation across subnational governments is effectively curtailed, a point emphasized by Joseph Ayee (2004) in his study of Ghana.

As a result, the authority subnational officials have over the administrative personnel who provide decentralized services constitutes one possible measure of administrative decentralization. At least two challenges arise, however, when such indicators are utilized. First, there may be considerable heterogeneity in the degree to which that authority is actually exercised throughout a country—in spite of universal rules and statutes. Second, measuring the responsiveness of governmental employees to subnational rather than national officials is not easy because it depends on making sense of bureaucratic career paths at a time when, in most countries, these have been substantially destabilized by the combined effects of decentralization and privatization.

The following indicators can be useful, however, in concluding with greater confidence that devolution has occurred, and not just deconcentration or delegation:

- Subnational elected officials have the right to hire and fire government workers in service sectors that have been decentralized and utilize those rights.

- Subnational governments, without permission from the central government, can and do fill open positions. Subnational governments set the minimum job qualifications for successful applicants.
- Subnational elected officials have the right to determine salary levels. Subnational elected officials can supplement salaries on a nonuniform basis (e.g., on the basis of performance).
- The number of positions of government employees at subnational levels is determined by the local government.
- Centrally deputed personnel do not play significant roles in the subnational budget process nor in the implementation of that budget.

While these indicators may help field officers assess the reach of administrative decentralization, it is also important to note that one has to be careful in interpreting such measures. As Smoke notes, "some countries that have instituted greater subnational control have backtracked after finding that poorly trained or corrupt local officials were abusing these powers in a way that wasted resources and abused public trust."[21]

The administrative decentralization indicators posited above can be useful in providing an overall picture of the independence of local governments and reflect the fact that scholars and analysts commonly categorize a country as being administratively centralized, deconcentrated, or devolved. Such characterizations can, however, be overly simplistic and are not focused on the most critical issue—delivery of local public services.[22] Institutional arrangements for public services tend to be service specific. Thus, a country may, for example, deconcentrate the administration of primary and secondary education, devolve the responsibility for health service administration, and keep the administration of agricultural extension services under the direct control of a ministry of agriculture. Hence, another approach to the measurement of administrative decentralization is sector based. In fact, the literature on administrative decentralization has probably made most progress when the focus is on individual service responsibilities rather than local public services in general.

It is commonly recognized that the provision of a local public service entails multiple activities as well as administrative decisions. For example, the provision of infrastructure services such as local roads, piped drinking water, or irrigation systems is likely to require activities such as planning and design of the system, construction, operation, and maintenance (Uphoff 1986, 63), only some of which may be the responsibility of subnational governments. In fact, even though it is common to find statutes which suggest that local governments have responsibility for the provision of a relatively long list of services (e.g., education, health, local roads, sanitation), in reality even where local governments do play critical roles in those services, it is highly unlikely and probably undesirable for all decisions and activities associated with a service to be solely the responsibility of local government. Some activities or decisions can minimize the likelihood of interjurisdictional spillover effects or take advantage of economies of scale; others permit utilization of scientific or technical information unlikely to be available at the local level.[23]

Realistic measurement of administrative decentralization should therefore encompass more than simply binary indicators of whether elected or locally appointed officials do or do not possess authority or responsibility over certain decisions. But adding to the complexity of such measurement is the fact that the list of decisions or activities over which local officials are to have authority can differ substantially across sectors. In fact, measurement of administrative decentralization has been attempted in various sectors, but is probably most fully developed in the education sector.

The most extensive database from which indicators of administrative decentralization in education have been constructed are from the Programme for International Student Assessment (PISA) of the Organisation for Economic Co-operation and Development (OECD). Three PISA surveys have been completed—in 2000 (which focused on reading achievement), 2003 (with a mathematics focus), and 2006 (where science learning was emphasized). Each survey included all of the OECD countries, but also a number of developing countries.[24] The survey administered tests to 4,500–10,000 students in each country; all students were approximately fifteen years of age. Of particular interest for the purpose of measuring decentralization are the surveys of school principals in the randomly selected public or private schools. Each principal was queried on the sources of funding for the school, student selection or admission criteria, resources available in the school as well who has the responsibility to make a number of administrative decisions, including the authority to hire or fire teachers, allocate budgets, and choose textbooks. While principals' perceptions of the degree to which they or others in the school possess autonomy over those decisions may differ within a specific administrative environment,[25] the responses still permit researchers and policymakers the opportunity to gauge relative decentralization of decisionmaking authority more realistically than relying entirely on written rules and ordinances.

These components of the PISA data have been utilized in a number of different studies that address the issue of how administrative decentralization affects test scores. Michael Fertig (2003) determined that, within German schools, greater school autonomy was significantly negatively related to test scores in the 2000 PISA. Esther Sui Chu Ho (2005) found no significant relationship between school autonomy and test scores of Hong Kong students in the 2004 math-oriented exam, but did find that teachers' participation in school decisions was positively and significantly related to test scores. Another study that relied on the PISA data, but only for OECD countries, is that of Douglas Sutherland and Robert Price (2007).[26]

Health is another sector in which efforts have been made to disaggregate the activities associated with administrative decentralization. One approach to the measurement of administrative decentralization in that sector was developed by Thomas Bossert (1998). The approach, based on the principal-agent model, focuses on a mapping of the decision space or "range of effective choice that is allowed by the central authorities (the principal) to be utilized by local authorities (the agents)" (Bossert 1998, 1518). He proceeds to define five different dimensions for the decision space—finance, service organizations, human resources, access rules, and governance rules—along with subcategories of decisions associated with each.

An illustration of how the approach was operationalized for Ghana, Zambia, Uganda, and the Philippines can be found in Thomas Bossert and Joel Beauvais (2002). While these four countries had recently "decentralized" portions of their health sector, each differed with respect to the degree that autonomy was permitted within the various components of the decision space. Unlike the previously discussed measures of education decentralization, the analysis by Bossert and Beauvais is based on a review of secondary sources rather than the perceptions of those directly involved in the sector. While no attempt was made to correlate systematically the various decentralization indicators with outcomes, some impressionistic outcomes relative to the efficiency and financial soundness, equity, and quality of health services were drawn by the authors. In any event, the decision space approach does permit policymakers and researchers the opportunity to go deeper into the complexities of administrative decentralization.

Some attempts have been made at disaggregating sector-based activities in areas other than education and health. Richard Robinson and David Stiedl (2001) bisect the administration of roads into finance and management responsibilities, with the latter further subdivided between road development and rehabilitation and road maintenance. They then argue that the management of either road development or maintenance should be further disaggregated to policymaking and planning on the one hand and actual operation on the other hand. Some of these activities are likely to be better candidates for some form of decentralization than are others; for example, the authors' case study of Zambia shows that local governments play little or no roles in either the planning or operations associated with road development (construction and rehabilitation) whereas the local governments have responsibility for planning and carrying out road maintenance. While the approach illustrated by Robinson and Stiedl does not permit the same degree of disaggregation of sector-related activities as for education and health, it does make clear that simple dichotomous indicators of administrative decentralization in a sector are likely to hide the complexities of the decentralization policies.

In a similar vein, the World Bank's Agricultural Knowledge and Information Systems (AKIS) Thematic Team suggests that the decentralization of agricultural extension be based on recognition of the multiple functions that encompass this service sector (World Bank 2000b). They include a wide variety of activities ranging from providing training market information to farmers to setting extension service policy and formulating strategies. Some of these activities are obviously most appropriate when centralized whereas others are inherently local in nature and thereby require some form of decentralized administration, including the possibility of privatization of service delivery.

The thrust of this sector-oriented literature on administrative decentralization is disaggregation of the administrative decisions that must be made in the delivery of a public service. Authority over some of these decisions may be retained centrally, some may be deconcentrated to regional or local offices, and some may be devolved to popularly elected local governments or even to the service delivery unit. This leads us to posit the following:

- Administrative decentralization can be approached on a disaggregated public service sector basis. Central to this approach is disaggregation of the administrative decisions critical to service outcomes.
- Determination of authority regarding the critical outcomes may be measured either on the basis of laws and regulations or on a de facto basis. The latter is obviously preferable as an indicator of administrative decentralization; however, it is possible that the indicator will not be uniform across all localities due to the specific circumstances or the degree of authority perceived by those actors themselves.
- Indicators of administrative decentralization of sectors are positive rather than normative given the recognition that absolute local authority over all administrative decisions is likely to be as inappropriate for public service outcomes as a totally centralized arrangement. Thus, the indicators are most useful when used to evaluate the efficacy of public services either across time within a country or across countries.

Fiscal Decentralization

Indicators of fiscal decentralization have probably been used in the academic and policy literature more extensively than either political or administrative decentralization measures. One likely reason for this is the longstanding desire by public finance economists to test hypotheses stemming from the theoretical predictions regarding the effects of decentralized fiscal arrangements on public service outcomes. But another, more practical reason is the availability of fiscal data over time both across countries as well as across jurisdictions within a country. Especially important in this regard is the compilation by the International Monetary Fund of aggregate fiscal data published in the annual *Government Finance Statistics* (*GFS*). These data have been used to test hypotheses regarding the apparent links between decentralization and a variety of other factors. One critical hypothesis concerns the effect of fiscal decentralization on the size of the public sector (relative to gross domestic product [GDP]). The so-called Leviathan hypothesis of Geoffrey Brennan and James M. Buchanan (1980) suggests that competition among subnational governments will create incentives that lead to small-sized public sectors and has been the subject of numerous studies using *GFS* data including Wallace Oates (1985), Jaber Ehdaie (1994), Jing Jin and Heng-fu Zou (2002), and Jonathan Rodden, Gunnar Eskeland, and Jennie Litvack (2003).

Another closely related hypothesis that has been tested with these data concerns the possible economic growth implications of decentralization. If fiscal decentralization leads to improved resource allocations, it may serve as a stimulant for increased economic growth; on the other hand, if subnational governments are not allocatively efficient due to such factors as lack of technical capacity, elite capture, or corruption, local fiscal powers may impede growth. Again, a variety of researchers have addressed this issue using the *GFS* data. Hamid Davoodi and Heng-fu Zou (1998) found that, while developed countries are more highly decentralized (in terms of subnational governments' share of total government spending) than are developing countries, decentralization is not found to be positively related to economic growth. Jorge Martinez-Vazquez and Robert McNab (2006) also use the *GFS* data and, although employing a slightly different underlying statistical model, obtain results similar to Davoodi and Zou.

The Martinez-Vazquez and McNab (2006) paper focuses on the effects that decentralization may have on inflation. In that sense, the model is in keeping with others who have used the *GFS* data to estimate effects of decentralization on macroeconomic stability. The concern by many fiscal economists is that subnational government spending can exacerbate macroeconomic business cycles. Two cross-sectional analyses focused on these issue include Luiz deMello (2000) and Kiichiro Fukasaku and Luiz deMello (1998).[27]

The academic and policy literature (including most of the cited studies) acknowledges that fiscal decentralization indicators, particularly as measured using aggregate cross-country data, are far from perfect. The imperfection stems from the fact that simple measures, such as the proportion of total public sector expenditures flowing through subnational governments or even the ratio of subnational government expenditures financed by own-source revenues, fail to capture the degree to which subnational governments truly have local fiscal autonomy. Indeed, Robert Ebel and Serdar Yilmaz (2003) demonstrate for nineteen countries that, when proper measures of fiscal decentralization are used, statistical results are altered significantly.

What are these "proper" measures of fiscal decentralization? In the basic theory of fiscal decentralization, a critical assumption that leads to the expectation of economically efficient outcomes is that, at the margin, local tax rates are set to reflect the marginal benefits derived by the local residents or taxpayers. But this requires the ability of subnational governments to have some control over tax rates or user tariffs or the definition of those revenues.[28] Thus, one important indicator is the degree to which subnational governments have autonomous control over their own revenues.[29] In many developing and transition countries, subnational governments are assigned "local" taxes, but the rates and bases of those taxes are fully defined and controlled by the central government. As such, these revenues should be viewed as shared taxes and are in fact really transfers from the central government, but with the allocation of the transfer based on where the taxes are collected.[30] Likewise, altering tariffs for user charges may require approval by the center, which means that the revenue is not fully under the control of the local government.

Autonomy in determining subnational expenditures is another necessary condition for fiscal decentralization. If subnational governments are simply delegated the task of carrying out local public service functions as the agent of the state, no real fiscal decentralization has occurred. For example, if the number of teachers in elementary schools, the individuals assigned to those slots, and their salaries are determined by a ministry of education, no real decentralization of the education functions has occurred, even though the salary funds flow through a local treasury. In similar vein, when central governments mandate that subnational governments carry out certain services that may or may not be demanded by local residents, the spending for those services cannot be considered fully decentralized.[31] Finally, there are instances in which the central government, either a ministry or even the legislature, must approve local annual budgets before they are considered final. Although such oversight review is often pro forma, even the threat of rejection of the budget diminishes the fiscal autonomy of local decisionmakers.

The more recent theoretical literature on fiscal decentralization has been termed a “second generation of fiscal federalism” by Yingyi Qian and Barry Wiengast (1997) and others.[32] One particularly critical feature of this literature is the importance of hard budget constraints (Rodden, Eskeland, and Litvack 2003; Rodden 2005). In the absence of such constraints, for example, where a national government provides additional transfers to bail out local or regional governments suffering from budgetary deficits, efficient allocations of subnational resources are unlikely to result. As the literature suggests, however, ensuring such constraints is not necessarily easy because elected officials at the central level who do not provide bailouts may be punished by voters who place blame on the center (Goodspeed 2002) or a central government determines that fiscal failures by a large local (e.g., New York City in the US context) or regional government will have undesirable consequences for the nation as a whole (Wildasin 1997).

A final indicator of fiscal decentralization is linked to the ability of decentralized local governments to finance infrastructure. Subnational borrowing is an important component of intergovernmental fiscal relations, and, as stated by Jameson Boex et al., “is necessary for local governments to extend infrastructure to meet the demands for infrastructure, particularly in urban areas” (2006, 23). Preferably such credit is allocated directly by private capital markets; however, since capital markets are often not strong in developing countries, alternative institutions can be used to allocate credit in manner not unlike a market. This requires a regulatory framework to decentralize borrowing powers. Credit-granting institutions that allocate funds on the basis of the fiscal performance of a local or regional government will reward good performers and punish poor performers through access to credit and through the interest rates that must be paid; as such, credit can also enhance local government performance and accountability. Borrowing by decentralized local governments can lead to more efficient outcomes than when capital infrastructure is funded through intergovernmental transfers.

This literature on fiscal decentralization leads to four suggested indicators:[33]

- Own-source revenues as percent of total subnational revenues where “own-source” revenues are restricted to those over which the subnational government retains rate- and base-setting autonomy.
- Locally controlled expenditures as percent of total public expenditures where mandated and pass-through expenditures that are made locally are excluded from the numerator.

- Subnational governments face a binding hard budget constraint.
- Subnational governments are permitted to obtain credit, but that credit is allocated through market or market-like mechanisms.

Integrating Indicators of Decentralization

Thanks to the disaggregating work of specialists who have focused, alternately, on the political, administrative, or fiscal dimensions of decentralization, we have a better understanding of the indicators that are useful in monitoring change along each of these dimensions. The challenge now is to use these indicators in a more integrated fashion in order to detect, at any one point in time, where the critical and timely interventions in support of decentralization can be made. This is important because movement in a decentralizing direction along one dimension does not mean that any movement is occurring in the other dimensions, or that it is occurring in the same direction (e.g., decentralization rather than centralization).

Indeed, there are good reasons not to expect political, fiscal, and administrative decentralization at the same time or in the same degree. [34] Precisely because national governments are often hesitant about decentralization and the loss of authority it might mean, they typically face incentives to agree to decentralizing changes in one dimension while preserving centralist practices or national government prerogatives in the other dimensions.[35] Evidence of the this type of politically rational behavior on the part of central governments is one of the most consistent findings in the literature on decentralization (Dickovick 2005; Falleti 2005; Manor 1999; Ribot 2002b; Wunsch 2001). Even central governments that have publicly committed to decentralize and that have demonstrated political will to make it happen can still face incentives to preserve their discretion over subnational governments. These powerful incentives mean that advocates of decentralization are smart, as a matter of course, to anticipate "stealth" centralizing behaviors by the center in at least some dimensions.

If politicians are able to make different decisions about whether to decentralize in each dimension, then it follows that a number of combinations of political, administrative, and fiscal decentralization are possible. Table 7.1 describes four particularly common combinations, as determined by different scores on each of decentralization's three main dimensions. Making reference to various country examples, the following paragraphs discuss the distinct political logic that produces and sustains these four combinations.

Combination A describes the position of a country whose central government has devolved fiscal resources and administrative responsibilities,

Table 7.1 Common Combinations of Political, Administrative, and Fiscal Decentralization

Common Combinations	Political Decentralization	Administrative Decentralization	Fiscal Decentralization
A	No	Yes	Yes
B	Yes	No	No
C	No	Yes	No
D	Yes	No	Yes

but retains political control over subnational officials. Numerous real-world examples illustrate the appeal of this position to the national government. From the 1970s on, several national governments under one-party rule in Africa trumpeted "decentralization revolutions," but over time it became clear that these were really only modest policies of deconcentration (Wunsch 1998). National party elites were willing to shift some administrative powers and enhanced fiscal autonomy to subnational governments, but not to augment their political independence from the governing party in substantive ways. In Latin America, beginning in the 1960s and continuing through the transitions to democracy in the 1980s, military-led governments exerted tight political control over subnational appointees, but at the same time shifted responsibility for schools and hospitals onto these appointed officials and gave them access to additional fiscal revenues (Eaton 2006a). More recently, China's Communist Party leadership has transferred to provincial governments the types of fiscal and administrative authorities they need to court and retain investors, without allowing a transition to subnational democracy (Montinola, Qian, and Weingast 1995).

In each case and to different degrees, subnational control over revenues and responsibilities increased, but the center successfully defended political control over subnational authorities. The increasingly widespread use of elections rather than appointments to fill subnational offices means that Combination A is less common than it was in the past and may become even less common in the future. However, for reasons that are discussed above (i.e., the use of electoral and party systems that enable national politicians to discipline subnational politicians), the holding of subnational elections may not move countries substantially away from this particular combination. For countries in which Combination A best describes the approach to decentralization, advocates of decentralization might prioritize such reforms as single member districts, smaller electoral districts, nonconcurrent elections, and local primaries to select candidates for local office.

Combination B marks a completely different, but equally rational, response by the center to the threats that decentralization often poses.

According to the logic of the decisionmaking that leads national politicians to embrace this combination, subnational officials can be selected through elections (e.g., political decentralization), but they cannot have significant decentralized control over fiscal revenues or administrative personnel. Getting national politicians to agree to elections in subnational units becomes much easier when they are assured that the central government will retain responsibility over administrative matters and fiscal revenues. This outcome all but guarantees that separately elected officials will be unable to use resources in ways that would challenge the political ambitions of politicians at the center.[36]

Salient examples of countries that have pursued this combination include Italy, where meaningful fiscal decentralization lagged behind the introduction of regional elections by some two decades (Putnam 1993). As Robert Putnam shows, the Italian case illustrates a dynamic according to which some politicians at the center may sign onto political decentralization only because they are confident they can successfully veto other forms of decentralization that would make subnational officials truly threatening. Chile is another country that demonstrates the logic of Combination B. In the eighty years that followed its civil war in 1891, Chile accrued one of the longest records of local democracy in the developing world without actually granting serious fiscal or administrative roles to municipal governments (Valenzuela 1977). Municipal governments were critical as sites of political contestation in which national political forces on the right, left, and center demonstrated their strength, but not as sites of governance. Since, as Ribot argues, "establishing accountable representation without powers is empty," advocates of decentralization in countries that have pursued Combination B should prioritize decentralization along the fiscal and administrative dimensions that are discussed above (2002b, 2).

Combination C marks an ideal position from the standpoint of national politicians in developing countries that are facing strong pressures to introduce and defend fiscal austerity through sustained budget cuts. One familiar dynamic that accounts for the appeal of this particular combination is the off-loading of unfunded expenditure responsibilities on subnational governments in the attempt to close national budget deficits. In this extreme position, national politicians share with subnational politicians neither political authority nor an independent stake in revenues. Instead, what is transferred is the responsibility to administer governmental services that can no longer be funded in a noninflationary way by the national government.

A prominent example of a national politician whose preferences vis-à-vis decentralization resembled Combination C is President Carlos Menem of Argentina (1989–1999), though he ultimately failed in his attempt to recentralize political and fiscal authority and simultaneously force administrative responsibilities onto provincial governments. Menem sought to recentralize political authority by exercising his right to intervene in (e.g., dismiss) elected provincial governments, and he certainly succeeded in transferring additional responsibilities over health and education to the provinces, but ultimately failed to recentralize fiscal authority (Eaton 2005). A similar dynamic can be identified in Russia under the centralizing rule of President Vladimir Putin, who successfully eliminated direct elections for regional governors and who sought to renegotiate the center's Byzantine set of bilateral fiscal contracts with individual subnational governments (Stoner-Weiss 2006).

In contrast to Combination C, where movement along the political and fiscal dimensions of decentralization lags behind the administrative dimension, in Combination D administrative decentralization lags far behind the much more significant transfer of political and fiscal authority to subnational governments. For example, this combination describes the status of decentralization in countries where national governments have agreed to subnational elections and revenue sharing while reserving the right to approve subnational expenditures above a certain (often quite low) threshold. Countries that pursue Combination D often appear to be more decentralized than they truly are, thanks in large part to the reality that acts of political and fiscal decentralization tend to be more visible than the more discrete administrative regulations that can keep subnational actors in check. For example, opponents of decentralization in Venezuela agreed to support the introduction of gubernatorial elections in the late 1980s because they believed that high levels of administrative centralization would enable them easily to continue their control over the subnational realm (Urdaneta, Martinez, and Lopez 1990). Other examples of Combination D include India, the Philippines, and South Africa; in each case, scholars have documented how administrative constraints over personnel and planning prevent subnational officials from fully capitalizing on their substantial political and fiscal authority (Jenkins 2003; Tapales 1993; Friedman and Kihato 2004).

Simply put, if we know that national governments often design decentralization in ways that will protect their ultimate control over subnational authorities, bringing such behaviors to light is much more likely when indicators of different types of decentralization are constantly matched against each other. For example, indicators of fiscal decentralization might be impressive, but substantially less so when crossed with indicators of administrative decentralization; in this case, subnational officials have resources, but not the control over administrative personnel they need in order to translate fiscal authority into the outcomes that voters demand. As another example, if elected mayors lack fiscal and administrative resources, this makes it harder for them to establish and defend their independence from traditional party bosses, thereby imperiling the very success of political decentralization. In effect, the failure to decentralize in all three dimensions can sabotage decentralization in any one dimension.

Conclusion

Whether decentralization "works" or not is, ultimately, an empirical question. It is also an enormously challenging one to answer. In the end, answers to this important question will certainly require that we improve our measurements of the dependent variable; in this case, the various goals that have motivated the adoption of decentralization. But assessing causal questions about the impact of decentralization will also require a more precise approach to the independent variable. As a result, we have concentrated in this chapter on those indicators that can be used to measure our independent variable: decentralization itself.

As is well documented in the literature, not only have multiple goals justified the adoption of decentralization (e.g., democracy, development, and security), but decentralization policies also occur in multiple dimensions. Traditionally, these dimensions have included political, administrative, and fiscal ones. The political dimension emphasizes the ability of local residents to directly or indirectly have a voice in public decisions; the administrative dimension concentrates on what level of government controls administrative decisionmaking either for individual public services or public services in general; and the fiscal dimension focuses on control over budget expenditure and revenue decisions. The discussion in this chapter suggests a variety of indicators for each of these dimensions such that it is possible to provide at least simple indicators of the extent of decentralization either across time within a single country or across a variety of countries. These can, in turn, be useful for policymakers and analysts alike.

Finally, in addition to developing useful indicators that are appropriate for each of the three main dimensions in which decentralization occurs, we have also advocated in this chapter for an integrated approach to the use of these indicators. Without the more integrated approach that we developed in the second half of the chapter, analysts will be hard pressed to assess accurately the more systemic qualities of decentralization. Thus, "making decentralization work" certainly requires the use of disaggregated indicators to collect information about political, administrative, and fiscal decentralization. But it simultaneously requires synthesizing this information in order to paint a bigger picture, one that accurately captures how decentralization is working or failing to work as a system of governance.

Notes

For detailed and constructive written comments on this chapter, we thank Ed Connerley, José Larios, Brian Levy, Andrew Selee, Paul Smoke, and two anonymous reviewers.

1. We use "subnational" rather than "local" to refer to the multiple levels of government below the national level. Use of the term "local" encourages analysts to focus exclusively on the lowest level of government (e.g., municipalities and villages) and to overlook the critical roles that intermediate-level governments have played in the ongoing wave of decentralization. Among other things, it encourages analysts to think of the relationship between national and local governments as the single axis of conflict over decentralization, and to neglect the important and often tense relations that connect multiple levels of subnational governments.

2. Studying decentralization as a multifaceted phenomenon stands in particular contrast to the (political science) literature on democracy, which by the end of the twentieth century had became quite narrowly focused on the political dimensions of democratization, as opposed to the economic and social dimensions that received more substantial attention in the past.

3. The Bardhan and Mookerjee volume includes studies of Pakistan (Cheema, Khwaja, and Qadir 2006) and China (Lin, Tao, and Liu 2006), both of which have had periodic alternations between more and less decentralized governance. Likewise, Wunsch (2001) provides evidence on the recentralization of various African states, and Eaton (2004a) reviews waves of decentralization and recentralization in Argentina, Brazil, Chile, and Uruguay over the course of the twentieth century.

4. As Smoke argues, the selective treatment of different dimensions of decentralization (political, administrative, fiscal) fails to "provide a solid basis for making informed judgments" about decentralization (2003, 8).

5. Exceptions include Brillantes and Cuachon (2002), who distinguish between fiscal, administrative, political, and economic decentralization; Smoke (2003) who distinguishes between fiscal, institutional, and political forms; and Treisman (2000) who distinguishes between structural, decision, resource, electoral, and institutional decentralization.

6. See Ndegwa (2002) for a discussion of the insufficiency of local elections in the African context.

7. The argument that subnational elections are insufficient repeats the argument made by Terry Karl and others that much of the theorizing about democratic transitions at the national level suffered from an "electoralist fallacy" (Karl 1995; Karl and Schmitter 1991).

8. In addition to electoral laws and internal party strength, the degree of political competition at the subnational level is an important factor to consider and one that varies independently of electoral incentives and party strength. We are grateful

to Paul Smoke for this point. For more on how and why the degree of political competition varies across subnational units, see Beer (2004) and Wibbels (2005).

9. For a more exhaustive treatment of these electoral issues, see Bland (Chapter 3). Bland finds that, even where electoral laws such as open list proportional representation appear to encourage responsiveness by subnational officials to their local constituents, persistent control by national party leaders can effectively limit this responsiveness.

10. See Hutchcroft's excellent and more thorough discussion of many of these points (2001) as well as Hiskey and Seligson (2003) for a critical analysis of recall mechanisms at the subnational level.

11. The ongoing and unresolved debate between advocates of presidential and parliamentary forms of government at the national level has its subnational counterpart (Cameron and Falleti 2005), but many of the supposed advantages of parliamentarism at the national level (e.g., fewer interbranch stalemates) appear to be less important at the subnational level.

12. As Ribot argues, central states often prefer party-list electoral systems at the subnational level (rather than single-member districts) in the attempt to create local institutions that are upwardly rather than downwardly accountable (2002a, 47).

13. Nonconcurrent subnational elections, however, can still function as a sort of midterm referendum on national government performance.

14. We are grateful to Andrew Selee for suggesting the importance of such an indicator.

15. Hiskey (Chapter 2) also argues for a strengthening of representative and not "simply" participatory institutions at the subnational level.

16. This is true not just in the context of presidential forms of subnational government, but also where parliamentary forms are used.

17. Wunsch and Ottemoeller note that newly established local councils in Uganda had a difficult time resisting domination by the executives as well as locally posted civil service personnel (2004, 199).

18. How to strengthen formal representative institutions at the subnational level depends in large part on the informal governance structures that are discussed in Ostrom, Picard, and Silverman (2006). As these authors argue, informal structures of governance are subject to considerable cross-regional variation.

19. For more on the "dark side" of civic engagement, see Armony (2004).

20. Andrews and Schroeder (2003) illustrate the differences between formal legislated models of decentralization and what actually occurs in various sub-Saharan African countries.

21. Paul Smoke, professor of international studies, Robert F. Wagner Graduate School of Public Service, New York University, personal communication with the author, Washington, DC, September 18, 2006.

22. As emphasized in Wunsch (1991), designing appropriate institutional arrangements for the delivery of local public services should begin with an analysis of the nature of the service along with the political, administrative, and cultural context in which the service is to be delivered. According to Wunsch, not only do individual services need to be analyzed to see what sort of institutional arrangement is appropriate for them, but individual services also should be disaggregated into their component parts, with varying institutional arrangements to fit the various components.

23. The desirability of combining scientific and local knowledge was recognized long ago by von Hayek (1945).

24. Fourteen non-OECD countries participated in the 2000 survey, ten participated in 2003, with twenty-seven included in the 2006 data.

25. That is, one principal may view his or her input in the budget process as trivial whereas a neighboring administrator may perceive his or her voice as influential, even though both operate within the same public education system.

26. The OECD has also compiled and published interesting data on the degree to which different levels of governments—central, state, provincial or regional, subregional, local—as well as schools are involved in a variety of administrative decisions, including organization of instruction, personnel management, planning and structures, and resource management. This permits the construction of a continuous composite indicator of administrative decentralization, although the value of the composite depends critically on the choice of weights given to each of the administrative decisions. One limitation of the data (OECD 2004) is that they are available for only twenty-five OECD countries rather than a broad cross-section of developed, developing, and transition economies.

27. The GFS data have also been used as a dependent variable to explain why different countries decentralize. See Arzaghi and Henderson (2005).

28. Local taxpayers must also realize that it is their locally elected leaders who are imposing those taxes. This is probably most obvious when the local government also has the authority to collect the tax.

29. For a more in-depth treatment of the design of revenue transfer systems, see Weingast (2006).

30. Stegarescu (2004) differentiates among four different types of tax-sharing arrangements, noting that it is feasible for the tax-sharing revenue split to be determined by the subnational government as in Canada and Switzerland or changes in the split to occur only after consent by subnational governments.

31. These indicators of fiscal decentralization are closely linked to the administrative decentralization indicators discussed above.

32. A recent review of this literature is found in Oates (2005). Note too that the term "fiscal federalism" is commonly used by economists in spite of the fact that the concepts are not restricted to federally organized states.

33. It should be noted that these indicators will not necessarily apply equally to all subnational governments in a country. For example, there may be substantial differences in the indicators for intermediate-level as opposed to local-level governments; likewise, there may be differences between urban and nonurban localities, which further complicates the task of deriving a single indicator.

34. Ndegwa (2002) contains estimates of decentralization indices in each of these three dimensions for thirty sub-Saharan African countries and illustrates how one index can be relatively high whereas others are low for the same country.

35. Dickovick's work on Senegal and South Africa is illustrative, where "subnational officials are now elected and receive revenue transfers, but remain limited by other measures, including low tax-raising capacity, tight central control over spending, limited access to capital markets, and even insecure legal rights in their own jurisdictions" (2005, 183). Similar findings regarding the limits placed on local autonomy in spite of decentralization policies are reported in the cases in Olowu and Wunsch (2004).

36. See Eaton (2004b), however, for the argument that political decentralization in the absence of fiscal and administrative decentralization may not be a very stable equilibrium. Even when national governments introduce subnational elections but decide to keep a tight rein on subnational finances, the introduction of elections itself can generate powerful and often irresistible pressures for administrative and fiscal autonomy from the individuals who win these elections. For a similar dynamic in Mexico, see Beer (2004).

8

Implementing Decentralization: Meeting Neglected Challenges

Paul Smoke

The chapters in this volume cover a broad variety of many of the most prominent themes and issues in the field of decentralization in developing and transition countries. We have seen that decentralization may have multiple goals of varying priority and that it is inherently a complex and challenging phenomenon. If decentralization is to work effectively, reform must be conceived in a way that is appropriate to the context in which it is being adopted, and careful attention to its various interrelated dimensions and elements is needed. This, of course, is a very tall order in highly politicized environments with varying interests and capacities, and there are many points in the reform trajectory when even well-intentioned and well-designed decentralization can go off track.

Although decentralization has not been studied in a sufficiently systematic way, the previous chapters demonstrate that we do know much more about making decentralization work than we used to. At the same time, there are critical aspects of decentralization that have not been adequately considered by decentralization researchers or practitioners. Perhaps the most important area of neglect is the implementation of decentralization. Implementation and related issues, such as capacity building and coordination, have been mentioned or suggested as important in a number of the chapters (see, for example, Kent Eaton and Ed Connerley, Chapter 1; Jonathan Hiskey, Chapter 2; and Derick Brinkerhoff and Omar Azfar, Chapter 4), but they have not been given sufficiently detailed consideration either in this volume or in the broader academic and practitioner literatures on decentralization.

The central argument of this chapter is that carefully considering implementation concerns could improve the effectiveness of decentralization. I first explore the types of dynamics underlying the limited way implementation is generally treated at present and review some of the problems that have commonly been encountered in practice. I then outline a range of issues relevant for considering how to implement decentralization more reflectively, strategically, and pragmatically, and I selectively compare a few country cases where a number of the considerable challenges associated with the implementation of decentralization have been dealt with to varying degrees. I conclude with a few broad observations regarding reform implementation and a recommendation for further policy research.

The Implementation Challenge

The implementation of decentralization—how and over what time period decentralization structures and processes are executed on the ground—is increasingly understood to be a critical determinant of its impacts and sustainability. Most of the decentralization literature, however, focuses heavily on the design of decentralization and devotes only limited effort to understanding its implementation. In recent years there has been growing, although still relatively limited, academic and practitioner attention given to the implementation and sequencing of decentralization.[1]

The variety of experiences with the implementation of decentralization has been great. In some countries, significant functions and resources have been rapidly devolved to subnational governments. Brazil and Argentina, for example, simultaneously devolved substantial administrative, fiscal, and political responsibilities to states and municipalities in the 1980s.[2] Indonesia's decentralization reform is often referred to as the "big bang approach" because elected local councils were rapidly created, given substantial functional responsibilities, and provided with 25 percent of net domestic revenue through two 1999 decentralization laws.[3] The decentralization in Uganda, which was defined by a new constitution (1995) and a robust local government statute (1997) made Ugandan local governments the most fiscally important in Africa, with about 30 percent of total public expenditures coming rapidly under their control.[4]

At the other end of the spectrum are countries in which decentralization is an official policy, but where the role that local governments play is quite modest and the process of decentralization has been relatively gradual. Cambodia, for example, rapidly created elected commune councils and provided them with new resources through an intergovernmental transfer program in 2002.[5] These commune councils, however, were not immediately empowered with major functions or independent revenues, and the initial transfers amounted to only 1.5 percent of the national budget and still do not exceed 2.5 percent. In Nicaragua, an official decentralization policy has been developed and significant intergovernmental transfers have been provided to municipalities, but a lack of clarity in specific functional responsibilities and weak capacities have limited the actual role that local governments independently play.[6] In several West African countries, decentralization has only modestly increased the functions of local governments and they are assuming new responsibilities slowly and erratically.[7]

In between the two extremes is a great variety of experience in terms of the importance of decentralization and the pace at which it is occurring. In South Africa, the postapartheid constitution and various decentralization laws give considerable powers and resources to local governments but, outside of major metropolitan areas, the assumption of these functions has been more limited and uneven.[8] The Thailand decentralization, which emerged in the 1990s, involved the creation of an elaborate and carefully sequenced reform process, but implementation has been extremely slow.[9] Chile stands out in Latin America as a case where local governments play an important role, but under rather heavy central guidance and control.[10]

Although the magnitude and speed of decentralization are very important, perhaps the most important factor in implementing decentralization is the specific strategy—or lack thereof—underlying it. A massive decentralization may be unambiguously desirable or politically inevitable in a particular country. If reforms are implemented too rapidly, however, problems may arise and could even result in efforts to recentralize. A number of analysts have argued that a more gradual, staged process could allow local governments—and central actors that have new roles under decentralization—the opportunity to acquire the experience and capacity they need to meet their obligations more effectively and responsibly, although of course a gradual process can also stall at an early stage.[11] In some cases, modest decentralizations, if successful, can lay the groundwork and provide momentum for more substantial efforts in the future.

Underlying Dynamics

The extent and pace of decentralization implementation in a particular country can be based on many factors, but five seem to be particularly important. First, as highlighted by Eaton and Connerley in Chapter 1 and discussed in other chapters (Hiskey, Chapter 2, and Gary Bland, Chapter 3), decentralization is inherently a political phenomenon, and political forces substantially determine the way decentralization is designed and how it is implemented. Second, pressure from international aid organizations has been an important factor underlying the impetus for and trajectory of decentralization in some aid-dependent developing countries that might otherwise have been reluctant to empower subnational governments in the way they have officially decided to do. Third, there has been a tendency to frame decentralization programs in many developing and transition countries on the basis of normative Western conceptual models, which embody explicit or implicit assumptions that may not always apply in the contexts of developing and transition countries and say little about implementation. Fourth, reluctant or competing central government agencies can slow or obstruct even appropriately crafted decentralization reforms during the implementation process. Finally, substantial capacity limitations at both central and subnational levels can constrain the implementation of even well-intentioned and well-designed decentralization efforts.

The Political Essence of Decentralization

The political nature of decentralization is reflected in a considerable academic literature on the politics of decentralization that is reviewed by Eaton and Connerley in Chapter 1.[12] In policy circles, the role of politics is often framed in terms of the need for adequate political will to decentralize.[13] The way that the term "political will" is often used by practitioners, however, implies commitment of a benevolent and unified central government to improving the lives of citizens by empowering locally elected governments to serve them. The motives behind decentralization, of course, are often much more complex and may be rather less benign. In addition, even strong political will is not sufficient for realizing decentralization reforms. Many countries that have developed strong constitutional and legal frameworks for decentralization often have only partially implemented them or undermined them in practice.

As highlighted in previous chapters, decentralization efforts in developing countries have not infrequently been responses to domestic political or economic crises.[14] They are often attempts by a ruling regime to appease aggrieved citizens and to maintain power. In some cases, strong subnational governments may use a crisis to place demands for greater powers on the central government. Given the perceived urgency to move forward quickly in crisis situations, there may be little opportunity or incentive for developing more than a superficial consensus on the form and process of decentralization. Weak or hasty consensus in turn may go hand in hand with limited understanding of basic principles and goals of decentralization, adoption of poorly designed frameworks, inadequate attention to implementation details, and indifferent support or outright resistance during implementation on the part of actors who perceive their interests as being poorly served or damaged by decentralization.

There are also important subnational political dimensions of decentralization, many of which are discussed in multiple previous chapters (see, especially, Eaton and Connerley, Chapter 1; Hiskey, Chapter 2; and Bland, Chapter 3).[15] Most critically, local governments must often learn as decentralization proceeds to act more autonomously and to be accountable in resource use to a constituency, and elected councilors must learn to work with civil servants who have historically taken their direction from above. Such fundamental changes are obviously fraught with political challenges that can vary substantially across local jurisdictions and affect the way decentralization unfolds on the ground. Local elites may drive political dynamics in their jurisdictions, and they may be involved in strong relationships with national bureaucratic and political elites. Broadening subnational political participation is often a complex challenge, as is developing a balance among the various subnational actors as well as between them and higher levels.

The Role of International Agencies in Shaping Reform

The often considerable role played by international development agencies or donors in promoting decentralization and the effect this has on implementation should not be overlooked in developing and transition countries.[16] Although they have arguably begun to shift behavior in recent years and there are cases of productive donor engagement, many major donors long supported primarily technical and formulaic approaches to decentralization, with inadequate consideration of whether they were politically and institutionally workable in the context of a particular country. These approaches can provide a useful starting point for analysis, but they have a narrow focus, and having been developed in the context of Western countries, are somewhat culture and institution specific.[17] They also focus on the attainment of normatively desirable outcomes with minimal consideration of the politics behind them or how to implement them.[18]

Beyond the broad role that donors play in defining and promoting decentralization reform in some countries, specific aspects of their behavior can be problematic. Despite rhetoric about institution building to implement sustainable decentralization, immediate donor interests are not always well served by genuine institutional reform. Such efforts can be time consuming and complex, and they may not initially require the large volume of resources or rapid disbursements that are often perceived as a key element of donor performance. In addition, donors often try to avoid the challenges of cross-sectoral and interjurisdictional coordination by defining projects and programs for specific sectors, ministries or subnational governments. The participating entities are then required to adopt mandated donor procedures for specific purposes, sometimes working through separate project or program implementation units. The approach often diverges from official government systems and procedures, and different donors have dissimilar approaches.

The adoption of inconsistent and separate mechanisms at a minimum complicates the implementation responsibilities of central and local officials and, in some cases, may undermine the development of a unified system for sustainable management of public sector functions. In certain cases, such behavior can also reinforce problematic competition among government agencies (as discussed below). There have been efforts undertaken in recent years to deal with these various concerns about donor behavior, but they remain pervasive to various degrees.

The Limitations of Dominant International Conceptual Norms

To the extent that the limitations of conventional analytical frameworks for decentralization noted above have been recognized in recent years, the main effect has been on the need to pay more attention to designing decentralization in context rather than to focus on implementation. Even a recently emerging focus on implementation in the decentralization literature has, with a few exceptions, a somewhat technocratic orientation, outlining a series of required reform steps with little guidance on how to deal with institutional and political realities.[19]

The technocratic approach in practice often results in unworkably comprehensive decentralization reforms that overwhelm capacity to adopt them at the central and local level (see more below). Massive reforms also threaten bureaucratic and political acceptance among central agencies that stand to lose power and resources. In cases where capacity or political constraints preclude moving rapidly, reform programs may focus only on limited (often technical) activities such as local government financial management reform. These minor activities may not be strategically connected to the broader set of reforms required for effective decentralization.

Another shortcoming of how the normative models are applied is the inadequate treatment of local government diversity within countries. Although variations in basic characteristics relevant for ideal systems (e.g., urban vs. rural, size and diversity of population) can be captured, there is rarely explicit attention given to varying capacities among local governments to assume functions according to the normative principles. It is common for decentralization reforms to treat all local governments (or categories) as if they had similar capacity. In fact, there are often considerable capacity differences among local governments, even those with a similar population, economic base, and so forth. Assigning major responsibilities to local governments with weak capacity invites failure while constraining competent local governments is counterproductive.

Bureaucratic Incentives and Competition

Decentralization often takes place in complex and poorly coordinated institutional environments.[20] A wide variety of central government agencies commonly have a role in fleshing out and implementing the often broad legal parameters of decentralization reforms. These include local government oversight ministries (local government, home affairs, interior, etc.), multisectoral or coordinating ministries with a government-wide mandate (finance, planning, civil service, etc.) and sectoral ministries involved in service delivery (education, health, transport, water, etc.).

Even if there is (or appears to be) broad national consensus for decentralization, these various agencies may have very different opinions regarding how far decentralization should go and what their role in the process should be. In some cases, central government agencies may overtly or covertly obstruct decentralization of major responsibilities when this reduces their political power and undermines their control over substantial resources. Such behavior can be related to the relationships between particular agencies and political parties or legislatures, but this need not be the case.

Another critical problem is that central agencies may have little or no incentive to work cooperatively, even though this is crucial for effective decentralization, which is inherently a multifaceted and multisectoral phenomenon. In some cases, powerful agencies may engage in direct competition for control of the decentralization agenda and the substantial internal and external resources that may be involved in its implementation.

Capacity Constraints

Although well known, well documented, and fairly well represented by the chapters in this volume, a discussion of the dynamics underlying the challenges of implementing decentralization would be incomplete without reiterating the common limitations of managerial and technical capacity at all levels of government in many developing and transition countries. Weak skills and inadequate or inappropriate training and capacity-building programs are pervasive. Lack of capacity is exacerbated by problematic civil service management, low salaries, and limited incentives for good performance. The processes of civil service reform and capacity building are inherently slow, and these aspects of reform tend not to be approached strategically.

The Logic of Strategic Implementation

As illustrated throughout this volume, decentralization often requires massive changes in the behavior of all actors involved. Central government actors must learn to reduce their control over local governments and develop the ability to undertake legitimate oversight or monitoring and to support the effective functioning of local governments. Local governments need to learn to adopt new systems and procedures and to function in different accountability environments. Citizens and businesses must learn to trust local governments and develop the capacity to hold their locally elected officials accountable to them. Even the best designed decentralization may not be effective if care is not given to how it is implemented and treats key actors.

Broad Approaches to Decentralization Reform

In recent years,[21] there has been an emerging modest attention to the implementation and sequencing of decentralization.[22] Implementation can be accomplished in a variety of ways, and it has both a national and a local dimension.

The national perspective. From the national perspective, there are several approaches to empowering local governments. At the most conventional extreme, the implementation of a national decentralization framework is the responsibility of central ministries and local governments. Each of these entities must become familiar with the framework, understand their role in it, develop appropriate capacity, and adopt its provisions as rapidly as possible. This could be called the "sink-or-swim approach" in the sense that it relies primarily on the independent behavioral adaptations of each of the relevant actors. Under this approach, the central government essentially adopts a hands-off stance, with little or no active effort to support decentralization beyond enforcement of the framework. Those local governments that cannot meet the requirements of the new system will fail to reap its benefits.

At the other extreme, a central government could pursue a highly proactive process for gradually implementing the provisions of a new decentralization framework. Under such an approach, no decentralization reforms are automatically implemented and no local government can of its own accord assume responsibilities for legally permissible functions. The framework is put into practice according to central decisions, and local governments must wait for central actions to receive powers and responsibilities in some sequence and at some pace that is entirely out of their control. This might be called the "paternalistic approach" to decentralization.

Neither of these extremes is likely to be entirely appropriate in most developing and transition countries. The sink-or-swim approach may work well for some developed urban areas where local governments have the level of capacity needed to assume new functions rapidly, citizens have sufficient capacity to hold local governments accountable to them, and the discipline of a hard budget constraint is institutionalized by the central government. Where local governments and citizens have weak capacity and central and local governments have limited political incentives to behave according to the new framework, the approach is not likely to be very effective. A purely paternalistic approach, however, is also highly problematic. In many developing and transition countries, at least a subset of local governments are capable of responsibly meeting decentralization requirements and managing their own affairs, and they should not be hampered from going about their business by restrictive central control over the adoption of their legal roles and responsibilities. The potential problems are compounded if the center is not using well-defined and transparently applied standards and processes in making decisions about what to decentralize and when.

In many decentralizing countries, a more strategic, asymmetric approach to decentralization could involve a judicious compromise between the two extreme approaches. This would require the central government to objectively differentiate among often highly dissimilar local governments. Those with higher levels of capacity can essentially be left to sink or swim while other local governments might be allowed to assume responsibilities only more gradually. These weaker local governments could also be targeted with appropriate capacity-building and technical assistance to help them adopt initial reforms and progressively move toward assuming more substantial functions and greater autonomy. Under such a "developmental" decentralization implementation strategy, the eventual target systems may be the same for all local governments, but the pace and specific path to realizing them need not be.

If properly structured, technical decentralization reforms can be linked to broader efforts to build capacity and governance progressively. The central government has considerable leverage in that it can use access to powers, resources, and technical assistance in a way that encourages the adoption of new functions, revenue sources, and operating procedures as well as the appropriate use of more robust accountability mechanisms and other types of reforms. From this perspective, local autonomy in developing environments should be at least partially earned. Immediate high levels of local government autonomy in the absence of a minimum of capacity to assume functions responsibly and some degree of accountability to local citizens is a well-documented recipe for poor performance. The specific situation, of course, will differ among developing countries that are at different stages. Some countries already have in place local government systems that they are trying to improve. Others are transferring portions of formally more centralized systems to local governments, sometimes along with staff. In still other cases, new systems and procedures are being created for new local governments. Such differences in the nature of the system—along with political and institutional factors elaborated on earlier—need to inform the strategy that would be developed in a particular country.

There are, however, risks to such an approach. It could be undermined by the political and bureaucratic dynamics outlined above, with politicized, subjective, nontransparent assessment of which local governments are ready to undertake specific functions. If there is not a clear process and momentum to move forward, some local governments might stall at early stages of reform that leave them with highly limited functions and autonomy. In addition, this approach assumes that the central government has the capacity and desire to manage decentralization in the way needed, and this volume has clearly demonstrated that reality can be rather different. Thus, it must be recognized that, despite its potential advantages over other approaches, the strategic developmental approach to implementing decentralization is fundamentally a technical approach that will work only if certain political conditions and capacity levels can be achieved. Given how poorly the sink-or-swim and paternalistic approaches have generally performed in developing and transition countries, a case can be made to consider the extent to which such an alternative approach might be feasible in a particular country.

The local perspective. From the local perspective, the notion of an implementation strategy takes on a different meaning than it does at the national level. Even the most capable local governments need to be strategic in implementing decentralization reforms that involve significant changes in the functions local governments undertake and in the level and nature of local taxes and fees. Trying to adopt too many reforms too quickly could overwhelm local government capacity and the political tolerance of local citizens for additional revenue burdens.

To offset the potential effects of overloading, a more gradual and strategic approach will often be justified. Simple and more politically acceptable reforms, for example, could be undertaken before more complex or controversial ones, which could be phased in later. For example, in places where new services are being undertaken by local governments, they could be rolled out over a period of time, either in terms of the aspects of service being decentralized (such as starting with local management of operations and maintenance before assuming fuller control over a function) or geographic coverage (such as starting in a few neighborhoods where good performance is likely before moving on to other areas). On the revenue side, new user charges, for example, could move gradually toward cost recovery in order to avoid harsh equity effects, undesirable reductions in basic service use, political resistance to large fee increases, and so forth. New systems and procedures being pushed by the center or considered by the local government could be tested through pilots, allowing evaluation and improvements before the reforms are more generally adopted.

Institutional innovations can be used, at least temporarily, to overcome some of the challenges to implementing reform. Adoption or tailoring of citizen engagement and oversight mechanisms can help to facilitate public acceptance of local revenue reforms, for example, and public education campaigns may facilitate improved citizen awareness and compliance.[23] User committees for specific services have sometimes been used to connect citizens to local government service delivery and associated revenue generation, although they can also be used to bypass and undermine local governments in certain circumstances.[24] Working with community groups on service delivery and revenue generation for local services like trash collection can benefit local governments, community groups, and individual citizens.

Capacity Building and Technical Assistance

Capacity building and technical assistance for both central and subnational actors is well recognized to be an important part of implementing decentralization, and a great deal of attention and significant resources are devoted to it. Capacity development is critical to decentralization reform and the need for capacity development is widespread in central and subnational governments (including both elected and appointed government officials), variously defined communities, civil society groups, and individual citizens. Typically, all of the actors involved in any specific decentralization reform effort must have the capacity to act differently than they have in the past if the full benefits of reform are to be realized.

Other chapters in this volume (Eaton and Connerley, Chapter 1; Hiskey, Chapter 2; and Brinkerhoff and Azfar, Chapter 4) note the problem of weak capacity and the challenges it creates for effective decentralization.

Capacity building and technical assistance, however, are often treated by central governments and donors in a standardized and mechanistic way.[25] General training is often provided for relevant central and local government staff as well as specific training for staff with particular responsibilities (e.g., finance staff receive special training and technical assistance in finance).

A logical starting point is to be clear about exactly what is meant by capacity building and technical assistance.[26] Such support can take the extremes of being either "supply-driven" (largely managed and provided by the central government or its agents) or "demand-driven" (tailored to the specific requests of local governments). Training for capacity enhancement can also be "classroom-style" or "on-the-job." Finally, capacity building and technical assistance can be provided solely to government entities or also to civil society (to help citizens to make effective use of their elected local governments).

Although formal statistics are not readily available, it seems fair to suggest that many developing and transition countries have continued to focus on relatively traditional supply-driven classroom-style training. There are certainly provisions in some countries for demand-driven capacity building, but there are no well-documented cases where a broad range of options are generally available to and pursued by local governments. In addition, there is a fairly heavy bias toward technical training, with a more limited focus on building the capacity of civil society for engaged governance and on the relationship between elected councilors and local government staff. Citizen training (such as that provided for participatory budgeting exercises), for example, is often provided in conjunction with or under the watchful eye of the local governments that citizens must learn to challenge and push to be accountable.

There is some limited emerging anecdotal evidence and a recognition that on-the-job training specifically demanded by local governments for particular tasks they are in the process of implementing is a better way of developing and retaining skills.[27] Thus, attending a general course at a training institute may be less useful than, or should at least be supplemented by, on-the-job training provided as local government employees are in the process of undertaking new functions. How capacity building is handled may well affect the ability of local governments to perform effectively.

Coordination

As noted above, decentralization and local government reform activities inherently involve various central government agencies, and there is almost invariably a lack of harmony among their views regarding reform.

Some but not all countries that undertake decentralization and local government reform programs institute some type of coordination mechanism to help ensure more effective design and implementation, but they vary widely in their nature, scope, and effectiveness.[28]

Some type of informal or semiformal cross-departmental mechanism to develop, coordinate, and implement decentralization policies and to mediate interdepartmental differences is common, but typically not very effective. Without effective coordination, reform efforts developed and managed by various departments may not support each other, and may even push the intergovernmental system in contradictory directions. This situation also leads to poor use of donor assistance provided to support reforms, as donors—or even different divisions of the same donor—may work primarily or exclusively with particular ministries without adequately consulting each other, thus reinforcing the problem and consequences of weak coordination among government departments.

It might be argued that the most reliable way to ensure smoother progress with decentralization reforms and to facilitate improved interdepartmental and donor coordination is to empower some relatively broad-based and politically credible body with formal responsibility for coordination, and to give this body the mechanisms required to enforce its authority. There are at least three types of mechanisms used to promote formal coordination.

One type is based on constitutional, legislative, or administrative provisions that give a single central government department the responsibility and power to coordinate all decentralization and local government reforms. This is particularly common in former British territories where relatively independent local government systems and ministries of local government were set up in the colonial era. In countries with different systems, a ministry of interior or home affairs, with traditional responsibility for internal security and administration, may evolve to serve a similar role. In many cases, however, single departments cannot coordinate effectively because they are seen as competitors and sometimes as inferiors in the government hierarchy by other ministries whose cooperation is required for successful decentralization. These other ministries may refuse to cooperate with plans and activities that they feel will reduce their own power or prestige. Single-department coordination responsibilities can work only if responsibilities of various agencies are reasonably clear, and if the coordinating department is well respected and adequately empowered to require compliance by other ministries. If functions are unclear, if the coordinating ministry is seen as biased or self-interested, or if the coordinating ministry has insufficient authority to enforce coordination, the arrangements may undermine coordination rather than promote it.

A second mechanism is to establish a formal interdepartmental body to oversee the development and implementation of intergovernmental fiscal reforms. Many interdepartmental mechanisms, however, have not fared well, degenerating into forums in which representatives of different departments argue with each other and, even if they come to certain agreements, fail to implement them. In many cases, these bodies are chaired by particular ministries that have the same legitimacy problems outlined above with respect to single-agency coordination mechanisms. To be effective, such mechanisms may need to be chaired by a neutral party or have a rotating leadership, and they also require strong, formal enforcement powers. Otherwise they are likely to be ineffective, a common fate with ad hoc interministerial coordinating committees that rely primarily on voluntary cooperation of members.

A third type of mechanism involves the appointment of a substantially independent body to coordinate local government reform activities. Such an arrangement reinforces the neutrality of the coordination mechanism and helps to raise it above interdepartmental politics. This type of mechanism, however, is rare. The State Finance Commissions, appointed by each state government in India to oversee the implementation of the seventy-fourth amendment to the constitution on municipal decentralization, approximate this type of arrangement. An example of a more independent, broad-based, and higher-level body is the National Decentralization Committee (NDC) in Thailand, which serves as the strategic policy development unit for decentralization. Its membership includes local government and nongovernmental organizations (NGOs) as well as central government representatives. The NDC played a key role in decentralization design and also has the mandate for monitoring and implementing decentralization reforms and, as appropriate, providing recommendations to the cabinet regarding further policy reform. Although the NDC was effective at developing a detailed implementation strategy, the momentum for decentralization has been tempered by various recent political events, and so it has been much less successful with implementation.

In summary, coordination is one of the most important and most poorly conducted aspects of decentralization. Regrettably, good performance is rare, partial, and temporary. There seem to be four key pitfalls. First, coordination mechanisms are often too informal, providing little pressure for participation on the various agencies from which cooperation is required for decentralization to succeed. Second, there are not uncommonly multiple coordination mechanisms with poorly specified and sometimes overlapping functions, and inadequate interaction with each other. Third, there is typically a lack of balanced responsibility among the various parties, with the all too common problem of assigning leadership to a single interested party, which undermines the willingness of the other partners to cooperate. Fourth, there is rarely sufficiently strong enforcement authority with such coordinating mechanisms. If decisions are made and there is no way to hold the concerned agencies to these agreements, there is no reason to expect effective coordination.

Selected Vignettes of Strategic and Nonstrategic Implementation

Although there has been no major, formal comparative study of how decentralization is implemented, it is possible to illustrate the range of practices—both desirable and problematic—by looking at a few countries. Four cases are briefly sketched here: (1) Cambodia, which introduced modest decentralization with some aspects of a creative implementation strategy; (2) Indonesia, which pursued a substantial big bang decentralization with no clearly articulated strategic planning for implementation; (3) Kenya, which has been trying to revitalize reasonably empowered but poorly performing local governments in a relatively strategic, but limited way; and (4) Uganda, which began a significant decentralization using both strategic and nonstrategic approaches to implementation, with the latter resulting in some nontrivial recentralization.

These cases are discussed comparatively beginning with an introduction to their contexts and decentralization policies. This is followed by a review of the strategy for implementation adopted by each, including capacity building and coordination.

Context

Decentralization is a new phenomenon in Cambodia, which operated under a highly centralized government system throughout its history.[29] A multilevel administrative structure was set up during the French colonial period, but it deteriorated during the protracted conflicts of the Khmer Rouge era, the Vietnamese occupation, and civil war. The 1991 peace accord and 1993 elections resulted in a fragile, multiparty power-sharing arrangement. This collapsed in a 1997 coup engineered by Hun Sen, whose Cambodia People's Party then won elections in 1998 and 2003. The emergence of a more stable political climate opened the door for decentralization. Newly in a position of strength and facing greater expectations from the public, the government began to shift from a focus on peace and stability to a greater concern with development. The inability of the state to deliver adequate basic services and the success of a local development initiative (see below) financed by donors led political leaders to see decentralization as a means to help fill this gap.

An element of decentralized administration was also introduced to Indonesia during its Dutch colonial period, although there was not a true local government system.[30] Building national unity through strong centralization was pursued after independence, a common practice in ethnically diverse former colonies. Centralized control was taken to an extreme under the authoritarian Suharto regime. Various donors promoted decentralization efforts in the 1970s and 1980s, but these never had genuine political traction and largely involved strengthening central ministries and their deconcentrated structures. The 1997 Asian economic crisis was a critical factor in the fall of Suharto, and this was followed by powerful events challenging national unity—the secession of the former province of East Timor and growing protests from natural resource endowed provinces about the outflow of their resources to Jakarta. The post-Suharto government pursued multiparty democratization and decentralization primarily as a strategy to hold the country together. The focus of the decentralization reform was on local governments, largely due to concerns that stronger ethnically identified provinces would push for separatism or federalism.

Local governance has enjoyed a long tradition in Kenya, both from the customs of its ethnic groups and from the formal local government system created during the British colonial era. [31] The colonial local governments were relatively empowered, but of course they served the colonists. They were retained but somewhat weakened in the name of national unity after independence, and many continued to provide some key services and to raise local revenues. Performance, however, generally declined over time. The center blamed this on the incompetence and corruption of local governments, who in turn blamed central government control and interference. The most important reason was likely a perceived political imperative to channel the majority of public resources through the central government budget and deconcentrated administration. The resumption of a multiparty system in 1992 helped to create space and some political pressure for improving the local government system.

Uganda had a less elaborately developed local government system than Kenya did during the colonial era.[32] The powers that local governments did enjoy were reduced by the 1967 republican constitution, and the system experienced the same types of problems that plagued Kenya in the postcolonial period. The overall system deteriorated as Uganda was enveloped in oppressive regimes with little interest in modern conventions of governance. The Idi Amin era effectively undermined the local government system. When Yoweri Museveni became president in 1986, he presided over a gradual public sector recovery that eventually involved local governments. Uganda did not until recently have a multiparty system like Kenya,[33] but the political desire for decentralization has been strong and largely homegrown. The desire to bring the country back from a long period of conflict and underdevelopment meant that Uganda, unlike many developing countries, did not move forward without building a relatively broad-based consensus on the general value of decentralization and the eventual form that the intergovernmental system should take.

Decentralization Policy

The foundation for decentralization in Cambodia was laid by donor relief efforts in the postconflict period. A series of donor projects to assist with refugee resettlement evolved into a local institutional development and capacity-building effort that later became an official government program.[34] In the political environment outlined above, the central government adapted the program's systems and procedures to create elected commune governments through legislation passed in 2001. Although this was an impressive progression, it was quite modest, focusing only on one lower tier of the administrative system. Provinces and municipalities remain deconcentrated entities that are integrated into the national budget, and the commune efforts cannot be considered true devolution. Communes have few formal functions and resources—the system is based on small and relatively unconditional intergovernmental transfers. There is, however, a major effort currently under way to strengthen the commune system and expand decentralization to other subnational levels.

Indonesia developed a substantial and advanced decentralization framework in the immediate post-Suharto period. A series of laws passed in 1999 and 2000 eliminated hierarchical relationships between local governments and higher levels, devolved considerable functions, provided significant fiscal transfers, and defined own revenues. Constitutional amendments in 2000 consolidated local government reforms. In 2004, however, new legislation weakened local government budgeting and civil service control, partly in reaction to problematic performance. On the fiscal side, the decentralization legislation devolves many public functions to local governments, but revenue decentralization is weak relative to their responsibilities. Many Indonesian local governments are highly dependent on the substantial intergovernmental transfers. The main program, the Dana Alokasi Umum (DAU), is a revenue-sharing fund capitalized by a minimum of 25 percent of national domestic revenues and largely targeted to the local level.

As Kenyan local governments have in principle been semiautonomous for some time (under a Local Government Act passed in 1967 and amended many times), there is no formal decentralization policy. The political conditions noted above, however, created some modest momentum for local government reform, and a series of new activities were started under the leadership of the Ministry of Local Government (MLG), which is legally responsible for local authorities. The process started by the MLG (discussed below) resulted in broader engagement from other central ministries and a progressive series of steps to improve local government systems, incentives, and performance.

In the self-driven, pro-reform environment of Uganda, the government developed a fairly robust formal framework for decentralization. The Local Governments Statute of 1993, 1995 Ugandan constitution, and Local Governments Act of 1997 provide considerable detail about local government powers and responsibilities. At the same time, there has been somewhat independent development of policies relevant for decentralization managed by the Ministry of Finance, Planning and Economic Development (MFPED) and a number of the sectoral ministries. These policies have had important implications for the way decentralization has unfolded.

Implementation Strategy

There are notable strategic elements of Cambodia's approach to decentralization. First, the predecentralization program conducted considerable experimentation with the development of administrative and fiscal systems and procedures over a period of years. By the time the decentralization law was passed, much had been learned and the systems generally worked fairly well. Second, the formal decentralization started in a highly limited way appropriate to a postconflict, fragile state situation. The assignment of limited formal functions to the communes and the provision of limited resources for them to provide new services prioritized through local participatory planning began a process of building local government credibility and capacity. Third, the total level of resources provided initially represented only about 1.5 percent of the total national budget. By devoting only modest resources to this effort, the fiscal risk to the state was limited. Finally, by building new systems from the bottom up and subjecting them to careful donor scrutiny, the commune system has been at least somewhat protected to date from the pervasive system of patronage that plagues the national government.

Although the broad structure of decentralization in Indonesia had politically strategic elements, such as the focus on local rather than provincial governments, Indonesia never established a coherent strategy for implementing its decentralization framework. Although the decentralization laws clearly defined broad functions and certain aspects of the system, operational details on many legally devolved functions have yet to be specified, local government revenue autonomy has remained weak, and subnational borrowing mechanisms have deteriorated. Perhaps most critically, there has been limited attention to building accountability. At the same time, certain aspects of the decentralization may have prevented damage that was widely expected under Indonesia's big bang reform. There were massive transfers of staff from the former deconcentrated bureaucracy to local governments, so service delivery did not fall apart, and a large portion of the intergovernmental transfers fund these personnel. Thus, some features of the new system, whether strategically intentional or not, constrained local government autonomy and limited some of the problems commonly experienced with significant, rapid decentralization.

Kenya's recent approaches to improving local government performance have exhibited some strategic implementation characteristics. The reforms were initiated with a program that piloted a practical, gradual, and systematic approach (as opposed to the type of normatively inspired, comprehensive approach discussed above). Broad common goals were defined, but exact steps and the implementation pace varied and were negotiated with individual local governments, placing some responsibility on them for what they agreed to undertake. Local governments that met goals they agreed to were rewarded in various ways, and performance generally improved considerably. After the successful pilot, the MLG received broader support to expand the approach through the interministerial Kenya Local Government Reform Program (KLGRP). Taking notice of MLG reforms and recognizing the need to improve public services, the Ministry of Finance (MOF) began to adopt larger fiscal system reforms, starting with small steps and moving on to larger ones such as the adoption of a significant new intergovernmental performance-based transfer program. Perhaps most significant from a strategic perspective, various reform components have been integrated in a larger program that provides performance incentives, both with respect to adopting new procedural reforms and enhancing service delivery and revenue generation. The process is structured to provide a realistic, gradual, and systematic path to reform that advances in a series of manageable, mutually reinforcing, coordinated steps.

Although Uganda developed a strong legal basis for decentralization, there has not been a pragmatic implementation process. Too many functions were initially transferred, at least officially, to local governments with limited capacity. There have been some strategic elements such as performance-based capital grants provided to local governments. Generally, however, little consideration was given to how to strategically implement and coordinate the multiple aspects of the system over time. Decentralization, in some sectors, has been slow because reluctant ministries impede progress while, in others, ministries attempting to comply with the law devolved functions too rapidly and overwhelmed local capacity. More emphasis has been given to developing intergovernmental transfers than to improving local revenues, and there are not adequate incentives in the transfer formulas to encourage the latter. In addition, there has been a weak link between the development of recurrent and capital budget decentralization. Perhaps most important, there has been an insufficient attempt to link the development of local administration and the development of local democracy.[35] Weak local government performance led to an increase in conditions placed on the use of intergovernmental transfers, partially reversing decentralization.

Capacity Building

Capacity building and technical assistance efforts for local governments in Cambodia have been carefully linked to the rollout of the overall system described above, and it has been directed not only to the local governments, but also to the higher-level government staff involved in the management of the system and the citizens who get involved in local participatory processes. Most of the capacity building has been done by trained local trainers, many from local NGOs, with support available from more experienced staff and consultants. Thus, there have been strategic aspects to the capacity-building efforts. They have, however, largely followed the supply-driven model, although local governments can request assistance when they need it. Moreover, the effectiveness of the capacity-building efforts immediately following the first commune elections was challenged by the need to serve many more communes than had to be covered during the predecentralization project period.

There is nothing particularly positive to note about local government capacity-building efforts in Indonesia. There is a national training body, and a subdivision of the Ministry of Home Affairs has official responsibility for local government capacity building. The reality, however, is extremely complex. Many individual ministries, often supported by different donor agencies, have multiple capacity-building and technical assistance programs that are largely uncoordinated. Some local governments also have the resources and motivation to pursue capacity building and technical support for their staff. But the great variety of current efforts has been highly fragmented and not closely linked to an overall capacity development strategy or the implementation of specific functions.

Historically, capacity building in Kenya has been very supply-driven. Local government staff members of various grades and positions were expected to attend formal training courses at the Government Training Institute-Mombassa. The KLGRP, however, included some innovative approaches to capacity building and technical assistance. A mobile MLG team worked closely with each participating local government to design a unique set of reforms to match their needs and link them to capacity development. In addition, the team helped local governments to implement the negotiated reforms and, as necessary, to modify them. Citizen participation was introduced as part of the process, and some task-specific training was provided for local officials on an as-needed basis. These, efforts, however, have not been broadly institutionalized.

As in Indonesia, there have been a great number of capacity-building efforts in Uganda provided by a number of government agencies, often with donor support. Over time, however, efforts have been consolidated to a greater extent under the Local Government Development Program (LGDP), a multidonor program of support. There have also been some demand-driven elements of capacity building. Most prominently, the performance-based capital transfers require that certain minimum performance conditions be met for a local government to receive funds. Local governments not meeting these conditions were awarded a capacity-building grant to help them get the assistance they needed to become eligible for the development grants.

Coordination

Coordination was not initially a substantial problem as decentralization unfolded in Cambodia. In the predecentralization stage, the early efforts were driven by a few donors who learned to work well together, and they developed a system for reasonably effective coordination of most major donors that has generally held together since the passage of the decentralization law. There are challenges and disagreements, but not to the extent often seen in other countries. The situation on the government side has been more problematic. During the predecentralization period and through the first local electoral cycle, decentralization to the communes was managed by an interministerial committee chaired by the Ministry of Interior (MOI), the National Committee to Support the Communes (NCSC), and the Seila Task Force (STF), a management structure set up when early donor efforts were adopted as a government program. Some other key ministries with relevant roles, such as the Ministry of Economy and Finance (MEF) and the Council on Administrative Reform (CAR), were not sufficiently engaged in developing the reform process, which they saw as an MOI effort. CAR's responsibilities were transferred to the MOI in 2004, but not coordinated with NCSC. In September 2006, the government created a new interministerial body, the National Committee for the Management of Democratic Development (NCDD), which folds the former responsibilities of the NCSC, CAR, STF, and other decentralization-related mechanisms under a single entity. This entity is chaired by the deputy prime minister and is thus technically above the individual ministry level, but the deputy prime minister is also the minister of interior. How this arrangement will work in practice remains to be seen.

In Indonesia, a ministerial-level Regional Autonomy Review Board (DPOD) was empowered to design decentralization policy and was in some broad ways effective, but subsequent leadership has been problematic. The Ministry of Home Affairs (MOHA) has the strongest official role, but other central agencies, such as the Ministry of Finance (MOF), National Planning Agency (BAPPENAS), and sectoral ministries, are important. Although these agencies serve together on a permanent secretariat, MOHA leadership is not sufficiently and broadly respected, so coordination remains weak and progress is ad hoc and erratic rather than strategic and progressive. The situation in Indonesia is complicated by persistently weak donor coordination. Although the Decentralization Support Facility (DSF) was set up to help coordinate donor support to decentralization and to better harmonize it with government policy, DSF has made only limited progress on these fronts to date.

Coordination of decentralization and local government reforms has never been a major consideration in Kenya. Responsibility for the local government system in Kenya is clearly under a single central agency, the MLG, although some sectoral ministries control certain local service roles. The MLG, however, has long been commonly seen as weak and somewhat biased, so that other ministries tend to be suspicious of its decisions, and it has little or no effective control over the MOF and sectoral ministries. In fact, in many respects, the MLG is subject to decisions by these other central agencies, so that it cannot fulfill its coordination responsibility.

When the MLG (with donor support) introduced reforms in the 1980s, other central agencies paid little attention. Only as the fiscal and political pressures outlined above mounted during the late 1990s and modest MLG efforts began to bear some fruit did the impetus for broader reform gather momentum and interministerial cooperation begin to improve (even though MLG authority has not) under the KLGRP, which has also helped to provide some donor coordination.

Coordination in Uganda has been difficult—a now defunct decentralization secretariat was set up under the MLG, which is not a sufficiently powerful ministry to play a coordination role. In the absence of effective leadership, the MFPED, which is wary of decentralization, began to play a stronger role, perhaps to the advantage of upward accountability (in terms of enforcing financial responsibility and local compliance with national poverty reduction strategy and Millennium Development Goals), but to the detriment of decentralization and local voice. There has been some talk of establishing a higher-level coordination body (under the Office of the President), but this has not happened to date. An independent body with a more limited scope is Uganda's Local Government Finance Commission (LGFC), which has considerable influence over all aspects of local government revenues and transfers. The LGFC is a broad-based independent body (set up by the constitution and further defined in the Local Governments Act) that reports directly to the president. As such, it is sometimes able to help resolve disputes on matters related to fiscal decentralization between the MLG and MFPED. There is a reasonably active donor coordination group on decentralization, but it has not dealt with the most basic coordination problems.

Concluding Comments

If policymakers and managers in developing and transition countries want decentralization to work more effectively, they need to pay greater attention to implementation. Decentralization is not an instantaneous act; on the contrary, it is typically a complex and lengthy process that often involves basic changes in attitudes and behaviors by actors at all levels of government as well as by citizens. Long-held mind-sets and behaviors change only with exposure to new ideas, appropriate information, adequate consultation, positive experiences, and sufficiently rewarding incentives. Thus, decentralization can be slow and challenging, and the way its implementation is approached can make all the difference in how productive and successful it ultimately is.

Unfortunately, there is no "best practice" regarding how to implement decentralization and, as noted above, this topic has not been given enough serious study to provide generalizable advice. Moreover, countries are so diverse in terms of context and the status of decentralization that the search for "best practice" is somewhat futile. The country cases briefly covered here, however, suggest a number of ideas about commonly important considerations. First, rushing the development of a broad decentralization policy and legal framework may be a political imperative, but rapid implementation may lead to poor performance and eventually backtracking on decentralization reforms. Some degree of experimentation with different approaches before finalizing decentralization policies may help to demonstrate progress and also allows some flexibility to define more workable systems and procedures.

Second, in trying to follow a pragmatic and sustainable path, difficult decisions will need to be made about which activities to undertake first. One often useful rule of thumb is that reforms with the greatest possibility of working effectively in a relatively limited time frame could be undertaken first where feasible. This may require identification of less complex activities that do not immediately and significantly threaten the tolerance of the central power base or overwhelm local capacity. In cases where local governance and capacity are especially weak, building local government credibility by meeting a few basic local priorities may be more important than the often recommended first steps in reform, such as the formal devolution of specific functions.

Third, strategically differentiating reform steps among local governments—on the basis of factors such as capacity and performance rather than size or classification—may better match reforms to needs and capacities. Some local governments have the competence to assume significant independent responsibilities while others may need more oversight and support. Reform steps may even be negotiated rather than dictated to local governments, making them more directly accountable for their performance. In addition, capacity building and technical assistance could be clearly tied to specific tasks that are being immediately undertaken. These and other aspects of an initially limited, gradual, strategic, and asymmetric approach may help to increase the probability of initial success, creating a positive foundation on which to build and sustain further decentralization reform in the future.

Fourth, the provision of information, education, and incentives for behavioral change is critical. All actors must understand how decentralization is to evolve and what is expected of them at each step. Incentives can help to ensure that central officials take the actions they need to, local governments behave consistently with new rules and procedures, and citizens begin to take more responsibility for articulating their expectations and disciplining local government performance.

Finally, coordination of decentralization implementation is essential. In many cases this has proven difficult to realize, but the clear problems generated by fragmented and inconsistent approaches to decentralization reform justify all feasible efforts to improve cooperation among key actors. Coordination of international development assistance for decentralization is just as important as coordinating government agencies, and it will generally be easier to accomplish if the government being provided support has a reasonably unified and coherent approach to implementing decentralization reform.

Although it is possible to consider how to use these various elements to approach decentralization productively in a particular case, it is equally important to honestly acknowledge that an implementation strategy as defined here is ultimately based significantly on a technical and managerial way of thinking about decentralization. In the final analysis, as repeatedly highlighted throughout this volume, politics drive decentralization and may frequently push the system in nonstrategic directions in pursuit of goals other than the official purposes for which decentralization is being undertaken. Well-informed and attentive policymakers and implementers, however, can attempt to frame the way decentralization is implemented in terms that both attract political support and bring about some of the expected benefits of decentralization. The realization of benefits, in turn, can create a momentum among citizens and government actors alike to continue and expand the reform process.

Unfortunately, much of what we currently know about implementing decentralization is largely anecdotal and conjectural. Policymakers and implementers would clearly benefit from a more systematic and robust review of the design and implementation of decentralization under different historical and political conditions. Better diagnosis of the key factors and dynamics involved in a particular country could provide a stronger basis for crafting and putting into practice reforms that help to realize and sustain the potential benefits of decentralization while reducing the likelihood that potential negative results will emerge. This is a key challenge for those seeking to make decentralization work in developing countries, and we need to embrace it in our future efforts in this exciting field of study and practice.

Notes

1. See, for example, Smoke (2003); World Bank (2005b); Bahl and Martinez-Vazquez (2006); Ebel and Weist (2006); Smoke (2007); and World Bank (2008a).
2. See, for example, Eaton and Dickovick (2006) and Gomez (2006).
3. Indonesia is discussed below and references are provided.
4. Uganda is discussed below and references are provided.
5. Cambodia is discussed below and references are provided.
6. Jerusalem (2008) reviews decentralization in Nicaragua.
7. Ribot (2004) discusses decentralization in a number of West African cases.
8. Bahl and Smoke (2003) cover a range of issues on decentralization in South Africa.
9. A review of the decentralization process in Thailand is provided in World Bank (2005b).
10. Chile is discussed in Smoke and Gomez (2006).
11. This literature and the arguments being made are cited and reviewed below.

12. The national politics of decentralization are discussed to varying degrees in Wunsch and Olowu (1990); Bird and Vaillancourt (1998); Litvack, Ahmed, and Bird (1998); Manor (1999); Burki, Perry, and Dillinger (1999); Cohen and Peterson (1999); Willis, Garman, and Haggard (1999); Ahmad and Tanzi (2002); Eaton (2002); Olowu and Wunsch (2004); Eaton (2004a); Bardhan and Mookherjee (2006a); Smoke, Gomez, and Peterson (2006); Cheema and Rondinelli (2007); Smoke (2007); and Eaton, Kaiser, and Smoke (2009).

13. For a more detailed discussion of this issue, see Smoke (2003).

14. Literature on this issue is reviewed in Smoke, Gomez, and Peterson (2006).

15. Useful discussions of democratic decentralization and accountability from various perspectives are provided in: Tendler (1997); Manor (1999); Blair (2000); Crook (2003); Olowu (2003); Olowu and Wunsch (2004); Shah and Thompson (2004); Ribot and Larson (2005); Blair (2006); Commins (2006); Ebel and Weist (2006); Platteau (2006); Shah (2006); Cheema and Rondinelli (2007); Manor (2007); and World Bank (2008b).

16. Many references cited in this chapter and in some other chapters in this volume touch on donor approaches to supporting decentralization reform. Some specific emphasis on donor behavior and coordination for decentralization is found in Smoke (2000) and Romeo (2003).

17. The fiscal federalism approach to decentralization has been particularly influential. Fiscal federalism is introduced in Oates (1972) and revisited in Oates (1999). Other work includes Shah (1994); Litvack, Ahmad, and Bird (1998); Bahl (2000); McClure and Martinez-Vazquez (2000); and Ebel and Taliercio (2005). Critiques include Prud'homme (1995); Tanzi (1996); Smoke (2001); Tanzi (2001); and Smoke (2006a). Recent literature on "second-generation" fiscal federalism includes Oates (2005) and Weingast (2006).

18. Donor approaches to decentralization are illustrated by UNDESA (2005); UNCDF (2006); USAID (2009); World Bank (2001a, 2004, 2005b, 2008a). Some of these more recent approaches go beyond formulaic approaches and include more strategic thinking.

19. The limitations of this approach are discussed in Prud'homme (1995); Tanzi (1996); Smoke (2001); Tanzi (2001); and Smoke (2006a). Examples of literature on implementation are provided in Smoke and Lewis (1996); Litvack, Ahmad, and Bird (1998); Burki, Perry, and Dillinger (1999); World Bank (2001a); Falleti (2005); Ebel and Weist (2006); Smoke (2006a); Bahl and Martinez-Vazquez (2006); Smoke (2007); World Bank (2008a); Eaton, Kaiser, and Smoke (2009).

20. Many of these weaknesses are elaborated in Leonard (1987); Smoke and Lewis (1996); Tendler (1997); Litvack, Ahmad, and Bird (1998); Cohen and Peterson (1999); and Smoke (2001).

21. This section is adapted from Smoke (2008a).

22. Literature that treats implementation in some prominent way includes: Smoke and Lewis (1996); Litvack, Ahmad, and Bird (1998); Burki, Perry, and Dillinger (1999); World Bank (2001a); Falleti (2005); Bahl and Martinez-Vazquez (2006); Ebel and Weist (2006); Smoke (2006a, 2007).

23. Empirical research on the politics of local government revenue generation is reviewed in Smoke (2008a).

24. Manor (2004b) provides a useful discussion of user committees.

25. Capacity building in the context of human resource management and transition to decentralization is discussed in Green (2005).

26. See Smoke (2008a) for a discussion of how capacity building is often treated by governments and donors.

27. See, for example, the discussion of the Kenya case below.

28. The discussion of coordination issues is drawn primarily from my personal experiences in multiple countries.

29. Cambodian decentralization is recent and formal literature is limited, so the analysis is partly based on interviews and observations. Relevant sources include Turner (2002); World Bank (2003); Blunt and Turner (2005); Smoke (2006b); Smoke and Taliercio (2007); and Smoke and Morrison (2008).

30. For a more detailed discussion of decentralization in Indonesia, see Hofman and Kaiser (2004); Lewis (2005); Kaiser, Pattinasarany, and Schulze (2006); and Malley (2009).

31. For a more detailed discussion of the evolution of decentralization and local government reform in Kenya, see Smoke (1993, 1994, 2004); Steffensen, Naitore, and Tideman (2004); and Smoke (2008b).

32. See Government of Uganda (2001); Francis and James (2003); Onyach-Olaa (2003); Steffensen, Naitore, and Tideman (2004); and Smoke (2008b) for more information on decentralization in Uganda.

33. Francis and James (2003) provide a useful discussion of Museveni's "nonparty" system known as the National Resistance Movement.

34. For more information on the foundational donor initiative, see "Cambodia's Recent History: CARERE 1" and "The Seila Initiative." Available at the UN Capital Development Fund Web site at www.uncdf.org.

35. Francis and James (2003) provide a review of local democracy and participation in Uganda.

References

Ackerman, John. 2004. "Co-governance for Accountability: Beyond 'Exit' and 'Voice.'" *World Development* 32 (3): 447–463.

Agrawal, Arun, and Krishna Gupta. 2005. "Decentralization and Participation: The Governance of Common Pool Resources in Nepal's Terai." *World Development* 33 (7): 1101–1114.

Agrawal, Arun, and Jesse C. Ribot. 1999. "Accountability in Decentralization: A Framework with South Asian and African Cases." *Journal of Developing Areas* 33 (Summer): 473–502.

Ahmad, Etisham, and Vito Tanzi. 2002. *Managing Fiscal Decentralization*. Oxford, UK: Routledge.

Alatas, Vivi, Lant Pritchett, and Anna Wetterberg. 2002. "Voice Lessons: Local Government Organizations, Social Organizations, and the Quality of Local Governance." Washington, DC: World Bank.

Andrews, Matthew, and Larry Schroeder. 2003. "Sectoral Decentralization and Intergovernmental Arrangements in Africa." *Public Administration and Development* 23 (1): 29–40.

Angeles, L. C., and F. Magno. 2004. "The Philippines: Decentralization, Local Governments, and Citizen Action." In Philip Oxhorn, Joseph S. Tulchin, and Andrew Selee, eds., *Decentralization, Democratic Governance, and Civil Society in Comparative Perspective: Africa, Asia, and Latin America*. Washington, DC: Wilson Center Press, 211–265.

Angell, Alan, Pamela Lowden, and Rosemary Thorp. 2001. *Decentralizing Development: The Political Economy of Institutional Change in Colombia and Chile*. Oxford: Oxford University Press.

Appadurai, Arjun. 2004. "The Capacity to Aspire: Culture and the Terms of Recognition." In Vijayendra Rao and Michael Walton, eds., *Culture and Public Action*. Palo Alto, CA: Stanford University Press, 59–84.

Armony, Ariel. 2004. *The Dubious Link: Civic Engagement and Democratization*. Palo Alto, CA: Stanford University Press.

Arzaghi, Mohammad, and J. Vernon Henderson. 2005. "Why Countries Are Fiscally Decentralizing." *Journal of Public Economics* 89 (7): 1157–1189.

Asante, R. 2004. *The Politics of Managing Ethnic Cleavages, Inequalities, Nation-Building and Democratization in Ghana.* New York: Transregional Center for Democratic Studies, the New School for Social Research.

Atallah, S. 1998. "Fiscal Decentralization in Lebanon." Paper prepared for the Governance: Efficiency and Participation workshop, Lebanese Center for Policy Studies, Marrakesh, Morocco, September 3–6, 1998.

Ayee, Joseph. 2004. "Ghana: A Top-Down Initiative." In Dele Olowu and James S. Wunch, eds., *Local Governance in Africa: The Challenges of Democratic Decentralization.* Boulder, CO: Lynne Rienner Publishers, 125–154.

Azfar, Omar. 2006. "Giving Citizens What They Want: Preference Matching and the Devolution of Public Service Delivery." Paper prepared for the Expert Group on Development Issues conference in Stockholm, Sweden, April 27–28, 2006.

Azfar, Omar, Satu Kahkonen, and Patrick Meagher. 2001. "Conditions for Effective Decentralized Governance: A Synthesis of Research Findings." College Park: IRIS Center, University of Maryland.

Bagadion, Benjamin U. 1997. "The National Irrigation Administration's Participatory Irrigation Management Program in the Philippines." In Anirudh Krisha, Norman Uphoff, and Milton J. Esman, eds., *Reasons for Hope: Instructive Experiences in Rural Development.* West Hartford, CT: Kumarian Press, 153–166.

Bahl, Roy. 2000. "How to Design a Fiscal Decentralization Program." In Shahid Yusuf, Weiping Wu, and Simon Evenett, eds., *Local Dynamics in an Era of Globalization.* Oxford: Oxford University Press: 94–100.

Bahl, Roy, and Jorge Martinez-Vazquez. 2006. "Sequencing Fiscal Decentralization." Washington, DC: World Bank.

Bahl, Roy, and Paul Smoke, eds. 2003. *Restructuring Local Government Finance in Developing Countries: Lessons from South Africa.* Cheltenham, UK: Edward Elgar.

Baiocchi, Gianpaolo. 2003. "Participation, Activism, and Politics: The Porto Alegre Experiment." In Archon Fung and Erik O. Wright, eds., *Deepening Democracy: Institutional Innovations in Empowered Participatory Governance.* London: Verso, 45–77.

Bandiaky, Solange. 2008. "Gender Inequality in Malidino Biodiversity Reserve, Senegal: Political Parties and the 'Village Approach.'" *Conservation and Society* 6 (1): 62–73.

Bardhan, Pranab. 1996. "Decentralised Development." *Indian Economic Review* 31 (2): 139–156.

———. 2002. "Decentralisation of Governance and Development." *Journal of Economic Perspectives* 16 (4): 185–205.

———. 2004. *Decentralization of Governance and Development.* Berkeley: Department of Economics, University of California.

Bardhan, Pranab, and Dilip Mookherjee. 2000. "Capture and Governance at Local and National Levels." *American Economic Review* 90 (2): 135–139.

———. 2005. "Decentralizing Antipoverty Program Delivery in Developing Countries." *Journal of Public Economics* 89 (4): 675–704.

———, eds. 2006a. *Decentralization and Local Governance in Developing Countries: A Comparative Perspective.* Cambridge, MA: MIT Press.

———. 2006b. "The Rise of Local Governance: An Overview." In Pranab Bardhan and Dilip Mookerjee, eds., *Decentralization and Local Governance in Devel-*

oping Countries: A Comparative Perspective. Cambridge, MA: MIT Press: 1–52.

Bates, Robert. 1981. *Markets and States in Tropical Africa*. Berkeley: University of California Press.

Beer, Caroline C. 2004. "Electoral Competition and Fiscal Decentralization in Mexico." In Alfred P. Montero and David J. Samuels, eds., *Decentralization and Democracy in Latin America*. Notre Dame, IN: University of Notre Dame Press, 180–200.

Beer, Caroline C., and Neil Mitchell. 2004. "Democracy and Human Rights: Elections or Social Capital?" *International Studies Quarterly* 48 (2): 293–312.

Benda-Beckmann, Franz von, and Keebet von Benda-Beckmann. 2006. "Changing One Is Changing All: Dynamics in the Adat-Islam-State Triangle." *Journal of Legal Pluralism and Unofficial Law* 53 (4): 239–270.

Benda-Beckmann, Franz von, Keebet von Benda-Beckmann, Julia Eckert, Fernanda Pirie, and Bertram Turner. 2003. "Vitality and Revitalisation of Tradition in Law: Going Back into the Past or Future-Oriented Development?" In Gunther Schlee and Bettina Mann, eds., *Max Planck Institute for Social Anthropology Report 2002–2003*. Halle/Saale, Germany: Max Planck Institute for Social Anthropology, 296–306.

Bergh, Sylvia. 2004. "Democratic Decentralisation and Local Participation: A Review of Recent Research." *Development in Practice* 14 (6): 780–790.

Berman, Sheri. 1997. "Civil Society and the Collapse of the Weimar Republic." *World Politics* 49 (3): 401–429.

Bermeo, Nancy. 2002. "The Import of Institutions." *Journal of Democracy* 13 (2): 96–110.

———. 2005. "Position Paper for the Working Group on Federalism, Conflict Prevention and Settlement." Paper prepared for the International Conference on Federalism in Brussels, Belgium, March 3–5, 2005.

Binswanger, Hans P., and Swaminathan S. Aiyar. 2003. "Scaling Up Community-Driven Development: Theoretical Underpinnings and Program Design Implications." Washington, DC: World Bank.

Bird, Richard, and Francois Vaillancourt, eds. 1998. *Fiscal Decentralization in Developing Countries*. Cambridge: Cambridge University Press.

Blair, Harry. 2000. "Participation and Accountability at the Periphery: Democratic Local Governance in Six Countries." *World Development* 28 (1): 21–39.

———. 2001. "Institutional Pluralism in Public Administration and Politics: Applications in Bolivia and Beyond." *Public Administration and Development* 21 (2): 119–129.

———. 2003. "Jump-Starting Democracy: Adult Civic Education and Democratic Participation in Three Countries." *Democratization* 10 (1): 53–76.

———. 2006. "Innovations in Participatory Local Governance." Background paper prepared for the 2008 World Public Sector Report, UN Department for Economic and Social Development, New York.

Bland, Gary. 2000. "The Popular Participation Law and the Emergence of Local Accountability." In *Bolivia: From Patronage to a Professional State: Bolivia Institutional and Governance Review*, vol. 2. Washington, DC: World Bank, 82–110.

———. 2007a. "Decentralization, Local Governance, and Conflict Mitigation in Latin America." In Derick Brinkerhoff, ed., *Governance in Post-Conflict Societies: Rebuilding Fragile States*. London: Routledge, 207–225.

———. 2007b. "The Transition to Democracy in Latin America." Paper prepared for the Southern Political Science Association meeting in New Orleans, LA, January 4–6, 2007.

Blaxall, John. 2004. "India's Self-Employed Women's Association (SEWA)—Empowerment Through Mobilization of Poor Women on a Large Scale." Washington, DC: World Bank.

Blunt, Peter, and Mark Turner. 2005. "Decentralisation, Democracy and Development in a Post-Conflict Society: Commune Councils in Cambodia." *Public Administration and Development* 25 (1): 75–87.

Boex, Jameson, Eunice Heredia-Ortiz, Jorge Martinez-Vazquez, Andrey Timofeev, and Guevara Yao. 2006. "Fighting Poverty Through Fiscal Decentralization." Report prepared for the US Agency on International Development. Atlanta, GA: Andrew Young School of Policy Studies. Available online at http://pdf.usaid.gov/pdf_docs/PNADH105.pdf.

Boone, Catherine. 2003. *Political Topographies of the African State: Territorial Authority and Institutional Choice.* Cambridge: Cambridge University Press.

Bossert, Thomas. 1998. "Analyzing the Decentralization of Health Systems in Developing Countries: Decision Space, Innovation and Performance." *Social Science and Medicine* 47 (10): 1513–1527.

Bossert, Thomas, and Joel Beauvais. 2002. "Decentralization of Health Systems in Ghana, Zambia, Uganda and the Philippines: A Comparative Analysis of Decision Space." *Health Policy and Planning* 17 (1): 14–31.

Brancati, Dawn. 2006. "Decentralization: Fueling the Fire or Dampening the Flames of Ethnic Conflict and Secessionism." *International Organization* 60 (3): 651–685.

Brautigam, Deborah. 2004. "The People's Budget? Politics, Participation and Pro-poor Policy." *Development Policy Review* 22 (6): 653–668.

Brennan, Geoffrey, and James M. Buchanan. 1980. *The Power to Tax: Analytical Foundations of Fiscal Constitution.* Cambridge: Cambridge University Press.

Brillantes, Alex, and Nora Cuachon. 2002. *Decentralization and Power Shift: An Imperative for Good Governance*, vol. 1. Manila, the Philippines: Center for Local and Regional Governance.

Brinkerhoff, Derick W. 2004. "Local Health and Education Services in Madagascar: The Impact of Remoteness on Poverty-Focused Service Delivery." Paper presented at the American Society for Public Administration conference in Portland, OR, March 27–30, 2004.

———. 2005. "Accountability and Good Governance: Concepts and Issues." In Ahmed Shafiqul Huque and Habib Zafarullah, eds., *International Development Governance.* New York: CRC Press, 269–288.

———, ed. 2007. *Governance in Post-Conflict Societies: Rebuilding Fragile States* London: Routledge.

Brinkerhoff, Derick W., and Arthur Goldsmith. 2004. "Good Governance, Clientelism and Patrimonialism: New Perspectives on Old Problems." *International Public Management Journal* 7 (2): 163–185.

———. 2005. "Institutional Dualism and International Development: A Revisionist Interpretation of Good Governance." *Administration and Society* 37 (2): 199–224.

Brinkerhoff, Derick W., and Charlotte Leighton. 2002. "Decentralization and Health System Reform: Issue in Brief." Washington, DC: US Agency for International Development.

Brinkerhoff, Derick W., and James Mayfield. 2005. "Democratic Governance in Iraq? Progress and Peril in Reforming State-Society Relations." *Public Administration and Development* 25 (1): 59–73.

Brinkerhoff, Jennifer M. 2002. *Partnership for International Development: Rhetoric or Results?* Boulder, CO: Lynne Rienner.

Brown, Michael, ed. 2003. *Grave New World: Security Challenges in the Twenty-First Century.* Washington, DC: Georgetown University Press.

Budlender, Debbie. 1998. "The South African Women's Budget Initiative." Background Paper No. 2. UN Development Programme, Women and Political Participation: 21st Century Challenges meeting in New York. Available online at http://magnet.undp.org/events/gender/india/Soutaf.htm.

Buhl, Dana. 1997. "Ripple in Still Water: Reflections by Activists on Local- and National-Level Work on Economic, Social and Cultural Rights." Washington, DC: Institute of International Education.

Burke, Edmund. 1774. "Speech at Bristol Previous to the Election." As quoted in *The* Founders' *Constitution*, vol. 1, chap. 13, Document 7. In *The Works of the Right Honourable Edmund Burke,* 6 vols. London: Henry G. Bohn, 1854–1856. Available online at http://press-pubs.uchicago.edu/founders/documents/v1ch13s7.html (accessed September 2006).

Burki, Shahid Javed, Guillermo Perry, and William Dillinger. 1999. "Beyond the Center: Decentralizing the State." Washington, DC: World Bank.

Cameron, Maxwell, and Tulia Falleti. 2005. "Federalism and the Subnational Separation of Powers." *Publius* 35 (2): 245–272.

Campbell, Timothy. 2003. *The Quiet Revolution: Decentralization and the Rise of Participation in Latin American Cities.* Pittsburgh, PA: University of Pittsburgh Press.

Campbell, Timothy, and Harald Fuhr, eds. 2004. *Leadership and Innovation in Subnational Government: Case Studies from Latin America.* Washington, DC: World Bank.

Careaga, Maite, and Barry R. Weingast. 2003. "Fiscal Federalism, Good Governance, and Economic Growth in Mexico." In Dani Rodrik, ed., *In Search of Prosperity: Analytic Narratives on Economic Growth.* Princeton, NJ: Princeton University Press, 399–438.

Carey, J. M., and M. S. Shugart. 1995. "Incentives to Cultivate a Personal Vote: A Rank Ordering of Electoral Formulas." *Electoral Studies* 14 (4): 417–439.

Center for Systemic Peace. 2009. *State Fragility and Warfare in the Global System 2009.* Severn, MD: Center for Systemic Peace. Available online at http://www.systemicpeace.org/warlist.htm.

Chanock, Martin. 1991. "Paradigms, Policies, and Property: A Review of the Customary Law of Land Tenure." In K. Mann and R. Roberts, eds., *Law in Colonial Africa.* Portsmouth, UK: Heinemann, 61–84.

Chattopadhyay, Raghabendra, and Esther Duflo. 2003. "The Impact of Reservation in the Panchayati Raj: Evidence from a Nationwide Randomized Experiment." Cambridge, MA: Massachusetts Institute of Technology.

Chaudhuri, Shubham. 2006."What Difference Does a Constitutional Amendment Make? The 1994 Panchayati Raj Act and the Attempt to Revitalize Rural Local Government in India." In Pranab Bardham and Dilip Mookherjee, eds., *Decentralization and Local Governance in Developing Countries: A Comparative Perspective*. Cambridge, MA: MIT Press, 153–201.

Cheema, Ali, Asim Ijaz Khwaja, and Adnan Qadir. 2006. "Local Government Reform in Pakistan: Context, Content, and Causes." In Pranab Bardhan and Dilip Mookerjee, eds., *Decentralization and Local Governance in Developing Countries: A Comparative Perspective.* Cambridge, MA: MIT Press, 257–284.

Cheema, G. Shabbir, and Dennis Rondinelli, eds. 2007. *Decentralizing Governance: Emerging Concepts and Practices*. Washington, DC: Brookings Institution Press.

Chhatre, Ashwini. 2008. "Political Articulation and Accountability in Decentralization: Theory and Evidence from India." *Conservation and Society* 6 (1): 12–23.

Chhibber, Pradeep K., and K. Køllman. 2004. *The Formation of National Party Systems: Federalism and Party Competition in Canada, Great Britain, India, and the United States*. Princeton, NJ: Princeton University Press.

Cohen, John M., and Stephen Peterson. 1999. *Administrative Decentralization in Developing Countries*. Boulder, CO: Lynne Rienner.

Collier, D., and S. Levitsky. 1997. "Democracy with Adjectives: Conceptual Innovation in Comparative Research." *World Politics* 49 (3): 430–451.

Collier, P. 2001. "Implications of Ethnic Diversity." *Economic Policy* 16 (32): 128–166.

Collier, P., and A. Hoeffler. 2000. "Greed and Grievance in Civil Wars." Washington, DC: World Bank.

Collier, P., Lani Elliott, Havard Hegre, Anke Hoeffler, Marta Reynal-Querol, and Nicholas Sambanis. 2003. *Breaking the Conflict Trap: Civil War and Development Policy.* Washington, DC: World Bank.

Comeau, Ludovic, Jr. 2003. "The Political Economy of Growth in Latin America and East Asia: Some Empirical Evidence." *The Economic Journal* 108: 44–59.

COMFREL. *See* Committee for Free and Fair Elections in Cambodia.

Commins, Stephen. 2006. "Community Participation in Service Delivery and Public Accountability: Advancing the MDGs." Background paper prepared for the *2007 World Public Sector Report*, UN Department for Economic and Social Development, New York.

Committee for Free and Fair Elections in Cambodia. 2006. "Election Reforms." Available online at http://www.comfrel.org/what_new.php?wnid=27.

Commonwealth Local Government Forum. 2005. "The Local Government System in Zambia." Update available online at http://www.clgf.org.uk/2005updates/Zambia.pdf.

Conyers, Diana. 2002. "Whose Elephants Are They? Decentralization of Control over Wildlife Management Through the CAMPFIRE Programme in Binga District, Zimbabwe." Washington, DC: World Resources Institute.

Coppedge, Michael. 1993. "Parties and Society in Mexico and Venezuela: Why Competition Matters." *Comparative Politics* 25 (3): 253–274.

Cornwall, Andrea, and John Gaventa. 2001. "Bridging the Gap: Citizenship, Participation and Accountability." Brighton, UK: University of Sussex.

Cornwall, Andrea, Henry Lucas, and Kath Pasteur, eds. 2000. "Accountability Through Participation: Developing Workable Partnership Models in the Health Sector." *IDS Bulletin* 31 (1): 1–13.

Coventry, Cowan. 1999. "The Bolivia Poverty Reduction Strategy Paper: A Preliminary Analysis of the Possibilities for Civil Society Participation." London: UK Department for International Development.

Craig, Gary, and Marjorie Mayo, eds. 1995. *Community Empowerment: A Reader in Participation and Development.* London: Zed Books.

Crook, Richard. 2003. "Decentralization and Poverty Reduction in Africa: The Politics of Local-Central Relations." *Public Administration and Development* 23 (1): 77–88.

Crook, Richard, and James Manor. 1998. *Democracy and Decentralization in Southeast Asia and West Africa: Participation, Accountability, and Performance.* Cambridge: Cambridge University Press.

Crook, Richard C., and Alan S. Sverrisson. 1999. "To What Extent Can Decentralized Forms of Government Enhance the Development of Pro-Poor Policies and Improve Poverty-Alleviation Outcomes?" Background paper prepared for the *World Development Report,* World Bank, Washington, DC, August 1999.

———. 2001. "Decentralization and Poverty Alleviation in Developing Countries: A Comparative Analysis or, Is West Bengal Unique?" Brighton, UK: Institute for Development Studies, University of Sussex.

Czajkowska, Beata, Judith Dunbar, Mike Keshishian, Caroline Sahley, and Kelley Strickland. 2005. "Assessment of the Serbian Community Revitalization Through Democratic Action Activity (CRDA)." Washington, DC: US Agency for International Development.

Dahl, R. 1971. *Polyarchy: Participation and Opposition.* New Haven, CT: Yale University Press.

———. 1982. *Dilemmas of Pluralist Democracy: Autonomy vs. Control.* New Haven, CT: Yale University Press.

Danielyan, E. 2005. "Local Elections Expose Weakness of Armenian Civil Society." *Eurasia Daily Monitor* 2 (182) (September 30). Available online at http://www.jamestown.org/programs/edm/single/?tx_ttnews%5Btt_news%5D=30926&tx_ttnews%5BbackPid%5D=176&no_cache=1.

Das Gupta, Monica, Helene Grandvoinnet, and Mattia Romani. 2004. "State-Community Synergies in Community-Driven Development." *Journal of Development Studies* 40 (3): 27–58.

Dauda, Carol L. 2004. "The Importance of de Facto Decentralization in Primary Education in Sub-Saharan Africa: PTAs and Local Accountability in Uganda." *Journal of Planning Education and Research* 24 (1): 28–40.

———. 2006. "Democracy and Decentralisation: Local Politics, Marginalisation and Political Accountability in Uganda and South Africa." *Public Administration and Development* 26 (4): 291–302.

———. 1989. *Working-Class Mobilization and Political Control: Venezuela and Mexico.* Lexington: University of Kentucky Press.

Davis, Gina, and Elinor Ostrom. 1991. "A Public Economy Approach to Education: Choice and Co-production." *International Political Science Review* 12 (4): 313–335.

Davoodi, Hamid, and Heng-fu Zou. 1998. "Fiscal Decentralization and Economic Growth: A Cross-Country Study." *Journal of Urban Economics* 43 (2): 244–257.

deMello, Luiz R. 2000. "Fiscal Decentralization and Intergovernmental Fiscal Relations: A Cross-Country Analysis." *World Development* 28 (2): 365–380.

DEMOS (Center for Democracy and Human Rights Studies). 2005. *Making Democracy Meaningful: Problems and Options in Indonesia.* Jakarta, Indonesia: DEMOS.

de Silva, K. M. 2000. "The Federal Option and Its Alternatives." In K. M. de Silva and G. H. Peiris, eds., *Pursuit of Peace in Sri Lanka: Past Failures and Future Prospects.* Kandy, Sri Lanka: International Centre for Ethnic Studies, 203–229.

Devas, Nick, and Ursula Grant. 2003. "Local Government Decision-Making—Citizen Participation and Local Accountability: Some Evidence from Kenya and Uganda." *Public Administration and Development* 23 (4): 307–316.

Diamond, Larry. 1997. "Introduction: In Search of Consolidation." In Larry Diamond, Marc F. Plattner, Yun-han Chu, and Hung-mao Tien, eds., *Consolidating the Third Wave Democracies: Regional Challenges.* Baltimore, MD: Johns Hopkins University Press, xiii–xlvii.

———. 1999. *Developing Democracy: Toward Consolidation.* Baltimore, MD: Johns Hopkins University Press.

Diamond, Larry, J. Hartlyn, J. Linz, and S. M. Lipset, eds. 1999. *Democracy in Developing Countries: Latin America.* Boulder, CO: Lynne Rienner.

Diamond, Larry, and Svetlana Tsalik. 1999. "Size and Democracy: The Case for Decentralization." In Larry Diamond, ed., *Developing Democracy.* Baltimore, MD: Johns Hopkins University Press, 117–160.

Dickovick, Tyler. 2005. "The Measure and Mismeasure of Decentralisation: Subnational Autonomy in Senegal and South Africa." *Journal of Modern African Studies* 43 (2): 183–210.

Diener, Ed, and Robert Biswas-Diener. 2005. "Psychological Empowerment and Subjective Well-Being." In Deepa Narayan, ed., *Measuring Empowerment: Cross-Disciplinary Perspectives.* Washington, DC: World Bank, 125–141.

Dietz, Henry, and David Meyers, eds. 2002. *Municipal Government and Democratization in Latin America.* Boulder, CO: Lynne Rienner.

Dillinger, William. 1994. "Decentralization and Its Implications for Service Delivery." Washington, DC: World Bank and UN Development Programme.

Easterly, W., and R. Levine. 1997. "Africa's Growth Tragedy: Policies and Ethnic Divisions." *Quarterly Journal of Economics* 112 (4): 1203–1250.

Easton, David. 1975. "A Re-assessment of the Concept of Political Support." *British Journal of Political Science* 5 (4): 435–457.

Eaton, Kent. 2001. "Political Obstacles to Decentralization: Evidence from Argentina and the Philippines." *Development and Change* 32 (1): 101–127.

———. 2002. *Politicians and Economic Reform in New Democracies: Argentina and the Philippines in the 1990s.* University Park: Penn State University Press.

———. 2004a. *Politics Beyond the Capital: The Design of Subnational Institutions in Latin America.* Palo Alto, CA: Stanford University Press.

———. 2004b. "Risky Business: Decentralization from Above in Chile and Uruguay." *Comparative Politics* 37 (1): 1–22.

———. 2005. "Menem and the Governors: Intergovernmental Relations in the 1990s." In Steven Levitsky and M. Victoria Murillo, eds., *Argentine Democracy: The Politics of Institutional Weakness.* University Park: Penn State University Press, 88–114.

———. 2006a. "Decentralization's Nondemocratic Roots: Authoritarianism and Subnational Reform in Latin America." *Latin American Politics and Society* 48 (1): 1–26.

———. 2006b. "The Downside of Decentralization: Armed Clientelism in Colombia." *Security Studies* 15 (4): 1–30.

Eaton, Kent, and Tyler Dickovick. 2006. "Decentralization and Re-centralization in Argentina and Brazil: The Menem and Cardoso Years." In Paul Smoke, Eduardo J. Gomez, and George E. Peterson, eds., *Decentralization in Asia and Latin America: Towards a Comparative Interdisciplinary Perspective.* Cheltenham, UK: Edward Elgar, 280–306.

Eaton, Kent, Kai Kaiser, and Paul Smoke. 2009. "The Political Economy of Decentralization Reforms in Developing Countries: A Development Partner Perspective." Draft paper prepared for the World Bank, Washington, DC.

Ebel, Robert, and Robert Taliercio. 2005. "Subnational Tax Policy and Administration in Developing Economies." *Tax Notes International* 37 (1): 919–936.

Ebel, Robert, and Dana Weist. 2006. "Sequencing Subnational Revenue Decentralization." Washington, DC: World Bank.

Ebel, Robert, and Serdar Yilmaz. 2003. "On the Measurement and Impact of Fiscal Decentralization." In Jorge Martinez-Vasquez and James Alm, eds., *Public Finance in Developing and Transitional Countries: Essays in Honor of Richard Bird.* Cheltenham, UK: Edward Elgar, 101–120.

Echeverri-Ghent, John. 1992. "Public Participation and Poverty Alleviation: The Experience of Reform Communists in India's West Bengal." *World Development* 20 (10): 1401–1422.

Eckert, Julia. 2006. "From Subjects to Citizens: Legalism from Below and the Homogenisation of the Legal Sphere." *Journal of Legal Pluralism and Unofficial Law* 53 (4): 45–76.

Ehdaie, Jaber. 1994. "Fiscal Decentralization and the Size of Government: An Extension with Evidence from Cross-Country Data." Washington, DC: World Bank.

Elazar, D. 1994. *Federal Systems of the World: A Handbook of Federal, Confederal and Autonomy Arrangements*, 2nd ed. London: Longman.

Engelbert, Pierre. 2002. "Patterns and Theories of Traditional Resurgence in Tropical Africa." *Mondes en Développement* 30 (118): 51–64.

Esty, Daniel C., Jack A. Goldstone, Ted Robert Gurr, Barbara Harff, Marc Levy, Geoffrey D. Dabelko, Pamela T. Surko, and Alan N. Unger. 1999. "The State Failure Project: Phase II Findings." In *Environmental Change and Security Project Report,* Project Report 5. Washington, DC: Woodrow Wilson Center, 49–72.

Evans, Peter. 1996. "Government Action, Social Capital and Development: Reviewing the Evidence on Synergy." *World Development* 24 (6): 1119–1132.

Faguet, Jean-Paul. 1997. "Decentralization and Local Government Performance." Rome: Food and Agriculture Organization.

———. 2001. "Does Decentralization Increase Responsiveness to Local Needs? Evidence from Bolivia." Washington, DC: World Bank.

Falleti, Tulia. 2005. "A Sequential Theory of Decentralization: Latin American Cases in Comparative Perspective." *American Political Science Review* 99 (3): 327–346.

Farrell, D. 2001. *Electoral Systems: A Comparative Introduction*. New York: Palgrave.

Fass, Simon M., and Gerrit M. Desloovere. 2004. "Chad: Governance at the Grassroots." In Dele Olowu and James S. Wunsch, eds., *Local Governance in Africa: The Challenges of Democratic Decentralization*. Boulder, CO: Lynne Rienner, 155–181.

Fearon, J. D., and D. D. Laitin. 2001. "Ethnicity, Insurgency and Civil War." Paper prepared for the American Political Science Association meeting in San Francisco, CA, September 1–4, 2001.

Ferguson, James. 1994. *The Anti-politics Machine: Development, Depoliticization, and Bureaucratic Power in Lesotho*. Minneapolis: University of Minnesota Press.

Fertig, Michael. 2003. "Who's to Blame? The Determinants of German Students' Achievement in the PISA 2000 Study." Discussion Paper IZA DP No. 739. Bonn, Germany: Forschungsinstitut zur Zukunft der Arbeit.

Fesler, James W. 1965. "Approaches to the Understanding of Decentralization." *Journal of Politics* 27 (3): 536–566.

Finkel, Steven E. 2003. "Can Democracy Be Taught?" *Journal of Democracy* 14 (4): 137–151.

Fiske, Edward. 1996. "Decentralization of Education: Politics and Consensus." Washington, DC: World Bank.

Food and Agriculture Organization. 2006. "FAO Experiences and Assets in Decentralization." In *The Online Sourcebook on Decentralization and Local Development*. Available online at http://www.ciesin.columbia.edu/decentralization/English/General/fao_experi.html(accessed August 1, 2006).

Foster, Andrew D., and Mark R. Rosenzweig. 2004. "Democratization and the Distribution of Local Public Goods in a Poor Rural Economy." Philadelphia: Penn Institute for Economic Research, University of Pennsylvania.

Fox, Jonathan. 1994. "Latin America's Emerging Local Politics," *Journal of Democracy* 5 (2): 105–116.

Fox, Jonathan, and Josefina Aranda. 1996. *Decentralization and Rural Development in Mexico: Community Participation in Oaxaca's Municipal Funds Program*. Monograph Series 42. San Diego: University of California, Center for U.S.-Mexican Studies.

Francis, Paul, and Robert James. 2003. "Balancing Rural Poverty Reduction and Citizen Participation: The Contradictions of Uganda's Decentralization Program." *World Development* 31 (2): 325–337.

Franco, Lynne M., Cheikh Mbengue, and Chris Atim. 2004. "Social Participation in the Development of Mutual Health Organizations in Senegal." Bethesda, MD: Abt Associates Inc.

Fraser, Nancy. 2000. "Rethinking Recognition." *New Left Review* 3 (May/June): 107–120.

Freedom House. 2009. *Freedom in the World: Annual Survey of Political Rights and Civil Liberties, 2009*. New York: Freedom House.

Friedman, Steven, and Caroline Kihato. 2004. "South Africa's Double Reform: Decentralization and the Transition from Apartheid." In Philip Oxhorn, Andrew Selee, and Joseph Tulchin, eds., *Decentralization, Democratic Governance, and Civil Society in Comparative Perspective: Africa, Asia, Latin America*. Washington, DC: Woodrow Wilson Center Press, 141–189.

Frye, Timothy. 1997. "A Politics of Institutional Choice: Post-Communist Presidencies." *Comparative Political Studies* 30 (5): 523–552.

Fukasaku, Kiichiro, and Luiz deMello. 1998. "Fiscal Decentralization and Macroeconomic Stability: The Experience of Large Developing and Transition Economies." In Kiichiro Fukasaku and Ricardo Hausmann, eds., *Democracy, Decentralization and Deficits in Latin America*. Paris: Organisation for Economic Co-operation and Development, 121–148.

Fung, Archon. 2006. *Empowered Participation: Reinventing Urban Democracy*. Princeton, NJ: Princeton University Press.

Fung, Archon, and Erik O. Wright, eds. 2003a. *Deepening Democracy: Institutional Innovations in Empowered Participatory Governance*. London: Verso.

———. 2003b. "Countervailing Power in Empowered Participatory Governance." In Archon Fung and Erik O. Wright, eds., *Deepening Democracy: Institutional Innovations in Empowered Participatory Governance*. London: Verso, 259–289.

Furniss, Norman. 1974. "The Practical Significance of Decentralization." *Journal of Politics* 36 (4): 958–982.

Gallup, J. 2002. "Cambodia's Electoral System: A Window of Opportunity for Reform." In Aurel Croissant, ed., *Electoral Politics in Southeast and East Asia*. Singapore: Friedrich Ebert Foundation, 25–73.

Garman, Christopher, Stephan Haggard, and Eliza Willis. 2001. "Fiscal Decentralization: A Political Theory with Latin American Cases." *World Politics* 53 (2): 205–236.

Gaventa, John. 1999. "Citizen Knowledge, Citizen Competence, and Democracy Building." In Stephen L. Elkin and Karol E. Sotan, eds., *Citizen Competence and Democratic Institutions*. University Park: Penn State Press, 49–67.

———. 2002. "Six Propositions on Participatory Local Governance." *Currents* 29: 29–35.

———. 2005. "Triumph, Deficit or Contestation? Deepening the 'Deepening Democracy' Debate." Brighton, UK: University of Sussex.

Gerring, John and Strom C. Thacker. 2004. "Political Institutions and Corruption: The Role of Unitarism and Parliamentarism." *British Journal of Political Science* 34 (2): 295–330.

Gervasoni, C. 2006. "A Rentier Theory of Subnational Democracy: The Politically Regressive Effects of Redistributive Fiscal Federalism." Paper prepared for the American Political Science Association meeting in Philadelphia, PA, August 31–September 3, 2006.

———. 2008. "Conceptualizing and Measuring Subnational Regimes: An Expert Survey Approach." Working Paper No. 23. Mexico City: Committee on Concepts and Methods, International Political Science Association, Center for Economic Research and Teaching (CIDE).

Geschiere, Peter, and Catherine Boone. 2003. "Crisis of Citizenship: New Modes in the Struggles over Belonging and Exclusion in Africa and Elsewhere."

Research concept sketch prepared for Social Science Research Council program, New York, November 2003.

Gibson, Edward L. 2005. "Boundary Control: Subnational Authoritarianism in Democratic Countries." *World Politic* 58 (October): 101–132.

Gibson, Edward, and Julieta Suarez-Cao. 2006–2007. "Competition and Power in Federalized Party Systems." Working Paper 1, Program in Comparative-Historical Social Science Working Paper Series. Evanston, IL: Northwestern University.

Gimishyan, M., and H. Manoukyan. 2003. "Case Study 1: Local Self-Governance in Armenia: Past, Present, and Future." In Igor Koryakov and Timothy Sisk, eds., *Democracy at the Local Level: A Guide for the South Caucasus*. Stockholm: International IDEA, 38–43.

Goetz, Ann Marie, and Rob Jenkins. 2001. "Hybrid Forms of Accountability: Citizen Engagement in Institutions of Public-Sector Oversight in India." *Public Management Review* 3 (3): 363–384.

———. 2004. *Reinventing Accountability: Making Democracy Work for Human Development*. London: Palgrave.

Goldfrank, Benjamin. 2007. "Lessons from Latin America's Experience with Participatory Budgeting." In Anwar Shah, ed., *Participatory Budgeting*. Washington, DC: World Bank Institute, 91–126.

Goldsmith, Arthur A., and Derick W. Brinkerhoff. 2004. "Strengthening Local Government Associations in Bulgaria." Washington, DC: RTI International.

Golola, M. 2001. "Decentralization, Local Bureaucracies and Service Delivery in Uganda." Discussion Paper No. 2001/115. Helsinki, Finland: World Institute for Development Economics Research, United Nations University.

Golooba-Mutebi, Frederick. 2005. "When Popular Participation Won't Improve Service Provision: Primary Health Care in Uganda." *Development Policy Review* 23 (2): 165–182.

Gomez, Eduardo J. 2006. "The Historical Institutional Genesis of Fiscal Decentralization Management: Lessons from Brazil." In Paul Smoke, Eduardo J. Gomez, and George E. Peterson, eds., *Decentralization in Asia and Latin America: Towards a Comparative Interdisciplinary Perspective*. Cheltenham, UK: Edward Elgar, 307–336.

Goodspeed, Timothy. 2002. "Bailouts in a Federation." *International Tax and Public Finance* 9 (4): 409–421.

Government of Uganda. 2001. *Fiscal Decentralization in Uganda: Draft Strategy Paper*. Kampala, Uganda: Decentralization Coordination Group.

Green, Amanda. 2005. "Managing Human Resources in a Decentralized Context." In *East Asia Decentralizes: Making Local Government Work*. Washington, DC: World Bank, 129–154.

Grindle, Merilee. 2007. *Going Local: Decentralisation, Democratization, and the Promise of Good Governance*. Princeton, NJ: Princeton University Press.

Guggenheim, Scott, Tatag Wiranto, Yogana Prasta, and Susan Wong. 2004. "Indonesia's Kecamatan Development Program: A Large-Scale Use of Community Development to Reduce Poverty." Washington, DC: World Bank.

Gurr, T. R. 1993. *Minorities at Risk: A Global Survey of Ethnopolitical Conflicts*. Washington, DC: US Institute of Peace.

———. 2000. *Peoples Versus States: Minorities at Risk in the New Century*. Washington, DC: US Institute of Peace.

Gutierrez, Eric, Aijaz Ahmad, Francisco L. Gonzales, Eliseo R. Mercado, Jr., Joel Rocamora, Marites Danguilan-Vitug, and Abdulwahab Guialal. 2000. *Rebels, Warlords and Ulama: A Reader on Muslim Separatism and the War in Southern Philippines*. Manila, the Philippines: Institute for Popular Democracy.

Habermas, Jürgen. 1991. *The Structural Transformation of the Public Sphere: An Inquiry into Categories of Bourgeois Society*. Cambridge, MA: MIT Press.

Hale, H. 2004. "Divided We Stand: Institutional Sources for Ethnofederal State Survival and Collapse." *World Politics* 56 (2): 165–193.

Halperin, Morton, Joseph Siegle, and Michael Weinstein. 2010. *The Democracy Advantage: How Democracies Promote Prosperity and Peace*, rev. ed. New York: Routledge.

Hara, Mafaniso. 2008. "Dilemmas of Democratic Decentralization in Mangochi District, Malawi: Interest and Mistrust in Fisheries Management." *Conservation and Society* 6 (1): 74–86.

Harrison, Kathryn, ed. 2006. *Racing to the Bottom: Provincial Interdependence in the Canadian Federation*. Vancouver: University of British Columbia Press.

Hartzell, Caroline, Matthew Hoddie, and Donald Rothchild. 2001. "Stabilizing the Peace after Civil War: An Investigation of Some Key Variables." *International Organization* 55 (1): 183–208.

Hegre, H., T. Ellingsen, S. Gates, and N. Gleditsch. 2001. "Toward a Democratic Civil Peace? Democracy, Political Change and Civil War, 1816–1992." *American Political Science Review* 95 (1): 33–48.

Heller, Patrick. 2001. "Moving the State: The Politics of Democratic Decentralization in Kerala, South Africa and Porto Alegre." *Politics and Society* 29 (1): 131–163.

Heller, Patrick, K. N. Harilal, and Shubham Chaudhuri. 2007. "Building Local Democracy: Evaluating the Impact of Decentralization in Kerala, India." *World Development* 35 (4): 626–648.

Hendrickse, M. 2005. "Local Government Elections." Presentation of the Independent Elections Commission in Pretoria, South Africa, 2005.

Hidayat, S., and H. Antlöv. 2004. "Decentralization and Regional Autonomy in Indonesia." In Philip Oxhorn, Joseph S. Tulchin, and Andrew Selee, eds., *Decentralization, Democratic Governance, and Civil Society in Comparative Perspective: Africa, Asia, and Latin America*. Washington, DC: Woodrow Wilson Center Press, 266–291.

Hirschman, Albert O. 1984. *Getting Ahead Collectively: Grassroots Experiences in Latin America*. New York: Pergamon Press.

Hiskey, Jonathan T. 2003. "Demand-Based Development and Local Electoral Environments in Mexico." *Comparative Politics* 36 (1): 41–59.

Hiskey, Jonathan T., and Shaun Bowler. 2005. "Local Context and Democratization in Mexico." *American Journal of Political Science* 49 (1): 57–71.

Hiskey, Jonathan T., and Mitchell A. Seligson. 2003. "Pitfalls of Power to the People: Decentralization, Local Government Performance and System Support in Bolivia." *Studies in Comparative International Development* 37 (4): 64–88.

Ho, Esther Sui Chu. 2005. "Effect of School Decentralization and School Climate on Student Mathematics Performance: The Case of Hong Kong." *Education Research for Policy and Practice* 4 (1): 47–64.

Hofman, Bert, and Kai Kaiser. 2004. "The Making of the Big Bang and Its Aftermath: A Political Economy Perspective." In James Alm, Jorge Martinez-Vazquez, and Sri Mulyani Indrawati, eds., *Reforming Intergovernmental Fis-*

cal Relations and the Rebuilding of Indonesia. Cheltenham, UK: Edward Elgar, 15–46.

Hommes, R. 1996. "Conflicts and Dilemmas of Decentralization." In Michael Bruno and Boris Pleskovic, eds., *Annual World Bank Conference on Development Economics 1995*. Washington, DC: World Bank, 331–362.

Hopkin, J. 2003. "Political Decentralization, Electoral Change, and Party Organizational Adaptation." *European Urban and Regional Studies* 10 (3): 227–237.

Horowitz, Donald. 1985. *Ethnic Groups in Conflict*. Berkeley: University of California.

Hutchcroft, Paul. 2001. "Centralization and Decentralization in Administration and Politics: Assessing Territorial Dimensions of Authority and Power." *Governance* 14 (1): 23–53.

Inman, Robert P. 2008. "Federalism's Values and the Value of Federalism." *CESifo Economic Studies* 53 (4): 522–560.

International IDEA. 2003. *Democracy at the Local Level: A Guide for the South Caucasus*. Stockholm, Sweden: International IDEA.

———. 2004. *Democracy at the Local Level in East and Southern Africa: Profiles in Governance*, Stockholm, Sweden: International IDEA.

Isin, Engin F., and Bryan S. Turner, eds. 2002. *Handbook of Citizenship Studies*. London: Sage.

Ito, Takeshi. 2007. "Institutional Choices in the Shadow of History: Decentralization in Indonesia." Washington, DC: World Resources Institute.

Ivanov, S. 2005. "Expanding Municipal Own Revenue." Paper prepared for the US Agency for International Development's Bulgaria Local Government Initiative, Sofia, Bulgaria, November 2005.

Jaggers, K., and T. R. Gurr. 1995. "Tracking Democracy's Third Wave with the Polity III Data." *Journal of Peace Research* 32 (4): 469–483.

Jenkins, Rob. 2003. "India's States and the Making of Foreign Economic Policy: The Limits of the Constituent Diplomacy Paradigm." *Publius* 33 (4): 63–81.

Jenkins, Rob, and Anne Marie Goetz. 1999. "Accounts and Accountability: Theoretical Implications of the Right-to-Information Movement in India." *Third World Quarterly* 20 (3): 603–622.

Jerusalem, Leila. 2008. "Decentralization in Nicaragua." Washington, DC: World Bank.

Jimenez, Emmanuel, and Yasuyuki Sawada. 1999. "Do Community-Managed Schools Work? An Evaluation of El Salvador's EDUCO Program." *World Bank Economic Review* 13 (3): 415–441.

Jin, Jing, and Heng-fu Zou. 2002. "How Does Fiscal Decentralization Affect Aggregate, National, and Subnational Government Size?" *Journal of Urban Economics* 52 (2): 270–293.

Johnson, Craig. 2001. "Local Democracy, Democratic Decentralisation and Rural Development: Theories, Challenges and Options for Policy." *Development Policy Review* 19 (4): 521–532.

Johnson, Ronald. 1995. "Decentralization Strategy Design: Complementary Perspectives on a Common Theme." Washington, DC: US Agency for International Development.

Jones, Mark. 1997. "Federalism and the Number of Parties in Argentine Congressional Elections." *Journal of Politics* 59 (2): 538–549.

Jones, Mark, and Scott Mainwaring. 2003. "The Nationalization of Parties and Party Systems: An Empirical Measure and an Application to the Americas." *Party Politics* 9 (2): 139–166.

Kaiser, Kai, Daan Pattinasarany, and Gunther Schulze. 2006. "Decentralization, Governance and Public Services in Indonesia." In Paul Smoke, Eduardo J. Gomez, and George E. Peterson, eds., *Decentralization in Asia and Latin America: Towards a Comparative Interdisciplinary Perspective.* Cheltenham, UK: Edward Elgar, 164–207.

Kakarala, Sitharamam. 2004. "The Challenge of Democratic Empowerment: A Special Report on Civil Society Building." Bangalore: India Regional Office, Humanist Institute for Cooperation with Developing Countries (HIVOS).

Karl, Terry. 1995. "The Hybrid Regimes of Central America." *Journal of Democracy* 6 (3): 72–86.

Karl, Terry, and Philippe Schmitter. 1991. "Modes of Transition in Southern and Eastern Europe and Southern and Central America." *International Social Science Journal* 5 (43): 269–284.

Kasper, Wolfgang. 1995. "Competitive Federalism: Promoting Freedom and Prosperity." Melbourne, Australia: Institute of Public Affairs.

Keech, William R. 1995. *Economic Politics: The Costs of Democracy*. New York: Cambridge University Press.

Key, V. O. 1966. *The Responsible Electorate: Rationality in Presidential Voting 1936–1960.* Cambridge, MA: Belknap Press.

Khemani, Stuti. 2006. "Can Information Campaigns Overcome Political Obstacles to Serving the Poor?" Paper presented at the Politics of Service Delivery in Democracies: Better Access for the Poor, Expert Group on Development Issues meeting in Lidingö, Sweden, April 27–28, 2006.

Kornblith, M., and D. H. Levine. 1995. "Venezuela: The Life and Times of the Party System." In Scott Mainwaring and Timothy R. Scully, eds., *Building Democratic Institutions: Party Systems in Latin America.* Palo Alto, CA: Stanford University Press, 37–71.

Kramer, Ralph M. 1969. *Participation of the Poor: Comparative Community Case Studies in the War on Poverty.* Englewood Cliffs, NJ: Prentice Hall.

Kymlicka, Will. 2002. *Contemporary Political Philosophy, An Introduction.* Oxford: Oxford University Press.

Lake, David, and Donald Rothchild. 1996. "Containing Fear: The Origins and Management of Ethnic Conflict." *International Security* 21 (2): 41–75.

———. 2005. "Territorial Decentralization and Civil War Settlements." In P. G. Roeder and D. Rothchild, eds., *Sustainable Peace: Power And Democracy After Civil Wars.* Ithaca, NY: Cornell University Press, 109–132.

Lankina, Tomila. 2004. *Governing the Locals: Local Self-Government and Ethnic Mobilization in Russia.* Lanham, MD: Rowman & Littlefield.

———. 2008. "'Fragmented Belonging' on Russia's Forested Western Frontier." *Conservation and Society* 6 (1): 24–34.

Lankina, Tomila, and Lullit Getachew. 2006. "A Geographic Incremental Theory of Democratization: Territory, Aid and Democracy in Post-Communist Regions." *World Politics* 58 (4): 536–582.

Lankina, Tomila, Anneke Hudalla, and Hellmut Wollmann. 2008. *Local Governance in Central and Eastern Europe: Comparing Performance in the Czech Republic, Hungary, Poland and Russia.* Basingstoke, UK: Palgrave MacMillan.

Larson, Anne. 2008. "Indigenous Peoples, Representation and Citizenship in Guatemalan Forestry." *Conservation and Society* 6 (1): 35–48.

Leonard, David K. 1987. "The Political Realities of African Management." *World Development* 15 (7): 899–910.

Lewis, Blane. 2005. Indonesian Local Government Spending, Taxing and Saving: An Explanation of Pre- and Post-decentralization Fiscal Outcomes." *Asian Economic Journal* 19 (3): 291–317.

Lijphart, A. 1999. *Patterns of Democracy: Government Forms and Performance in Thirty-Six Countries*. New Haven, CT: Yale University Press.

Lin, Jutin Yifu, Ran Tao, and Mingxing Liu. 2006. "Decentralization and Local Governance in China's Economic Transition." In Pranab Bardhan and Dilip Mookerjee, eds., *Decentralization and Local Governance in Developing Countries: A Comparative Perspective*. Cambridge, MA: MIT Press, 305–328.

Lipset, S. M., ed. 1995. *Encyclopedia on Democracy*. Washington, DC: Congressional Quarterly.

Litvack, Jennie, Junaid Ahmad, and Richard Bird. 1998. "Rethinking Decentralization in Developing Countries." Washington, DC: World Bank.

Local Government Forum Working Group. 2005. "Expanding Municipal Own Revenue." Issue paper prepared for the Bulgaria Local Government Initiative, a USAID-sponsored project implemented by RTI International. Sofia, November.

Luppia, Arthur. 2001. "Delegation of Power: Agency Theory." In Neil J. Smelser and Paul B. Baltes, eds., *International Encyclopedia of the Social and Behavioral Sciences*, vol. 5. Oxford, UK: Elsevier Science Ltd., 3375–3377.

Luppia, Arthur, and Matthew T. McCubbins. 1998. *The Democratic Dilemma: Can Citizens Learn What They Need to Know?* New York: Cambridge University Press.

MacPherson, C. B. 1978. *Property: Mainstream and Critical Positions*. Toronto, ON, Canada: University of Toronto Press.

Mainwaring, Scott, and Timothy R. Scully, eds. 1995. *Building Democratic Institutions: Party Systems in Latin America*. Palo Alto, CA: Stanford University Press.

———. 2008. "Latin America: Eight Lessons for Governance." *Journal of Democracy* 19 (3): 113–127.

Malley, Michael. 2003. "New Rules, Old Structures and the Limits of Democratic Decentralisation." In Edward Aspinall and Greg Fealy, eds., *Local Power and Politics in Indonesia: Decentralisation and Democratisation*. Singapore: Institute of Southeast Asian Studies, 102–116.

———. 2009. "Decentralization and Democratic Transition in Indonesia," In Gary Bland and Cynthia Arnson, eds., *Democratic Deficits: Addressing Challenges to Sustainability and Consolidation around the World*. Woodrow Wilson International Center for Scholars, 135–145.

Mamdani, Mahmood. 1996. *Citizen and Subject: Contemporary Africa and the Legacy of Late Colonialism*. Princeton, NJ: Princeton University Press.

Manin, Bernard, Adam Przeworski, and Susan Stokes. 1999. "Elections and Representation." In Adam Przeworski, Susan Stokes, and Bernard Manin, eds., *Democracy, Accountability and Representation*. Cambridge: Cambridge University Press, 29–53.

Manor, James. 1999. *The Political Economy of Democratic Decentralization*. Washington, DC: World Bank.

———. 2004a. "Democratization with Inclusion: Political Reforms and People's Empowerment at the Grassroots." *Journal of Human Development* 5 (1): 5–29.

———. 2004b. "User Committees: A Potentially Damaging Second Wave of Decentralization?" *European Journal of Development Research* 16 (1): 192–213.

———. 2006. "Extending Services over the Last Mile: Bridging the Gap Between Intermediate and Local." Paper presented at the Politics of Service Delivery in Democracies: Better Access for the Poor, Expert Group on Development Issues meeting in Lidingö, Sweden, April 27–28, 2006.

———. 2007. "Strategies to Promote Effective Participation." Background paper prepared for the *2007 World Public Sector Report*, UN Department for Economic and Social Development, New York.

Mansuri, Ghazala, and Vijayendra Rao. 2003. "Evaluating Community-Driven Development: A Review of the Evidence." First draft report, Development Research Group. Washington, DC: World Bank.

———. 2004. "Community-Based and -Driven Development: A Critical Review." *World Bank Research Observer* 19 (1): 1–39.

Markell, Patchen. 2000. "The Recognition of Politics: A Comment on Emcke and Tully." *Constellations* 7 (4): 496–506.

Marshall, Monty. 2002. "Measuring the Societal Impact of War." In F. Hampson and D. Malone, eds., *Reaction to Conflict Prevention: Opportunities for the UN System*. Boulder, CO: Lynne Rienner, 63–104.

———. 2009. *Polity IV Project: Political Regime Characteristics and Transitions, 1800–2008*. Severn, MD: Center for Systemic Peace. Available online at http://www.systemicpeace.org/polity/polity4.htm.

Marshall, M., and T. R. Gurr. 2005. *Peace and Conflict: A Global Survey of Armed Conflicts, Self-Determination Movements and Democracy*. College Park: Center for International Development and Conflict Management, University of Maryland.

Marshall, M., and K. Jaggers. 2000. *Polity IV Project Codebook*. College Park: Center for International Development and Conflict Management, University of Maryland.

Martinez-Vazquez, Jorge, and Robert McNab. 2006. "Fiscal Decentralization, Macrostability and Growth." *Hacienda Publica Espanola/Revista de Economia Publica* 179 (4): 25–49.

Mawhood, Philip. 1983. *Local Government in the Third World*. Chichester, UK: John Wiley.

McClure, Charles E., and Jorge Martinez-Vasquez. 2000. *The Assignment of Revenues and Expenditures in Intergovernmental Fiscal Relations*. Washington, DC: World Bank.

McGarry, J., and B. O'Leary. 2002. *Federation as a Method of Ethnic Conflict Regulation*. Ottawa, ON, Canada: Forum of Federations.

McGee, Rosemary. 2000. "Participation in Poverty Reduction Strategies: A Synthesis of Experience with Participatory Approaches to Policy Design, Implementation and Monitoring." With Andy Norton. Brighton, UK: University of Sussex.

McNulty, Stephanie L. 2006. "Empowering Civil Society: Decentralizing the State and Increasing Local Participation in Peru." PhD dissertation, George Washington University, Washington, DC.

Migdal, Joel S. 1988. *Strong Societies and Weak States: State-Society Relations and State Capabilities in the Third World.* Princeton, NJ: Princeton University Press.

Miller, Gary J. 2005. "The Political Evolution of Principal-Agent Models." *Annual Review of Political Science* 8: 203–225.

Molina, J., and J. Hernández. 1998. "Sistemas electorales subnacionales en América Latina." In Dieter Nohlen, Sonia Picado, and Daniel Zovatto, eds., *Tratado de Derecho Electoral Comparado en America Latina.* Mexico City: Instituto Interamericano de Derechos Humanos/Centro de Asesoría y Promoción Electoral, Fondo de Cultura Económica de México (IIDH/CAPEL), Universidad de Heidelberg, Instituto Federal Electoral de Mexico (IFE), Tribunal Electoral del Poder Judidicial de la Federación de México (TRIFE), and Fondo de Cultura Económica de México. Available online at http://www.iidh.ed.cr/BibliotecaWeb/Varios/DocumentosHtml/Indice-Tratado.htm?Comunidad=200&Tipo=387&URL=%2FBibliotecaWeb%2FVarios%2FDocumentosHtml%2FIndice-Tratado.htm&Barra=1&DocID=1817.

Mongbo, Roch. 2008. "State Building and Local Democracy in Benin: Two Cases of Decentralized Forest Management." *Conservation and Society* 6 (1): 49–61.

Montalvo, Daniel. 2009. "Citizen Satisfaction with Municipal Services." *AmericasBarometer Insights,* No. 28. Nashville: Latin America Public Opinion Project., Vanderbilt University.

Montero, A. P. 2002. *Shifting States in Global Markets: Subnational Industrial Policy in Contemporary Brazil and Spain.* University Park: Penn State University Press.

Montero, A. P., and D. J. Samuels. 2004. *Decentralization and Democracy in Latin America.* Notre Dame, IN: University of Notre Dame Press.

Montinola, Gabriella, Yingyi Qian, and Barry Weingast. 1995. "Federalism Chinese Style: The Political Basis for Economic Success in China." *World Politics* 48 (1): 50–81.

Moore, Sally Falk. 1986. *Social Facts and Fabrications: "Customary" Law on Kilimanjaro, 1880–1980.* Cambridge: Cambridge University Press.

Muriaas, Ragnhild L. 2005. "Chiefs in Local Democracy: Framework for Analysing Local Governance in East and Southern Africa." Paper presented at the National Conference in Political Science in Hurdalsjoen, Norway, January 5–7, 2005.

Namara, Agrippinah, and Xavier Nsabagasani. 2003. "Decentralization and Wildlife Management: Development rights or shedding responsibility? Bwindi Impenetrable National Park, Uganda." Environmental Governance in Africa Working Paper No. 9, World Resources Institute, Washington, DC. Available online at http://pdf.wri.org/eaa_agrippinah.pdf.

Narayan, Deepa, ed. 2002. *Empowerment and Poverty Reduction: A Sourcebook.* Washington, DC: World Bank.

———, ed. 2005. *Measuring Empowerment: Cross-Disciplinary Perspectives.* Washington, DC: World Bank.

National Progressive Primary Health Care Network. 1998. "Community Involvement in Hospitals: Key Findings and Recommendations." Cape Town, South Africa: National Progressive Primary Health Care Network (NPHCN).

Ndegwa, Stephen N. 2002. "Decentralization in Africa: A Stocktaking Survey." Washington, DC: World Bank.

Nelson, Joan. 2006. "Unpacking the Concept of Social Sector Reform." Paper presented at the Politics of Service Delivery in Democracies: Better Access for the Poor, Expert Group on Development Issues meeting in Lidingö, Sweden, April 27–28, 2006.

Nickson, R. Andrew. 1995. *Local Government in Latin America.* Boulder, CO: Lynne Rienner.

Nijenhuis, Karin. 2003. "Does Decentralization Serve Everyone? The Struggle for Power in a Malian Village." *European Journal of Development Research* 15 (2): 67–92.

NPPHCN. *See* National Progressive Primary Health Care Network.

Ntsebeza, Lungisile. 2005. "Democratic Decentralisation and Traditional Authority: Dilemmas of Land Administration in Rural South Africa." In Jesse C. Ribot and Anne Larson, eds., *Decentralization of Natural Resources: Experiences in Africa, Asia and Latin America.* London: Frank Cass, 71–89.

Nylen, William. 2002. "Testing the Empowerment Thesis: The Participatory Budget in Belo Horizonte and Betim, Brazil." *Comparative Politics* 34 (2): 127–140.

Oates, Wallace. 1972. *Fiscal Federalism.* New York: Harcourt Brace Jovanovich.

———. 1985. "Searching for Leviathan: An Empirical Study," *American Economic Review* 75 (4):748–757.

———. 1999. "An Essay on Fiscal Federalism." *Journal of Economic Literature* 38 (3): 1120–1149.

———. 2005. "Toward a Second-Generation Theory of Fiscal Federalism." *International Tax and Public Finance* 12 (4): 349–373.

O'Donnell, Guillermo, Jorge Vargas Cullell, and Osvaldo Iazzetta. 2004. *The Quality of Democracy: Theory and Applications.* Notre Dame, IN: University of Notre Dame Press.

Olken, Benjamin A. 2005. "Monitoring Corruption: Evidence from a Field Experiment in Indonesia." Cambridge, MA: National Bureau of Economic Research.

Olowu, Dele. 2003. "Local Institutional and Political Structures and Processes: Recent Experience in Africa." *Public Administration and Development* 23 (1): 41–52.

Olowu, Dele, and James S. Wunsch. 2004. *Local Governance in Africa: The Challenge of Democratic Decentralization.* Boulder, CO: Lynne Rienner.

Olson, Mancur. 1965. *The Logic of Collective Action: Public Goods and the Theory of Groups.* Cambridge, MA: Harvard University Press.

———. 1982. *The Rise and Decline of Nations.* New Haven, CT: Yale University Press.

Oneal, J., and B. Russett. 2001. *Triangulating Peace.* New York: Norton & Norton.

O'Neill, Kathleen. 2003. "Decentralization as an Electoral Strategy." *Comparative Political Studies* 36 (9): 1068–1091.

———. 2005. *Decentralizing the State: Elections, Parties and Local Power in the Andes.* New York: Cambridge University Press.

Onyach-Olaa, Martin. 2003. "The Challenges of Implementing Decentralization: Recent Experiences in Uganda." *Public Administration and Development* 23 (1): 105–113.

Organisation for Economic Co-operation and Development. 2004. *Education at a Glance: OECD Indicators, 2004.* Paris: Organisation for Economic Co-operation and Development (OECD).

Ostrom, Elinor. 1990. *Governing the Commons: The Evolution of Institutions for Collective Action.* Cambridge: Cambridge University Press.

———. 1996. "Crossing the Great Divide; Coproduction, Synergy, and Development." *World Development* 24: 1073–1087.

———. 2000. "The Danger of Self-Evident Truths." *PS: Political Science and Politics* 33 (1): 33–44.

———. 2005. *Understanding Institutional Diversity.* Princeton, NJ: Princeton University Press.

Ostrom, Elinor, Lou Picard, and Jerry Silverman. 2006. "Regional Variations in Local Governance." Washington, DC: Office of Democracy and Governance, US Agency for International Development.

Oxhorn, Philip, Joseph S. Tulchin, and Andrew D. Selee, eds. 2004. *Decentralization, Democratic Governance, and Civil Society in Comparative Perspective: Africa, Asia, and Latin America.* Baltimore, MD: Johns Hopkins University Press.

Pateman, Carole. 1970. *Participation and Democratic Theory.* Cambridge: Cambridge University Press.

Paul, Samuel, and Sita Sekhar. 2000. *Benchmarking Urban Services: The Second Report Card on Bangalore.* Bangalore, India: Public Affairs Centre.

Pitkin, Hanna. 1967. *The Concept of Representation.* Los Angeles: University of California Press.

Platteau, Jean-Philippe. 2006. "Pitfalls of Participatory Development." Background paper prepared for the *2007 World Public Sector Report*, UN Department for Economic and Social Development, New York.

Poiré, A. 2000. "Do Electoral Institutions Affect Party Discipline? or Nominations Rule! Comparative Evidence on the Impact of Nomination Procedures on Party Discipline." Paper prepared for the Latin American Studies Association meeting in Miami, FL, March 16–18, 2000.

Political Risk Services. 2006. *International Country Risk Guide.* Annual ratings 1982–2005, East Syracuse, New York. Available online at http://wwwl.prsgroup.com/ICRG.aspx.

Posen, B. 1993. The Security Dilemma and Ethnic Conflict. *Survival* 35 (1): 27–47.

Poteete, Amy. 2007. "How National Political Competition Affects Natural Resource Policy: The Case of Community-Based Natural Resource Management in Botswana." Paper presented at the Canadian Political Science Association conference in Saskatoon, SK, Canada, May 30–June 1, 2007.

Povinelli, Elizabeth A. 2002. *The Cunning of Recognition: Indigenous Alterities and the Making of Australian Multiculturalism.* Durham, NC: Duke University Press.

Powell, Bingham. 1982. *Contemporary Democracies: Participation, Stability and Violence.* Cambridge, MA: Harvard University Press.

Powell, G. B., Jr. 2000. *Elections as Instruments of Democracy: Majoritarian and Proportional Vision.* New Haven, CT: Yale University Press.

Pozzoni, Barbara, and Nalini Kumar. 2005. "A Review of the Literature on Participatory Approaches to Local Development for an Evaluation of the Effectiveness of World Bank Support for Community-Based and -Driven Development Approaches." Washington, DC: World Bank.

Prichett, Lant, and Michael Woolcock. 2004. "Solutions When the Solution Is the Problem: Arraying the Disarray in Development." *World Development* 32 (2): 191–212.

Prud'homme, Remy. 1995. "The Dangers of Decentralization." *World Bank Research Observer* 10 (2): 201–220.

Przeworski, Adam, Guillermo O'Donnell, and Philippe Schmitter. 1986. *Transitions from Authoritarian Rule*. Baltimore, MD: Johns Hopkins University Press.

Putnam, Robert. 1993. *Making Democracy Work: Civic Traditions in Modern Italy*. Princeton, NJ: Princeton University Press.

Qian, Yingyi, and Barry Wiengast. 1997. "Federalism as a Commitment to Preserving Market Incentives." *Journal of Economic Perspectives* 11 (4): 83–92.

Querubín, C., M. F. Sánchez, and I. Kure. 1998. "Dinámica de las Elecciones Populares de Alcaldes, 1988–1997." In Andrés Dávila and Ana María Bejarano, eds., *Elecciones y Democracia en Colombia 1997–1998*. Bogotá, Colombia: Universidad de los Andes y Fundación Social, 117–140.

Rao, Vijayendra, and Ana M. Ibáñez. 2003. "The Social Impact of Social Funds in Jamaica: A Mixed-Methods Analysis of Participation, Targeting, and Collective Action in Community-Driven Development." Washington, DC: World Bank.

Reinikka, Ritva, and Jakob Svensson. 2004. "Local Capture: Evidence from a Central Government Transfer Program in Uganda." *Quarterly Journal of Economics* 119 (2): 679–705.

Rhodes, Sybil. 2003. "Progressive Pragmatism as a Governance Model: An In-Depth Look at Porto Alegre, Brazil." In Susan Eckstein and Timothy Wickham-Crowley, eds., *What Justice? Whose Justice? Fighting for Fairness in Latin America*. Berkeley: University of California Press, 217–232.

Ribot, Jesse C. 1999. "Decentralization and Participation in Sahelian Forestry: Legal Instruments of Central Political-Administrative Control." *Africa* 69 (1): 23–65.

———. 2002a. "African Decentralization: Local Actors, Powers, and Accountability." Geneva, Switzerland: UN Research Institute for Social Development.

———. 2002b. "Democratic Decentralization of Natural Resources: Institutionalizing Popular Participation." Washington, DC: World Resources Institute.

———. 2003. "Democratic Decentralization of Natural Resources: Institutional Choice and Discretionary Power Transfers in Sub-Saharan Africa." *Public Administration and Development* 23 (1): 53–65.

———. 2004. *Waiting for Democracy: The Politics of Choice in Natural Resource Decentralization*. Washington, DC: World Resources Institute.

———. 2006. "Choose Democracy: Environmentalists' Socio-political Responsibility." *Global Environmental Change* 16 (2): 115–119.

Ribot, Jesse C., and Anne Larson, eds. 2005. *Democratic Decentralization Through a Natural Resource Lens*. Oxford, UK: Routledge.

Riker, William H. 1964. *Federalism: Origin, Operation, and Significance*. Boston: Little, Brown.

Roberts, K. M. Forthcoming. *Political Parties in Latin America's Neoliberal Era*. New York: Cambridge University Press.

Robinson, Richard, and David Stiedl. 2001. "Decentralization of Road Administration: Case Studies in Africa and Asia." *Public Administration and Development* 21 (1): 53–64.
Rodden, Jonathan. 2005. *Hamilton's Paradox: The Promise and Peril of Fiscal Federalism.* New York: Cambridge University Press.
Rodden, Jonathan, Gunnar S. Eskeland, and Jennie Litvack, eds. 2003. *Fiscal Decentralization and the Challenge of Hard Budget Constraints.* Cambridge, MA: MIT Press.
Rodrik, Dani. 1999. *The New Global Economy and Developing Countries: Making Openness Work.* Washington, DC: Overseas Development Council.
———, ed. 2003. *In Search of Prosperity: Analytics Narratives on Economic Growth.* Princeton, NJ: Princeton University Press.
Roeder, P. 1991. "Soviet Federalism and Ethnic Mobilization." *World Politics* 43 (2): 196–232.
Romeo, Leonardo. 1996. *Local Development Funds: Promoting Decentralized Planning and Financing of Rural Development.* Policy Series, United Nations Capital Development Fund.
———. 2003. "The Role of External Assistance in Supporting Decentralization Reform." *Public Administration and Development* 23 (1): 89–96.
Romeo, Leonardo G., and Luc Spyckerelle. 2004. "Decentralization Reforms and Commune-Level Services in Cambodia." Case study presented at the Local Government and Pro-Poor Service Delivery workshop, Asian Development Bank, Manila, the Philippines, February 9–13, 2004.
Rondinelli, Dennis. 1989. "Decentralizing Public Services in Developing Countries: Issues and Opportunities." *Journal of Social, Political and Economic Studies* 14 (1): 77–97.
Rose-Ackerman, Susan, and Jonathan Rodden. 1997. "Does Federalism Preserve Markets?" *Virginia Law Review* 83 (7): 1521–1572.
Rowland, Allison, M. 2001. "Population as a Determinant of Variation in Local Outcomes Under Decentralization: Illustrations from Small Municipalities in Bolivia and Mexico." *World Development* 29 (8): 1373–1389.
Rubin, Edward. 2005. "The Myth of Accountability and the Anti-administrative Impulse." *Michigan Law Review* 103 (8): 2073–2136.
Rummel, R. J. 1994. *Death by Government.* New Brunswick, NJ: Transaction.
Rustow, Dankwart A. 1970. "Transitions to Democracy: Toward a Dynamic Model." *Comparative Politics* 2 (3): 337–363.
Ryan, J. 2004. "Decentralization and Democratic Instability: The Case of Costa Rica." *Public Administration Review* 64 (1): 81–91.
Saideman, S., and R. W. Ayres. 2000. "Determining the Causes of Irredentism: Logit Analyses of Minorities at Risk Data from the 1980s and 1990s." *Journal of Politics* 62 (4): 1126–1144.
Saideman, S., D. Lanoue, M. Campenni, and S. Stanton. 2002. "Democratization, Political Institutions, and Ethnic Conflict: A Pooled Time-Series Analysis, 1985–1998." *Comparative Political Studies* 35 (1): 103–129.
Sambanis, N. 2002. "Preventing Violent Civil Conflict: The Scope and Limits of Government Action." Background paper for *World Development Report 2003: Dynamic Development in a Sustainable World.* Washington, DC: World Bank.
Samuels, David. 2000. "The Gubernatorial Coattails Effect: Federalism and Congressional Elections in Brazil." *Journal of Politics* 62 (1): 240–253.

Sartori, Giovanni. 1976. *Parties and Party Systems: A Framework for Analysis.* New York: Cambridge University Press.

———. 1997. *Comparative Constitutional Engineering: An Inquiry into Structures, Incentives and Outcomes.* New York: NYU Press.

Schedler, Andreas. 1999. "Conceptualizing Accountability." In Andreas Schedler, Larry Diamond, and Marc F. Plattner, eds., *The Self-Restraining State: Power and Accountability in New Democracies.* Boulder, CO: Lynne Rienner, 13–28.

Schmitter, P. C., and T. L. Karl. 1991. "What Democracy Is. . . . And Is Not." *Journal of Democracy* 2 (3): 75–89.

Schneider, Aaron. 2003. "Decentralization: Conceptualization and Measurement." *Studies in Comparative International Development* 38 (3): 32–56.

Schou, A., and M. Haug. 2005. *Decentralisation in Conflict and Post-Conflict Situations.* Working Paper 139, Norwegian Institute for Urban and Regional Research, Oslo.

Schroeder, Larry. 2003. "Mechanisms for Strengthening Local Accountability." Washington, DC: World Bank.

Schumpeter, Joseph A. 1943. *Capitalism, Socialism, and Democracy.* Reprint, London: George Allen & Unwin, 1976.

Seligson, Mitchell A. 2005. "The Latin American Public Opinion Project: Corruption Victimization, 2004." In Diana Rodriguez, Gerard Waite, and Toby Wolfe, eds., *Global Corruption Report 2005.* Ann Arbor: Pluto Press, in association with Transparency International, 282–284.

———. 2006. "The Measurement and Impact of Corruption Victimization: Survey Evidence from Latin America." *World Development* 34 (2): 381–404.

Seligson, Mitchell A., and John A. Booth, eds. 1979. *Political Participation in Latin America: Politics and the Poor.* New York: Holmes & Meier.

Shah, Anwar. 1994. "The Reform of Intergovernmental Fiscal Relations in Developing and Emerging Market Economies." *Policy Research Working Paper* No. 23. Washington, DC: World Bank.

———. 2006. "Corruption and Decentralized Public Governance." Washington, DC: World Bank.

Shah, Anwar, and Theresa Thompson. 2004. "Implementing Decentralized Local Governance: A Treacherous Road with Potholes, Detours, and Road Closures." Washington, DC: World Bank.

Shatkin, Gavin. 2000. "Obstacles to Empowerment: Local Politics and Civil Society in Metropolitan Manila, the Philippines." *Urban Studies* 37 (12): 2357–2375.

Shawkat Ali, A. M. M. 1987. "Decentralization for Development: Experiment in Local Government Administration in Bangladesh." *Asian Surve* 27 (7): 787–799.

Shleifer, Andrei, and Robert W. Vishny. 1998. *The Grabbing Hand: Government Pathologies and Their Cures.* Cambridge, MA: Harvard University Press.

Shugart, M. S., and J. M. Carey. 1992. *Presidents and Assemblies: Constitutional Design and Electoral Dynamics.* New York: Cambridge University Press.

Sidel, John. 1999. *Capital, Coercion, and Crime: Bossism in the Philippines.* Palo Alto, CA: Stanford University Press.

Siegle, J., and P. O'Mahony. 2006. "Assessing the Merits of Decentralization as a Conflict-Mitigating Strategy." Washington, DC: Office of Democracy and Governance, US Agency for International Development.

Silverman, Jerry M. 2004. "The Missing Link: Creating Mutual Dependencies Between the Poor and the State." *International Public Management Journal* 7 (2): 227–247.

Smith, Benjamin. 2008. "The Origins of Regional Autonomy in Indonesia: Experts and the Marketing of Political Interests." *Journal of East Asian Studies* 8 (2): 211–234.

Smoke, Paul. 1993. "Local Government Fiscal Reform in Developing Countries: Lessons from Kenya." *World Development* 21 (6): 901–923.

———. 1994. *Local Government Finance in Developing Countries: The Case of Kenya*. Oxford: Oxford University Press.

———. 2000. "Strategic Fiscal Decentralization in Developing Countries: Learning from Recent Innovations." In Shahid Yusuf, Weiping Wu, and Simon J. Evenett, eds., *Local Dynamics in an Era of Globalization*. Oxford: Oxford University Press, 101–109.

———. 2001. *Fiscal Decentralization in Developing Countries: A Review of Current Concepts and Practice*. Geneva, Switzerland: UN Research Institute for Social Development.

———. 2003. "Decentralization in Africa: Goals, Dimensions, Myths and Challenges." *Public Administration and Development* 23 (1): 1–17.

———. 2004. "Erosion and Reform from the Center in Kenya." In Dele Olowu and James S. Wunsch, eds., *Local Governance in Africa: The Challenge of Decentralization*. Boulder, CO: Lynne Rienner, 211–236.

———. 2006a. "Fiscal Decentralization Policy in Developing Countries: Bridging Theory and Reality." In Yusuf Bangura and George Larbi, eds., *Public Sector Reform in Developing Countries*. London: Palgrave-Macmillan, 195–227.

———. 2006b. "Cambodia's Nascent Decentralization: From Donor Experiment to Sustainable Government System?" In Paul Smoke, Eduardo J. Gomez, and George E. Peterson, eds., *Decentralization in Asia and Latin America: Towards a Comparative Interdisciplinary Perspective*. Cheltenham, UK: Edward Elgar, 63–87.

———. 2007. "Fiscal Decentralization and Intergovernmental Relations in Developing Countries: Navigating a Viable Path to Reform." In G. Shabbir Cheema and Dennis Rondinelli, eds., *Decentralized Governance: Emerging Concepts and Practice*. Washington, DC: Brookings Institution, 131–155.

———. 2008a. "Local Revenues Under Fiscal Decentralization in Developing Countries: Linking Policy Reform, Governance and Capacity." In Gregory K. Ingram and Yu-Hung Hong, eds., *Fiscal Decentralization and Land Policies*. Cambridge, MA: Lincoln Institute of Land Policy, 380–68.

———. 2008b. "The Evolution of Subnational Development Planning Under Decentralization Reforms in Kenya And Uganda." In Victoria A. Beard, Faranak Miraftab, and Christopher Silver, eds., *Planning and Decentralization: Contested Spaces for Public Action in the Global South*. Abingdon, UK: Routledge, 89–105.

Smoke, Paul, and Eduardo Gomez. 2006. "The Dynamics of Decentralization in Asia and Latin America: Towards a Comparative Interdisciplinary Perspective." In Paul Smoke, Eduardo J. Gomez, and George E. Peterson, eds., *Decentralization in Asia and Latin America: Towards a Comparative Interdisciplinary Perspective*. Cheltenham, UK: Edward Elgar, 339–367.

Smoke, Paul, Eduardo J. Gomez, and George E. Peterson, eds. 2006. *Decentralization in Asia and Latin America: Towards a Comparative Interdisciplinary Perspective.* Cheltenham, UK: Edward Elgar.

Smoke, Paul, and Blane Lewis. 1996. "Fiscal Decentralization in Indonesia: A New Approach to an Old Idea." *World Development* 24 (8): 1281–1299.

Smoke, Paul, and Joanne Morrison. 2008. "Decentralization in Cambodia: Consolidating Central Power or Building Accountability from Below?" Paper prepared for the Decentralization in Difficult Environments conference, Andrew Young School of Policy Studies, Georgia State University, Atlanta, GA, September 2009.

Smoke, Paul, and Robert Taliercio. 2007. "Aid, Public Finance and Accountability: Cambodian Dilemmas." In James Boyce and Madalene O'Donnell, eds., *Peace and the Public Purse: Economic Policies for Postwar Statebuilding.* Boulder, CO: Lynne Rienner, 55–84.

Snyder, Jack. 2000. *From Voting to Violence: Democratization and Nationalist Conflict.* W. W. Norton & Co.

Snyder, Richard. 2001. "Scaling Down: The Subnational Comparative Method." *Studies in Comparative International Development* 36 (1): 93–110.

Sparke, M. 2004. "Passports into Credit Cards: On the Borders and Spaces of Neoliberal Citizenship." In J. S. Migdal, ed., *Boundaries and Belonging: States and Societies in the Struggle to Shape Identities and Local Practices.* Cambridge: Cambridge University Press.

Spierenburg, Marja. 1995. *The Role of the Mhondoro Cult in the Struggle for Control Over Land in Dande (Northern Zimbabwe): Social Commentaries and the Influence of Adherents.* NRM Occasional Paper Series, Centre for Applied Social Sciences, University of Zimbabwe, Harare, and Amsterdam School for Social Science Research, Amsterdam, October 1995.

Spierenburg, Marja, Conrad Steenkamp, and Harry Wels. 2008. "Enclosing the Local for the Global Commons: Community Land Rights in the Great Limpopo Transfrontier Conservation Area." *Conservation and Society* 6 (1): 87–97.

Steffensen, Jesper, Harriet Naitore, and Per Tideman. 2004. "A Comparative Analysis of Decentralization in Kenya, Tanzania and Uganda. Report to the World Bank." Copenhagen, Denmark: Nordic Consulting Group.

Stegarescu, Dan. 2004. "Public Sector Decentralization: Measurement Concepts and Recent International Trends." Discussion Paper No. 04-74. Mannheim, Germany: Zentrum fur Europaische Wirtschaftsforschung GmbH (Centre for European Economic Research). Available online at ftp://ftp.zew.de/pub/zew-docs/dp/dp0474.pdf.

Stepan, Alfred. 2001. *Arguing Comparative Politics.* Oxford: Oxford University Press.

Stoner-Weiss, Kathryn. 1997. *Local Heroes: The Political Economy of Russian Regional Governance.* Princeton, NJ: Princeton University Press.

———. 2004. "Russia: Managing Territorial Cleavages Under Dual Transitions." In Ugo Amoretti and Nancy Bermeo, eds., *Federalism and Territorial Cleavages.* Baltimore, MD: Johns Hopkins University Press.

———. 2006. *Resisting the State: Reform and Retrenchment in Post-Soviet Russia.* New York: Cambridge University Press.

Strom, Kaare. 1992. "Democracy as Political Competition." *American Behavioral Scientist* 35 (4–5): 375–396.

Swinburn, Gwen. 2006. "Local Economic Development: LED Quick Reference Guide." Washington, DC: World Bank

Sutherland, Douglas, and Robert Price. 2007. "Linkages Between Performance and Institutions in the Primary and Secondary Education Sector." *OECD Economics Department Working Papers,* No. 558.

Tang, Shui Yan. 1992. *Institutions and Collective Action: Self-Governance in Irrigation.* San Francisco, CA: Institute for Contemporary Studies Press.

Tanzi, Vito. 1996. "Fiscal Federalism and Decentralization: A Review of Some Efficiency and Macroeconomic Aspects." In *Proceedings of the 1995 Annual World Bank Conference on Development Economics*, 295–316.

———. 2001. "Pitfalls on the Road to Fiscal Decentralization." Global Policy Program Working Paper No. 19. Washington, DC: Carnegie Endowment for International Peace.

Tapales, Proserpina. 1993. *Devolution and Empowerment: The Local Government Code of 1991 and Local Autonomy in the Philippines.* Quezon City: University of the Philippines Press.

Taylor, Charles. 1994. "The Politics of Recognition." In A. Guttman, ed., *Multiculturalism.* Princeton, NJ: Princeton University Press, 25–74.

Tendler, Judith. 1997. *Good Government in the Tropics*. Baltimore, MD: Johns Hopkins University Press.

Thomson, James T., ed. 2004. *Mali, Botswana, Namibia, and Malawi: Institutional Aspects of Renewable Natural Resources Governance and Management Through Special Districts.* Burlington, VT: ARD Inc.

Thun, Eric. 2004. "Keeping Up with the Jones': Decentralization, Policy Imitation and Industrial Development in China." *World Development* 38 (2): 1289–1308.

Tiebout, Charles M. 1956. "A Pure Theory of Local Expenditures." *Journal of Political Economy* 64 (5): 416–424.

Tomasi, Mariano, and Federico Weinschelbaum. 2003. "Centralization vs. Decentralization: A Principal-Agent Analysis." Leitner Working Paper 2003–02. New Haven, CT: Leitner Program in International and Comparative Political Economy, Yale University.

Toni, Fabiano. 2007. "Party Politics, Social Movements, and Local Democracy: Institutional Choices in the Brazilian Amazon." Washington, DC: World Resources Institute.

Transparency International. 2006. *Corruption Perceptions Index 2006*. Berlin, Germany: Transparency International. Available online at http://www.transparency.org/policy_research/surveys_indices/cpi/2006.

Treisman, Daniel. 2000. *Decentralization and the Quality of Government.* Los Angeles: University of California.

———. 2002. *Defining and Measuring Decentralization: A Global Perspective.* Los Angeles: University of California.

———. 2007. *The Architecture of Government: Rethinking Political Decentralization*. Cambridge: Cambridge University Press.

Tully, James. 2000. "Struggles over Recognition and Distribution." *Constellations* 7 (4): 469–482.

Turner, Mark. 2002. "Whatever Happened to Deconcentration? Recent Initiatives in Cambodia." *Public Administration and Development* 22 (3): 353–364.

UN Capital Development Fund. 2006. *Delivering the Goods: Building Local Government Capacity to Achieve the Millennium Development Goals.* New York: UN Capital Development Fund (UNCDF).

UN Department for Economic and Social Affairs. 2005. *Decentralized Governance.* New York: UN Department for Economic and Social Affairs (UNDESA).

UN Development Programme. 2002. *Human Development Report 2002: Deepening Democracy in a Fragmented World.* New York: Oxford University Press.

———. 2004. *Decentralized Governance for Development: A Combined Practice Note on Decentralization, Local Governance and Urban/Rural Development.* New York: UN Development Programme (UNDP).

———. 2006. "Decentralization: Lebanon." Available online at http://www.pogar.org/countries/decentralization.asp?cid=9.

———. 2007. "Report on the 2007 Commune Council Elections in Cambodia." Phnom Penh: UNDP Cambodia.

Uphoff, Norman. 1986. *Local Institutional Development: An Analytical Sourcebook with Cases.* West Hartford, CT: Kumarian Press.

Urdaneta, Alberto, Leopoldo Martinez, and Margarita Lopez Maya. 1990. *Venezuela: Centralizacion y Descentralizacion del Estado.* Caracas: Centro de Estudios del Desarrollo (CENDES).

US Agency for International Development. 2000. *Decentralization and Democratic Local Governance Programming Handbook.* Washington, DC: US Agency for International Development.

———. 2006. "Making Cities Work Assessment and Implementation Toolkit: Local Economic Development." Washington, DC: US Agency for International Development.

———. 2009. *Democratic Decentralization Programming Handbook.* Washington, DC: US Agency for International Development.

USAID. *See* US Agency for International Development.

Uwimana, Antoinette, and Dean Swerdlin. 2007. "Local Politics and Health: Performance-Based Contracts (Imihigo) Between Mayors and the President and Impact on Selected Health Indicators in Rwanda." Paper presented at the American Public Health Association conference in Washington, DC, November 6, 2007.

Valenzuela, Arturo. 1977. *Political Brokers in Chile: Local Governments in a Centralized Polity.* Durham, NC: Duke University Press.

Van Cott, Donna. 2008. *Radical Democracy in the Andes.* Cambridge: Cambridge University Press.

Varshney, Ashutosh. 2002. *Ethnic Conflict and Civic Life: Hindus and Muslims in India.* New Haven, CT: Yale University Press.

Vetter, Angelika. 2002. "Local Political Competence in Europe: A Resource of Legitimacy for Higher Levels of Government?" *International Journal of Public Opinion Research* 14 (1): 3–18.

von Hayek, Friedrich A. 1945. "The Use of Knowledge in Society." *American Economic Review* 35 (4): 519–530.

Walter, Barbara. 1999. "Designing Transitions from Civil War: Demobilization, Democratization and Commitments to Peace." *International Security* 24 (1): 127–155.

Wampler, Brian. 2007. *Participatory Budgeting in Brazil: Contestation, Cooperation and Accountability*. University Park: Penn State University Press.

Wedeman, Andrew. 2003. *From Mao to Market: Rent Seeking, Local Protectionism and Marketization in China*. New York: Cambridge University Press.

Weingast, Barry R. 1995. "The Economic Role of Political Institutions: Market-Preserving Federalism and Economic Development." *Journal of Law, Economics and Organization* 11 (1): 1–31.

———. 2006. Second *Generation Fiscal Federalism: Implications for Decentralized Democratic Governance and Economic Development*. Washington, DC: US Agency for International Development.

White, Roland, and Paul Smoke. 2005. *East Asia Decentralizes: Making Local Government Work*. Washington, DC: World Bank

Wibbels, Erik. 2005. *Federalism and the Market: Intergovernmental Conflict and Economic Reform in the Developing World*. New York: Cambridge University Press.

Wildasin, David E. 1997. "Externalities and Bailouts: Hard and Soft Budget Constrains in Intergovernmental Fiscal Relations." *Policy Research Working Paper*, No. 1843. Washington DC: World Bank.

Willis, Eliza, Christopher Garman, and Stephan Haggard. 1999. "The Politics of Decentralization in Latin America." *Latin American Research Review* 34 (1): 7–56.

Work, Robertson. 2002. "Overview of Decentralisation Worldwide: A Stepping Stone to Improved Governance and Human Development." Paper presented at the International Conference on Decentralisation in Manila, the Philippines, July 25–27, 2002.

World Bank. 2000a. *World Development Report 1999/2000: Entering the 21st Century: The Changing Development Landscape*. Oxford: Oxford University Press.

———. 2000b. "Decentralizing Agricultural Extension: Lessons and Good Practice." Washington, DC: World Bank.

———. 2001a. "Decentralization in the Transition Economies: Challenges and the Road Ahead." Washington, DC: World Bank.

———. 2001b. "Morocco: Municipal Management and Decentralization." World Bank Team Report. Washington, DC: World Bank.

———. 2002. "Project Appraisal Document on a Proposed Loan in the Amount of US$ 400 Million to the United Mexican States for Municipal Development in Rural Areas Project." Washington, DC: World Bank.

———. 2003. "Integrated Fiduciary Assessment and Public Expenditure Review for Cambodia." Washington, DC: World Bank.

———. 2004. *World Development Report: Making Services Work for the Poor*. Washington, DC: World Bank.

———. 2005a. "Exploring Partnerships Between Communities and Local Governments in Community-Driven Development: A Framework." Washington, DC: World Bank.

———. 2005b. *East Asia Decentralizes: Making Local Government Work*. Washington, DC: World Bank.

———. 2007. *World Development Indicators 2007*. Washington, DC: World Bank.

———. 2008a. "Decentralization in Client Countries: An Evaluation of World Bank Support 1990–2007." Washington, DC: World Bank.
———. 2008b. "Local Government Discretion and Accountability: Application of a Local Governance Framework." Washington, DC: World Bank.
Wright, Angus, and Wendy Wolford. 2003. *To Inherit the Earth: The Landless Movement and the Struggle for a New Brazil.* Oakland, CA: Food First Books.
Wunsch, James S. 1991. "Institutional Analysis and Decentralization: Developing an Analytical Framework for Effective Third World Administrative Reform." *Public Administration and Development* 11 (5): 431–451.
———. 1998. "Decentralization, Local Governance and the Democratic Transition in Southern Africa: A Comparative Analysis." *African Studies Quarterly: The Online Journal for African Studies* 2 (1). Available online at http://web.africa.ufl.edu/asq/v2/v2i1a2.htm.
———. 2001. "Decentralization, Local Governance and 'Recentralization' in Africa." *Public Administration and Development* 21 (4): 277–288.
Wunsch, James S., and Dele Olowu. 1990. *The Failure of the Centralized State: Institutions and Self-Governance in Africa.* Boulder, CO: Westview Press.
———. 1996. "Regime Transformation from Below: Decentralization, Local Governance, and Democratic Reform in Nigeria." *Studies in Comparative International Development* 31 (4): 66–82.
Wunsch, James S., and Dan Ottemoeller. 2004. "Uganda: Multiple Levels of Local Governance." In Dele Olowu and James S. Wunch, eds., *Local Governance in Africa: The Challenge of Democratic Decentralization.* Boulder, CO: Lynne Rienner, 181–210.
Xiaoyi, Wang. 2007. "Undermining Grassland Management Through Centralized Environmental Policies in Inner Mongolia." Washington, DC: World Resources Institute.

The Contributors

The late **Omar Azfar** was associate professor of economics at the Department of Public Management at the John Jay College of Criminal Justice of the City University of New York. He was an expert on corruption, decentralization, and other aspects of governance, and routinely gave advice to the World Bank, the US Agency for International Development (USAID), and other development agencies. His coedited book (with Charles A. Cadwell) *Market-Augmenting Government: The Institutional Foundations for Prosperity* advances the idea that markets work best when governments provide an effective legal infrastructure that allows exchange to be voluntary and reliable. He published articles on corruption and other topics in the political economy of development.

Gary Bland is fellow at RTI International, an applied research and development institute based in North Carolina. A senior public policy and democratic governance specialist, he has worked most closely and written extensively on decentralization and the development of public sector institutions, primarily in Latin America. For nearly five years he served as director of RTI's Center for Democratic Governance. Prior to joining RTI, he was a fellow and decentralization adviser at the Center for Democracy and Governance at USAID. Earlier he worked at the Latin American Program of the Woodrow Wilson International Center for Scholars and at the US House of Representatives. He has been a private consultant to the Inter-American Development Bank, the World Bank, and other organizations. His most recent research and publications have addressed decentralization, conflict, and democratic deficits in Latin America.

Derick W. Brinkerhoff is distinguished fellow in international public management with RTI International and an associate faculty member at George Washington University's Trachtenberg School of Public Policy and Public Administration. He is a specialist in policy implementation, strategic management, democracy and governance, decentralization, civil society and nongovernmental organizations, and organizational change. He has published extensively, including eight books and numerous articles and book chapters.

Ashwini Chhatre is assistant professor in the Department of Geography at the University of Illinois at Urbana-Champaign's School of Earth, Society, and Environment. During 2006–2007, he was a Giorgio Ruffolo postdoctoral fellow in sustainability science at the Center for International Development, Harvard University. He spent eleven years organizing communities around the democratic governance of, and local rights to, natural resources in India. His interests include political ecology, the outcomes and impacts of democratic politics, the role of institutions in preference formation, and the use of combined quantitative and qualitative research methodologies.

Ed Connerley is senior adviser for decentralization and subnational governance in the Office of Democracy and Governance at USAID. He provides technical leadership and field support to USAID missions throughout the world. He has undertaken consulting assignments to improve democracy and governance in approximately forty countries worldwide and he has held faculty positions at US and Brazilian universities. He has published several book chapters and journal articles in the *Public Administration Review* and the *International Journal of Public Administration.*

Kent Eaton is professor of politics and director of the Center for Global, International, and Regional Studies at the University of California, Santa Cruz. He is the author of *Politicians and Economic Reform in New Democracies: Argentina and the Philippines in the 1990s* and *Politics Beyond the Capital: The Design of Subnational Institutions in South America*. His recent publications on subnational politics, decentralization, and federalism have appeared in *Comparative Politics*, *Latin American Research Review*, *Politics and Society*, *Security Studies*, and *World Politics*. Before joining the faculty at U.C. Santa Cruz, he taught at the Woodrow Wilson School of Public and International Affairs at Princeton University and at the Naval Postgraduate School in Monterey, California.

Jonathan T. Hiskey is associate professor of political science at Vanderbilt University. His work has focused primarily on issues related to the political economy of local development in Latin America as well as the development implications of political transitions taking place across the region. He is the author of numerous articles on these topics in such journals as the *American Journal of Political Science*, *Comparative Politics*, and *Latin American Research Review*. His current work looks at the political implications of migration in sending communities across Latin America.

Tomila Lankina is senior research fellow and lecturer at De Montfort University in the UK. Previously she was a researcher at the World Resources Institute in Washington, DC, a visiting fellow at the Woodrow Wilson International Center for Scholars, a research fellow at Humboldt University in Berlin, and a postdoctoral fellow at Stanford University. She is the author of *Governing the Locals: Local Self-Government and Ethnic Mobilization in Russia* and coauthor (with Anneke Hudalla and Hellmut Wollmann) of *Decentralization and Local Performance in Central and Eastern Europe*. She has published in *World Politics*, *Post-Soviet Affairs*, *Europe-Asia Studies*, *Social Research*, *Conservation and Society*, and other journals.

Patrick O'Mahony currently serves as chief of party on the USAID Afghanistan Local Governance and Community Development Program. He has managed postconflict reconstruction and state-building programs for the UN Department of Peacekeeping Operations and USAID in Iraq, Afghanistan, Bosnia, Kosovo, Serbia, Croatia, and Macedonia.

Jesse C. Ribot is associate professor of geography and director of the Social Dimensions of Environmental Policy Initiative at the University of Illinois. Previously, he was senior associate in the Institutions and Governance program at the World Resources Institute from 1999 to 2008. He has been a fellow at the Max Planck Institute for Social Anthropology, a Woodrow Wilson International Center for Scholars fellow, a MacArthur fellow at the Harvard Center for Population and Development Studies, and a fellow at the Yale Program in Agrarian Studies. From 1990 to 1994, he lectured on environment and development policy and planning in the Department of Urban Studies and Planning at the Massachusetts Institute of Technology. Over the past two decades, he has conducted numerous studies for the World Bank, USAID, and the UN. He conducts research on decentralization and democratic local government, natural resource tenure and access, distribution along natural resource commodity chains, and vulnerability in the face of climate and environmental change.

Larry Schroeder is professor of public administration at the Maxwell School, Syracuse University, and is a public finance economist with primary interest in state and local public finance and financial management. He has conducted research on a variety of state and local government fiscal issues both in the United States and abroad, particularly in developing and transition economies. His research focuses on problems associated with financing the construction and maintenance of public infrastructure in these environments as well as the broader issues of decentralization, intergovernmental fiscal relations, and the effects of institutional arrangements on the provision of public services. He is the coauthor of several books and has written a large number of articles addressing these subjects. He has consulted with and led policy research projects in numerous countries, especially in South and Southeast Asia, but also in Africa and Eastern Europe.

Joseph Siegle is director of research at the Africa Center for Strategic Studies of the National Defense University and a senior research scholar at the University of Maryland's Center for International and Security Studies. Previously he was Douglas Dillon Fellow at the Council on Foreign Relations, and worked for many years as a development practitioner in some twenty countries around the world in both conflict and postconflict contexts. He has published widely on the economic and security implications of democratic transitions, and coauthored (with Morton Halperin and Michael Weinstein) *The Democracy Advantage: How Democracies Promote Prosperity and Peace.*

Paul Smoke is professor and director of International Programs at the Robert F. Wagner Graduate School of Public Service at New York University. His main research and policy interests include public sector reform and decentralization, with a particular focus on East and Southern Africa and Southeast Asia. He previously taught at the Massachusetts Institute of Technology, and worked with the Harvard Institute for International Development. He has written or edited several books, most recently (with George Peterson and Eduardo Gomez, eds.) *Decentralization in Asia and Latin America: Towards a Comparative Interdisciplinary Perspective*. He has published in a variety of journals, including *World Development*, *Public Administration and Development*, *International Journal of Public Administration*, *Economic Development Quarterly*, and *Third World Planning Review*. He has also worked extensively with international development agencies.

Index

About the Book

It is increasingly difficult to find developing countries whose leaders have not debated or implemented some type of decentralization reform. But has decentralization worked? Does it actually help a country to deepen democratic governance, promote economic development, or enhance public security? Under what conditions does it justify the enthusiasm of those who have pushed so successfully for its adoption?

The authors of this volume sift through the accumulating evidence to assess how well decentralization has fared. Focusing on consequences rather than causes, their goal is to inform future interventions in support of decentralized governance by showcasing some of the important trade-offs that it has generated so far.

Ed Connerley is senior adviser for decentralization and local governance in the USAID Office of Democracy and Governance, providing technical leadership and field support for AID missions around the world. **Kent Eaton** is professor of politics at the University of California, Santa Cruz. He is author of *Politics Beyond the Capital: The Design of Subnational Institutions in South America* and *Politicians and Economic Reform in New Democracies: Argentina and the Philippines in the 1990s*. **Paul Smoke** is professor of international studies in the Robert F. Wagner Graduate School of Public Service at New York University. His most recent book is *Decentralization in Asia and Latin America: Towards a Comparative Interdisciplinary Perspective*.